PRAISE FOR
MISS ME WITH THAT

"In this revealing debut, erstwhile Bachelorette Lindsay offers a blistering critique of the Bachelor franchise while reflecting on her racial identity, turbulent relationships, and life as a reality-TV personality. . . . Lindsay's many fans will devour this entertaining exposé."

—*Publishers Weekly*

MISS ME WITH THAT

HOT TAKES, HELPFUL TIDBITS, AND A FEW HARD TRUTHS

RACHEL LINDSAY

with Sofia Quintero

BALLANTINE BOOKS
New York

2022 Ballantine Books Trade Paperback Edition

Copyright © 2022 by Rachel Lindsay

Published in the United States by Ballantine Books, an imprint of Random House, a division of Penguin Random House LLC, New York.

BALLANTINE is a registered trademark and the colophon is a trademark of Penguin Random House LLC.

Originally published in hardcover in the United States by Ballantine Books, an imprint of Random House, a division of Penguin Random House LLC, in 2022.

ISBN 978-0-593-35709-5
Ebook ISBN 978-0-593-35708-8

Printed in the United States of America on acid-free paper

randomhousebooks.com

9 8 7 6 5 4 3 2 1

This book is dedicated to the wild at heart kept in cages.

CONTENTS

CONTENTS

THIS IS NOT A FAIRY TALE

On August 7, 2017, more than seven million people watched me accept a marriage proposal on *The Bachelorette*. They tuned in almost every Monday night for almost three months to witness the very emotional process of my meeting, getting to know, and ultimately sending home thirty men. After watching genuine connections, tense conflicts, and heartbreaking farewells, fans think they know me.

When you watched me on TV, you might have seen someone who had it all together—an intelligent and mature woman who was secure within herself, knew what she wanted, and refused to suffer anyone whose own agenda got in the way. Privileged upbringing, attorney-at-law, and actually married to the man I chose on the show? It can be easy to think that my life is a fairy tale.

But my journey to love began long before those eleven episodes. To truly understand the desires, motives, and reasons behind the decisions I made on *The Bachelorette,* you have to know my story before I ever followed that whim to audition for a show I'd never watched. My biggest hope is that when you finish reading *Miss Me with That,* you'll realize that I'm not so different from you. I *don't* have it all together. In fact, right before I signed on to be a contestant on *The Bachelor* . . . Girl, I was the epitome of untogether.

So much so that had the man I wanted to marry at the time asked me not to do the show, I would have passed on the opportunity (and probably be living that mediocre life my critics love to keep threatening me with). But I appreciate how much you wanted me to win, and I want to reciprocate the love by sharing the journey behind the journey so you can win, too. I want you to know me at my worst so you can learn from my experiences and realize that no matter how complicated you might be, you can have the life you dream for yourself. You absolutely deserve it.

Note to *The Bachelor* fans: Let me warn you that this is not your typical *Bachelor* book. When I share anything about the show that I haven't disclosed before (and we can all agree I have had tons to say), my intention isn't to spill the tea. C'mon, you already know that I'm going to be honest about what I think and feel about the franchise. Just understand that my intention is not to gossip about or hurt your favorites. If anything, I expose no one more than myself. I make a genuine effort to own my mistakes and regrets as readily as I express my concerns and resentments. I wrote this book with an open heart and I hope you read it with an open mind.

Miss Me with That is about how I went from pursuing a life of other people's design to becoming clear about what I wanted for myself and finding the courage to pursue my authentic desires. I wrote it to share the experiences and work it took to become the woman you see on TV or might hear on a podcast. Not to present myself as some paragon of success, because I assure you that I remain a work in progress. If anything, as you read, I want you to think, "Damn, Rachel was a hot mess, but at least she was always willing to clean her shit up."

I chose the title *Miss Me with That* because it's a phrase I've been prone to say on the two podcasts I cohosted after appearing on *The*

Bachelor and *The Bachelorette*—*Bachelor Happy Hour* with fellow alum Becca Kufrin and *Higher Learning,* where Van Lathan and I discuss the latest in hot topics, politics, current affairs, and sports, and how they impact Black culture. Whether a gentle pushback or a forceful argument, saying "Miss me with that" is my way of calling bullshit. In other words, I use it a lot. Especially about serious topics like justice and equality and to my haters (and I've got plenty for you, too, since I know you're here, too).

Contrary to popular belief, the best gift I ever received was not a wedding ring. It was the permission I gave myself to be imperfect and grow from some less-than-flattering experiences. If you think that my transparency can be of service to you in any way, turn the page. If not, you know the saying . . . you can miss me with that.

RACHEL'S LIFE PLAN (AGE 18)

- **AGE 18**: Graduate from First Baptist Academy and move from Dallas, Texas, to New York City to attend New York University. (Who needs a gap year?) While in college, meet my future husband—an Omega football player. (Refer to the list on page 48 for other qualifications.)

- **AGE 22**: Graduate from New York University with a BA in political science. Then promptly move to Southern California and begin law school. First choice is Loyola Marymount, but Pepperdine or UCLA would be great, too.

- **AGE 25**: Graduate from law school with a specialization in sports and entertainment law. Then start my career as a sports agent at CAA, WME, or IMG.

- **AGE 26**: Get engaged to my future husband. (Even though I know the proposal is coming, he still manages to surprise me.)

- **AGE 27**: Get married. (This age gives me the perfect amount of time to spend two years with my husband traveling the world before we have any kids.) The idea of walking down the church aisle in a white dress with all eyes on me and then pouring my heart out at the altar is *mortifying*. We're eloping. Just immediate family at the courthouse followed by a huge reunion-style celebration.

- **AGE 29**: Give birth to the first of four children. Two is not enough. As the second of three, I want to spare my child that middle child syndrome, so four it is. Maybe more.

GROWING UP LINDSAY

I recently learned that I came into this world fighting for my life. Literally.

I was in Houston visiting my mom's side of the family . . . grandmother, aunts, uncles, and cousins. We typically gather around my grandmother's kitchen table for hours to talk, laugh, and gossip. We were talking about my unusual life path when my Aunt Jetta shared that she knew I was destined for greatness because of how I came into this world. "You know you almost didn't make it, right?" she said.

"I'm sorry, what?" My aunt explained that when my mother was twelve weeks pregnant with me, she stood as a bridesmaid in a friend's wedding. From the congregation, my grandmother watched as my mother slumped over the piano. Mom fainted and later discovered that she was spotting. She almost lost me, and the doctor insisted she remain bedridden until she had me. Having never heard this, I looked at my mother. "Mom?"

She shrugged. "I thought I told you that story."

Meet the Lindsays. We're reluctant to share information. Even family business that pertains to you. (The Lindsay group chat is probably ablaze right now since we're not even two chapters in, and I've already shared too much.)

Learning about the circumstances surrounding my birth made me realize that we rarely question how we came into this world, what a delicate process coming to life is, and how easily things can go wrong. The story rocked me, making me consider my life and its purpose from a different angle. I almost never existed, but I did, which means I'm here for a reason.

According to Mom, I already showed a temper at three weeks old. She was changing me when I balled up my fist and growled at her. Now, *that* doesn't surprise me. As a Lindsay, I would be expected to succeed no matter the odds, so of course, I was born ready for any challenge or fight. Success included excelling at school, establishing a respectable career, and raising a family—all under the guidance of the Church—just as my parents had.

My father grew up one of eleven children on a farm in Beeville, Texas. His was one of the only Black families in a small community, and at the age of five, Dad learned how to work the land. While my grandmother coddled my father and his siblings, Pa-Pa was all about tough love. At a time when it was unheard of for African Americans to own land, my grandfather accumulated hundreds of acres of real estate that remain in our family to this day. Educational and economic success was paramount to my grandfather, and he ingrained in all his children an expectation that they would achieve these things. The Lindsay side of my family is reserved and private, and my father is no exception. (While my father did meet the final three men during my *Bachelorette* hometown visit to Dallas, he chose not to appear on camera. More about his take on Bryan, Peter, and Eric when the time comes.)

Meanwhile, my mother hails from a family with a radically different vibe. She grew up in a family of seven in Houston's Fifth Ward and then moved to South Park. In other words, the inner city. My relatives on my mother's side could not care less where I went to school or what my GPA was. They are more open with their feelings, the life of any party, and the kind of kinfolk that burst in when you're in the bathroom because *Privacy? What's that? We're family!* While I feel blessed to have been raised with my father's professional ethic and discipline, my emotional temperament comes from my mother's family.

My female cousins on my mother's side are more like sisters to me. Unlike the cousins on the Lindsay side, who are much older than I am and spread throughout the country, they all lived in Houston, and we are all close in age. I spent summers with my maternal cousins, having sleepovers, watching movies, dancing to Michael Jackson and Prince, and talking about boys. I feel so fortunate to have had the experience of forging strong female ties from the start.

My mother's extended family lived in Homer, Louisiana, where both my grandparents are from. My granddaddy's side still lives there. I can close my eyes and see the red clay, dirt roads, and slender trees. I can smell the fresh scent of the country and feel the hot sun kissing my skin. Like my father's side of the family, the Sheltons lived on acres and acres of land that they owned. Initially, we traveled to Homer every other year for a family reunion. Then, as we grew older and our schedules became hectic, the biannual reunion gave way to an annual trail ride through our family's property (including a pivotal one that I'll eventually tell you about). Homer represents freedom to me. While there, we didn't watch television, play video games, or scroll on our phones (mostly because there's no signal). Instead we immersed ourselves in the outdoors and family, chasing one another, playing dominoes, spades, and volleyball, and riding horses. I cherished every single second of those summers with my cousins, grandparents, and great-aunts and -uncles. Even as I now reminisce, I miss those priceless and defining moments. Summers in Homer taught me where I came from and who I am. This is why I describe myself as having a city-girl swag with a country-girl spirit. I look back at those times with a strong sense of pride; Beeville, Homer, and Houston made me.

My parents met when she was a sophomore in college and he was a second-year law student at the University of Texas at Austin. I always joke with my mom that she knew exactly what she was doing, snatching up a future lawyer while she was in college. They became engaged and married upon Mom's graduation. With my own love story being such a public one, it occurred to me that I had never learned about my parents' engagement, so I recently asked my mom how they got engaged. Although they had been dating for two and a half years and had expressed their love for each other, Dad still caught Mom off-guard when he proposed. They were sitting in his car after a date when he asked her to marry him. She cried and said yes.

After completing law school, Dad passed the bar and became a practicing attorney. My parents were living in Austin when my mother scored a great job opportunity with Arco as a computer programmer; she would be earning more than my father and had to move to Dallas. So what did my alpha male father do?

He moved to Dallas with her. He moved *for* her, putting aside his pride and ego to benefit their growing family. This selfless act always resonated with me. In the future my father's example became a reason why one relationship failed and another succeeded. But that story is for another essay.

At first, my father struggled in Dallas. In the seventies, nobody was hiring Black attorneys, and it took him months to find a job despite having attended one of the nation's top law schools. Just as Dad was about to hang up his shingle and start his own practice, somebody told him that the City of Dallas was hiring Black lawyers. Naturally, Dad applied and got the job. He also promised himself that if he didn't triple his salary in one year, he would resign. Not only did my father achieve his goal, he eventually advanced from assistant city attorney to be appointed by the city council as the City Attorney . . . Dallas's first Black City Attorney. I did not realize it at the time but firsts seem to run in this family. In this role, he oversaw all the city's attorneys and legal matters involving the City of Dallas. After seven years in that position, he was appointed by President Bill Clinton to be a United States District Judge of the United States District Court for the Northern District of Texas. He is the first Black person to serve on the federal district court in the Northern District.

While the public sees this commanding figure, his family knows him as a tender, funny, and respectful man. Think Philip Banks, Will Smith's uncle and surrogate father on *The Fresh Prince of Bel-Air*. When I began seeking a partner who would not hold my successes against me, I would learn how high my father set the bar and how rare a man like him is.

But we're not the Bankses, and don't call me a Cosby kid. People see the daughter of a federal judge and computer programmer and presume I grew up like a Huxtable. Miss me with that. Yes, I grew up privileged, but my economic advantages didn't spare me from life's hard lessons. As the first in their families to attend college, both my parents were raised to work hard for everything they had, and they were intent on instilling in my sisters and me the same drive. We were expected to strive just as they had. The Lindsay imprint is powerful. In the same spirit in which my grandfather raised him, Dad refused to baby me. I remember spending summers in Beeville doing the same chores my father had done decades before . . . working the land, building fences, and feeding the cattle/horses. When my sisters and I succeeded at something, he would say, "Well, you're a Lindsay. That's what you're supposed to do."

My sisters and I are each four and a half years apart. When I entered high school, Constance started college, and when I went off to college, Heather began high school. That's classic Lindsay pragmatism: planning each pregnancy so they did not have to pay more than one child's college tuition at a time (because we had *better* be finished in four years before the next one enrolled). The age difference allowed my sisters and me both to admire and annoy one another in equal measure. Constance and Heather are nine years apart, which makes their relationship with each other quite different from the one each has with me. Pretty much protective big sister and adoring baby sister between those two. As the middle child between them, however, I both received and dished out regular doses of admiration and annoyance.

Extroverted and fashionable, Constance always knows the latest trends—what styles to wear, where the hotspots are, who is relevant and why. Since childhood my oldest sister has been comfortable with the spotlight and enjoys the finer things in life. One time she called from the top of the stairs, "Look at me!" Once all eyes were on her, Constance proceeded to slide down the banister until she knocked over a lamp. She takes her role as the oldest quite seriously and is very protective of her family. (Exhibit A: the ninth episode of my season on *The Bachelorette* when I brought my future husband, Bryan, to Dallas to meet my family. The mama bear in my older sister was on full display. She cut him no slack.) She fought for me when not ordering me around. Constance is the Kim Kardashian of our clan.

Meanwhile, my younger sister, Heather, is more like Kourtney. When Constance was putting Bryan through the wringer on camera, my younger sister refused to film and wasn't even there. In the infamous words of Kim Kardashian, "She is the least exciting to look at." I actually say this because Heather is stunning. Breathtaking even, and yet you just may never know how exciting she truly is. The few social media profiles she has are set to private. A homebody who prefers to keep to herself, she can be quite sociable and make it seem natural when, truth is, it takes her some effort. While I itched to get out of the house, Heather was and still is content to stay home with her favorite TV marathons.

Which makes me Khloé. As the middle child and a shameless extrovert, socializing comes second nature to me. Meeting and talking to new people has always energized me.

One trait that my sisters and I share is sensitivity, with one major caveat. I do have some rough edges, and as a straight shooter, I speak my mind without much thought as to how it might make others feel. (Shocking, I know.) My soft spots are social issues, not personal conflicts. Funny that middle children are reputed to be peacemakers, because if there's drama in my family, I tend to be in the starring role. As I told my brother-in-law Alex after a contentious dinner conversation during Bryan's hometown visit, I'm chill 'til I'm not. You're not going to hurt my feelings because of the way you speak to me. But four-year-old Rachel could bring eight-year-old Constance to tears.

We have evidence of this called the Infamous Video. While Heather lay in her crib, my mother recorded a routine that Constance and I were performing. In true Rachel fashion, I got bored midway through the routine and decided to do my own thing. I stopped singing and headed over to Heather's crib. "Rachel, sing!" ordered Constance. I ignored her. "Rachel!" She jammed the off button on the stereo and cut the music.

Meanwhile, my mother continued shooting and even laughed. "And this is what always happens."

"Mom, Rachel won't sing," Constance cried. "She won't do it right."

Mom panned the camera to me and zoomed in on the evil smile on my face. *Got her. Again. Every single time.* My mother turned the camera back on Constance in time to catch her fit. She took off her house shoes and threw them about. My sister glared at me, and I just grinned back like the Cheshire cat.

Good times.

I very much looked up to Constance. But as much as I admired her, I knew she was sensitive and I knew how to push her buttons. She'd boss me around, and I'd rebel against her authority in true sisterly fashion.

I grew up as a tomboy who hated all the girly stuff. I didn't want to wear dresses or skirts, and, least of all, stockings. (To this day, I have to take deep breaths to calm myself when putting them on.) From pre-K to twelfth grade, I attended First Baptist Academy, a small, predominantly white parochial school where my mother was a teacher and I was only one of the few Black students. Starting in preschool, my mom sent me to school in red tights. I felt like I couldn't breathe in them, and by the time she picked me up at the end of the school day, I would have ripped holes in my tights. That got me a spanking. (Clair Huxtable would never . . . nor would Aunt Viv.) Mom said it made me look like they couldn't afford to buy me new tights and as if she didn't know how to dress me properly. To be a Black child attending a predominantly white school in ripped stockings could play into my teachers' and classmates' stereotypical notions, and my mother would have none of that.

When I was six, my parents enrolled me in a summer track program not only to increase my exposure and interactions with other Black people (remember, I spent the bulk of my days at a predominantly white school) but also to start instilling the lesson of mind over matter. During track practice, I trained to run the 100, the 200, and the 400 (also known as the quarter mile). The quarter is a sprint of an ungodly length that takes your entire body to run. You know you've run a good 400 if, when you cross the finish line, you can barely stand. From a young age, I spent my summers training to compete two hours each day in the middle of the blazing Texas heat, internalizing the belief that if I sharpened my mind, I could push my body past any physical limitations I thought it had. If you had the will, there was little you could not achieve, and as a Lindsay, your will was presumed infinite.

I wanted very much to please my parents, and I remember vividly how hard I would tackle that quarter mile every meet. No matter what other commitments he might have had, my dad was at every one, pushing me from the sidelines to go harder. The referee would fire the gun, and I'd blast out of the blocks, rounding the curve of the first hundred meters and winning the straight. Then when I reached the 200 mark, the pain would hit. Heart in my throat, lungs on fire, legs trembling as I rounded the curve to the 300 mark. My stamina draining, I would hit the final stretch and look for my father. Without fail, there Dad would be, yelling at me through the fence between the stands and the straightaway. "Kick it, Rachel, kick it! Give it all you've got!" At the sound of his command I somehow would conjure something deep within me that propelled me those last hundred meters toward the finish line. I'd burst over the finish line and practically collapse and remember that I was a Lindsay; I had pushed through the pain, and I had prevailed. I won the medal. My father expected me to succeed, and because I could count on his support, I wanted to meet his expectations. The quarter mile is a brutal race, and I was good at it. It became my best distance . . . and I hated running it. But not more than I loved making my father proud.

Dad overcame barriers and blazed trails. As if it were not enough to be a first-generation college student and graduate from a great law school, my father became the first Black person appointed as the City Attorney of Dallas when I was seven years old. *That's my daddy.* I often accompanied my father to his huge office on the seventh floor of city hall and watched with awe and pride as city council members and the mayor himself drifted in and out of his office. When not camping under the massive conference table, I was skimming through the leather-bound volumes on his shelves and stacks of documents in red ropes on his desk. Without comprehending a word of what I was reading, I understood my father's work to be meaningful. I knew that Daddy was a lawyer just like Ben Matlock.

I was obsessed with *Matlock* as a child. Every week I looked forward to hanging out with him and following his investigation. And Matlock wasn't just an attorney; he was a crime solver! *That's what I want to do.* Between Dad and *Matlock* (one of the few television shows that my parents allowed my sisters and me to watch), I decided then I wanted to be a lawyer when I grew up. And that thrilled my parents.

If you buy into birth order theory, you might attribute my

desire to please others, especially my parents, to my being a middle child. The classic theory states that when parents have a second child, they relax in their approach to parenting. With some experience under their belt, they loosen their grip, but they may also be less attentive. To get their parents' attention, the second child pulls out the stops to please them, and that desire to please often extends to other people, from teachers to friends. In fact, the second child thrives on friendships and develops large social circles, aims to keep the peace yet sometimes rebels. We value our independence, tend to be melodramatic, and find creative ways to get attention.

Guilty as charged. Looking back at my childhood in Dallas, I can see how being the second of three daughters contributed to my strong drive to achieve professional goals and create social connections. I started young, performing every Disney movie scene and making my dolls, and my sisters, play their respective parts. My approach to life essentially became Work hard, party harder.

(And as for rebellion and melodrama . . . wait for it.)

That said, middle children also face stigmas that contradict these traits. Theoretically, because we don't get the attention usually lavished on the cherished firstborn or the adorable youngest, we stay under the radar. Being overlooked allows us to dodge great expectations, and consequently, we're perceived to be underachievers with underdeveloped social skills.

Miss me with *those* middle child myths. Sounds to me like motivation to stand out. If you don't believe me, ask Jennifer Lopez, Michael Jordan, or Warren Buffett. With my older sister Constance being the Pretty One, and my younger sister Heather becoming the Smart One, I had a subconscious drive to carve out a space for myself as the Cool One.

However, being "cool" is far easier said than done when you're growing up in one of the strongholds of the Bible Belt, where evangelicalism, Protestantism, and social conservatism reign supreme. I attended Bible classes throughout the year and during summer vacation, played piano in Sunday school, sang in the choir, was on the youth usher board, and praise-danced (which is just as it sounds—using music and movement as a form of worship unique to the Black Church—and involves a variety of styles, from jazz to mime). Through workshops, events, and youth groups, I ate, breathed, and lived the Christianity of my elders. I was religion, and religion was me. In other words, I was a goody two-shoes who always walked the line (until I began to rebel).

I was popular at First Baptist (no hard feat). When I joined the basketball team, I took on the nickname Big Rach to intimidate my opponents on the court. It complemented my outrageous temper. I pushed opponents, talked trash, made excessive fouls, threatened to fight . . . I was Dennis Rodman in a ponytail.

At the end of the school day, my popularity stayed behind at First Baptist. I went home to an overwhelmingly Black neighborhood in Oak Cliff in southwestern Dallas where the Black kids didn't accept me. That's right. The first Black Bachelorette was the proverbial ugly duckling until high school. In fact, many of the Black boys who teased me during my middle school years had big crushes on Constance. They teased me about how I spoke and called me "white girl." Meanwhile, I would look in the mirror and think *How?* Staring back at me was a short Black girl with a big forehead. Sticking out of my little two-piece track outfit were these tiny arms and legs and a potbelly of baby fat I was still trying to run off. Not only was my forehead much bigger than my sisters', my summertime cornrows made it stand out even more. No wonder this boy ran up to me, cupped my forehead, and started singing, "I got the whooole world in my hands . . ." (I laugh about it now, but when I was ten, I was devastated. Little shit did that IN FRONT of all the neighborhood kids!) After enjoying eight hours of coolness amid my white classmates, coming home to other Black kids to whom I was persona non grata was so painful.

And Constance wonders why I cried so much. With her flawless bangs and ponytail, she had all the style and cool friends, and all I had to offer was awkwardness. I ran to my older sister a lot, hoping she'd take care of me, that some of her swag would rub off and people would leave me alone. In typical older sister fashion, Constance didn't want me around, never mind me copying her. (And this is why, for a time, I was very conscientious about not treating Heather the same way. Then I eventually did blossom into the Cool One, and that child had to stay away from me. I don't make the rules.)

When I started high school, three things happened that changed everything. One, puberty. Two, my first boyfriend. Three, a life-changing trip at the age of fifteen to visit Constance at the Spelman-Morehouse homecoming. A major part of my transformation from the awkward duckling to the cool chick was the development of my racial identity. Despite living in a majority Black neighborhood and attending a small Black church, my school, First Baptist Academy, dominated my young life. There were about eighty kids in my graduating class, and only seven or eight of us were Black. Let's do the math. Approximately 180 days in a school year, 7 hours in a school day . . . that's 1,260 hours per year steeped in whiteness.

First Baptist had a basketball gym it made available to the public, and the kids from the performing arts school down the block regularly played there. A girlfriend and I befriended some kids at Booker T. Washington High School for the Performing and Visual Arts, which boasted famous alums like Erykah Badu and Norah Jones, among others. Soon we were dating two friends from Arts Magnet, as we called it. I gravitated to Karim, who was both Black and Persian, making him at once familiar and intriguing.

The most captivating thing about these public school boys was the way they expressed themselves. As a girl forced to wear a uniform every day, I loved the way Karim spoke and dressed. His entire family was artistic. His mother taught dance at Arts Magnet, and his sister studied dance there as well. Karim was an actor, while his older brother worked behind the scenes.

I went to all of Karim's performances—whether stage productions at Arts Magnet or the poetry club. Watching the poets perform spoken word inspired me to write. I'd write poems and rhymes and read them to Karim over the phone. He introduced me to neo-soul artists like Erykah Badu and Jill Scott. We would speak every day for long spells, and our relationship freed my mind and broke up the monotony of my life. Without him my days would have been nothing more than church and school. Even my extracurricular activities—namely basketball and piano—were linked to those institutions. Every time I hung out with Karim and his circle, I escaped the bubble where *I* was the diversity experience. Like Alice in Wonderland, whenever I crossed the threshold into his magical world, I never knew what adventure awaited me on the other side. Karim's everyday life was a field trip for me, the parochial school girl getting to hang out with the cool kids from *Fame*. I loved how they both welcomed and challenged me. With them I felt free.

My dad, however, was not a fan of Karim. (Surprise, surprise.) First, his appearance was so unpredictable. One day Karim could show up at my house with a long, dark ponytail, then the next his hair was bleached blond and pulled into two curly Afro puffs. Also, my parents kept us in a protective bubble and strictly limited our access to popular culture. R-rated movies and explicit music were off-limits, as was much of television (especially reality TV). They were, indeed, attempting to raise us as Cosby kids, and here came these Arts Magnet schoolboys, exposing me to ideas and environments that I soaked up like a sponge. To my father's dismay, I invited Karim to my homecoming dance. No way I would wear a dress like everyone else. Instead, Karim and I decided to dress alike. We braided our hair into cornrows, bought canes, and donned pinstripe suits with hats. I just knew I was so cool showing up at First Baptist with my public school boyfriend, dressed like pimps. I knew exactly what I was doing—rebelling.

But then Karim showed up an hour and a half late to pick me up. This was before the ubiquity of cellphones, so I had no idea why he was delayed or if he was coming at all. I just sat there in my suit with my cane, waiting while my father seethed. When Karim finally arrived with flowers in hand, I instantly forgave him and couldn't wait to get to the dance. Meanwhile, Dad gave him the death glare. *How dare you have my child waiting for you for over ninety minutes without a good excuse!* Noting the look on my father's face, Karim mumbled something about car trouble, and we were out the door. We had a fabulous time. (I'm still surprised that I was allowed to go!)

I sometimes lied about my whereabouts to hang out with Karim. And because I was a terrible older sister, I once made the mistake of taking Heather with me when she was only twelve. A mistake not because I was a bad role model, but because the girl ratted me out. I had told my parents we were at the mall only for Heather to blurt out over the dinner table, "I really love Karim's room."

"How do you know what Karim's room looks like?" said Dad.

I lied about having seen Karim's room, but not because we were doing anything sexual. We never did anything more than kiss, and we usually hung out with a group of friends. I lied to avoid the hassle of my parents' disapproval, though lying made the problem worse. It gave the false impression that something more was going on between Karim and me, especially because I was so infatuated with him.

And like most teenage infatuations, Karim and I were not meant to be. We even broke up for the most clichéd reason. Of course Karim wanted to have sex with me, but I was never going to do that. Despite my infatuation with him and my penchant for rebellion, I remained grounded in my Christian faith and had no intention of giving up my virginity before marriage. His senior prom landed on the same day as my junior prom. Karim told me that he couldn't go to my prom with me, and we decided to attend our respective dances without each other. Then a friend of Karim's showed up at my prom. "It's messed up that you're here by yourself," he said. "Only reason Karim didn't take you to his prom was because he wanted to take this other girl. A girl he knew that he could get from her what he can't get from you." I sure knew how to pick them, ladies. And sadly this was only the beginning.

And just like that we were done. No confrontation with Karim. No tears over him. More like *Fuck you. I'm glad I never gave you what you wanted if this is how you were capable of treating me.*

Thanks and goodbye. Oh, yeah . . . fuck you. (Okay, maybe not fuck you. I didn't talk like that back then. But you can't tell me I didn't feel it.)

Karim and I would cross paths as adults and make our peace. It was easy not just because so many years had passed but because I always appreciated the things I learned from our young love. My initial motivation for dating him was to rebel, and yet through our youthful romance, my free spirit and artistic side blossomed.

Hailing from a family without artists, however, it would be decades before I gave myself permission to follow the creative impulses I had as a child. The Lindsays do not pursue media or entertainment as pastimes, never mind professions. My first experience of coming into my own, however, did involve culture—defining Blackness on my own terms.

ALL BLACK EVERYTHING

Merely by describing yourself as black you have started on a road towards emancipation . . .

—Steve Biko

Raise your hand if you've ever watched *The Cosby Show.* (It's okay to admit it. Millions of people across race and age made Dr. Heathcliff Huxtable "America's favorite dad." Very few of us, however, had any idea how his creator was conducting himself off set.) Despite not being a Cosby kid, I grew up watching and relating to the Huxtables because they resembled my own family. While not as affluent as Clair and Cliff, my parents were upper-middle-class professionals with traditional values. They also had several daughters, each as different as can be.

Now raise your hand if you've ever watched the show *Thea.* Had you even heard of *Thea* until now? My *Higher Learning* podcast cohost Van Lathan (who insists I'm a Cosby kid—miss me, Van) grew up in Baton Rouge, Louisiana, watching *Thea.* Starring stand-up comedian Thea Vidale, this short-lived sitcom followed a widowed mother raising four children in Houston, Texas, while working as a supermarket cashier by day and running a beauty salon from her front porch at night. Although it was canceled after only nineteen episodes, *Thea* made television history as the first time an African American female comedian starred in a series named after her.

Thea's bashful and only daughter, Danesha Turrell, was played by a teenage Brandy Norwood. I, too, watched *Thea,* and I was no Danesha. But I was a far cry from Vanessa Huxtable. (Van, stop.) Like many Black children growing up in racially divided environments, I struggled to find a place where I could be both authentic and accepted. My complicated journey to being able to stand in a Blackness defined on my terms began at the age of four, but first some context.

Raise your hand if you've heard of the Clark doll experiment.

In the 1940s, married African American psychologists Kenneth and Mamie Clark designed and implemented several experiments to study the psychological effects of segregation on African American children. They handed Black children between the ages of three and seven four dolls. The dolls were identical, except that two were white and two were dark-skinned. The Clarks asked the children a series of questions about the dolls to gauge their preference:

Which dolls are nice?
Which dolls are bad?
Which doll is most like you?

The majority of the children not only preferred the white dolls to the Black dolls, they labeled the Black dolls "bad" and claimed that the white dolls looked most like them. As chief counsel of the NAACP, Thurgood Marshall asked the Clarks to repeat their doll experiment as he prepared to argue *Briggs v. Elliott,* the first of five cases that eventually would be argued before the Supreme Court as

Brown v. Board of Education. In other words, the Clark doll test was integral in overthrowing the "separate but equal" doctrine of *Plessy v. Ferguson* and ending the legal segregation of public schools.

Had four-year-old Rachel participated in a re-creation of the Clark doll experiment, I, too, would have preferred the white dolls. While my parents certainly bought me a Black Cabbage Patch doll, I wanted the same toys my friends had, and most of my friends were white. In fact, when my parents told me that my mother was pregnant with my younger sister, Heather, I said, "If she's not white or purple, I'm not going to love her."

I'm embarrassed by this to this day, but I admit it because I doubt I'm alone in having said something like this.

Anti-Blackness is ubiquitous and insidious, and Black people are not immune. Despite my parents' steady involvement in Black culture and causes, I still internalized it. They were a deacon and deaconess in our church and leaders in the community, and my sister and I were always accompanying them on some mission, whether it was visiting the elderly at the nursing home, handing out flyers for a community meeting, or getting out the vote during election season. Mom and Dad also were among the parents who fought for my school to recognize Martin Luther King, Jr. Day and took us to the library to learn about Black history. Whether they were telling stories about our grandparents over dinner, mentoring youth, advocating through their work, or participating at church or school, both my mother and father were always asserting themselves as proud Black people.

But I still wanted my little sister to look like one of my white baby dolls.

Even as my parents valued the Christian education that First Baptist provided my sisters and me, they were fully aware that its religious priorities and socioeconomic composition would severely limit my exploration of Black culture and history. They wanted their daughters to know who we were racially as well as religiously. So in addition to the usual reasons parents enroll their kids in extracurricular activities, this oversaturation of white culture just might have prompted mine to register me in Black organizations.

Just saying.

In addition to signing me up for that summer track program where my team was all Black, my parents enrolled me in Jack and Jill. For those of you unfamiliar with it, Jack and Jill's a national membership organization with 252 chapters representing more than 40,000 Black families across the United States. It was created by a group of twenty-one African American mothers in Philadelphia during the Great Depression with the intention of "establishing a social and cultural union for their children" and "preparing its members with a valuable adulthood by ingraining leadership qualities."

Anyway, that's what the website says, but let me put it this way. One day a kid at school asked me, "Rachel, what exactly is Jack and Jill?"

I said, "It's a country club for Black people."

Yeah, I said it. Then I ran off before she could ask me anything else, because I *hated* Jack and Jill and didn't want to be associated with it. Ask me about it, and I'd pull a Mariah Carey: *No, I don't know them.* (I've kept my participation in Jack and Jill from Van, who's now never going to let me hear the end of this, but I'll happily take yet another L for those of you who can relate to this struggle.)

If you were a member of Black Twitter in the summer of 2016 (I was offline auditioning for a show you might've heard of), you might have seen #GrowingUpJackandJill. What began as a celebration of the organization soon turned into criticism. On one side, you had former members appreciating the opportunities they received through Jack and Jill, everything from college tours to scholarships. On the other side, detractors blasted the organization for its elitism.

While it's a membership organization, Jack and Jill is not the Y. You can't just join because you're Black and can afford the chapter fees. The organization is an exclusive society requiring certain qualifications for admission. Applicants must be nominated by two current members to even be considered. Then you *might* be invited to join. Suffice it to say, the people who can vouch for you must also be members of the Black "elite" (I hate the concept of elitism). It's no coincidence that the children enrolled in Jack and Jill are the sons and daughters of doctors, lawyers, and business executives. Despite no explicit income requirement, your profession, connections, and, yes, your appearance matter. In a 1998 interview with *The New York Times,* the then executive director of the national organization made no bones about the fact that members had to at least have a bachelor's degree and be able to afford fees for such activities like horseback riding and skiing. (Now can you understand why I wasn't trying to let those kids who were teasing me know I was a member and kept Van in the dark for so long?) Let's just say this is a whole different look for an organization that began organizing swimming parties for their children because the segregation of the late thirties banned them from public pools.

And while the kids in the Dallas chapter were a range of skin tones and hair textures, the founding of Jack and Jill was not untouched by the colorism of its time. The Black community in the U.S. has made great strides in overcoming the divisive ideas we internalized during slavery, but we still have a ways to go. The evolution of the natural hair movement from the 1960s to today and Dr. Yaba Blay's #PrettyPeriod as a clapback to the backhanded compliment *You're pretty for a dark-skinned girl* are just a few efforts to dismantle the colorism we inherited from white colonialists who pitted our enslaved ancestors against one another. (Even though fair-skinned Africans were allowed to work in the home while their dark-skinned brethren were exploited in the fields, no one escaped brutality.) Still, as a culture, we have yet to shake off centuries of vile tests used to measure our Blackness—the paper bag test, the comb test, the pencil test. I'm so disheartened by the way we have progressed from using phenotypical features to socioeconomic status as a way to disparage one another.

According to a *MadameNoire* article on #GrowingUpJackandJill, the organization enjoyed a surge in popularity in the nineties. Apparently my parents were among many who were raising their children in predominantly white environments and turned to Jack and Jill in a desire to preserve their cultural identity. They felt compelled to immerse Constance, Heather, and me in Black culture and concluded that living in a Black neighborhood, attending a Black church, and registering us for a Black track program every summer could not trump the experience of attending an all-white private school. So they put us in Jack and Jill when I started middle school, aka my awkward phase. The organization serves children as young as two, and so by the time I joined, most of the kids in my chapter were practically *born* into it. Having grown up together, the girls all knew one another and did not invite me into their long-standing clique.

Now, I don't believe Jack and Jill was created to emulate white elitist organizations. How can I when I'm a member of a Black sorority that some accuse of doing that very thing? However, we can't deny, as the saying goes, that membership has its privileges for kids and parents alike. While the children become friends and have fun, their parents network for business opportunities. Another way that Jack and Jill mimics similar institutions in the white community is in its traditional gender divide in responsibilities. Whether or not they work outside the home, the mothers are expected to be very active and organize all the programs. My defection from Jack and Jill gave Mom a short reprieve, but once my younger sister became involved, she had to resume her involvement. Meanwhile, my father continued to play his role: paying the annual dues and activity fees.

This always felt weird to me. My parents came from humble beginnings, and damn, these people were bougie! Mom and Dad must have had no idea when they applied for membership. I was so embarrassed to be affiliated with Jack and Jill that I eventually began to rebel. "You put me in this thing to meet other Black kids, but they're no different from everyone at First Baptist," I remember saying once. "They all go to private school with white people, too. Like, where's the Black diversity here?"

Yes, this is how I spoke when I was thirteen.

At first, I fell back on my other activities, such as sports and piano, as an excuse to avoid Jack and Jill programs, but by the time I was in high school, I flat-out refused to attend. The exceptions were the few events that were open to the public, to which I'd invite my friends and hang out with them. I had certain friends that I knew would never be invited to join Jack and Jill, so I hid my affiliation from them. That was how much I resented the exclusivity of the organization.

I find that Jack and Jill perpetuates a harmful notion: *My Black is better than yours.* And this makes no sense to me. How can any

Black person take pride in having a white person tell them, *Oh, but you're not like other Black people*? Such people may fit the Eurocentric beauty standards, make a lot of money, or otherwise have proximity to whiteness, and those attributes may make them different from other Black people. However, none can override the single trait that makes them different from *white people*.

But let me acknowledge the positive things. The extracurricular activities offered by Jack and Jill greatly increased my exposure to other Black kids. In fact, through Jack and Jill I met two of my dearest friends, Mark and Trey, and we are close to this day. Trey is a year younger than me, and our moms are best friends. Trey saw potential in me long before I saw it in myself. We have always supported each other throughout the years, and our professional paths have even crossed, giving us the opportunity to work together. Trey is one of my most loyal and encouraging friends; I don't know if I would have achieved some of my accomplishments without his support. When we met at twelve years old, Mark attended public school but was privileged like me. He played football at a popular high school, and even though I played basketball for First Baptist, I much preferred to go to his games. When I didn't have a game to play, you could find me in the stands cheering him on and then hanging out with everybody after the game at the local Sonic or Whataburger. Mark introduced me to a classmate whom I nicknamed Twin because we clicked instantly and were so much alike. Fortunately, my parents liked Mark and Twin a lot. I'd spend the weekends at Mark's house with Twin and his friends, and during the summers, we would watch sports and movies and go to Joe Pool Lake, where we rented WaveRunners and Jet Skis, played the summer jams, and ate barbecue.

At track, however, the other Black kids constantly teased me because of how I talked and where I went to school, which was too white by their standards. If they ever cut me any slack, it was thanks to my older sister Constance's popularity. (Then I got promoted to "Constance's little sister.") But for the most part, it was very hard for me to make friends with other Black kids. Wherever I went I somehow managed to make an acquaintance—thank God for the single person who was willing to be nice to me—but the others just could or would not embrace me.

Okay, I need to address something. Some Black folks who have never experienced this can be oblivious or dismissive about how painful it is to have your own people reject you. The loneliness that overtakes you when you're alienated by the ones you assumed would embrace you is like no other. It is difficult for other relationships to fill the void that that rejection creates. Especially over something trivial like the way you express yourself or the things you enjoy, instead of meaningful choices like the way you treat other people. They sit on social media presuming that if you were teased this way as a child, it had to be because you turned up your nose at other Black people because they didn't watch *Friends* or listen to Hanson or have other interests associated with whiteness. To justify the alienation of other Black people—usually *children*—from their own community, they reach to argue that you must have done something to deserve the comeuppance. In my personal experience, I also think the other Black kids rejected me because they equated being successful with betraying the culture. I did not measure up to their level of Blackness, and being different from the norm was something to be ashamed of, not celebrated.

Miss me with your presumptions and take your racial essentialism with you. I wasn't looking down on anyone. On the contrary, I was a crybaby (more on this when I tell you about my first time in therapy) desperate to fit in with my Black peers. I even started to lie about where I went to school and tried to alter the way I spoke, using African American Vernacular English and changing the way I pronounced my words. It only invited more teasing. That is, if I risked opening my mouth at all. I grew very shy and uncomfortable around the Black people I encountered, when they were the ones whom I most wanted to be with.

Since I was rejected by Black kids, I found myself hanging out more with white kids at school, and I became popular. Or so I thought. I believed they accepted me, but as I look back, I recognize the ways I withheld aspects of my personality from white people so they'd feel comfortable around me. Just as I lied to the Black kids about where I went to school, I hid where I lived from my white classmates. At one time its own town, Oak Cliff is a huge, predominantly Black neighborhood on the southern side of Dallas where my parents still reside. It has some beautiful areas that the news media ignores, preferring to report on every negative thing that occurs there. I was so afraid of my white classmates finding out that I lived there and bombarding me with their ignorant questions: *Oh my God, you live in Oak Cliff? You live in the ghetto? Like, that's the 'hood!* To avoid that, I would say I lived farther out in the suburbs. I also watched the shows my white classmates watched, got the toys they played with (although my parents were sure to get me Addy, the first Black American Girl doll. Of five historical dolls meant to highlight the American Girl's positive achievements, the best the Black one could do was become strong and independent after escaping slavery).

As much as I call out the racism of the *Bachelor* franchise, I still have Black detractors question my Blackness. They learn about my predominantly white schooling, my upbringing, my circle of friends, or my husband and assume that not only am I always comfortable with white people, I prefer their company to that of other Black people. But if growing up with a survival instinct to put white people at ease in my presence isn't Exhibit A in defense of my Blackness, what is?

No, really . . . what the fuck is?

On second thought, don't tell me. Instead let me tell you how we walk that Black unity talk. Let me tell you about the Black people who did embrace me just as I was and the beautiful impact their acceptance had on my life.

First, let me tell you about Robby J.

When I started middle school, Robby J moved to Dallas, and we met because Constance was friends with his cousin, whom she met through *smirk* Jack and Jill. Robby was the first Black person who gave me permission to be Black in my unique way. "I really like the way you talk," he said soon after meeting me. "You shouldn't try to change it." Robby attended the neighborhood school and took me under his wing, exposing me to the Black culture I couldn't get at First Baptist or from the Black kids who rejected me. He expanded my knowledge of sports and rap music and taught me how to freestyle (Big Rach had bars and still does. Please see my *Wild 'N Out* appearance for further reference). During the summers, Robby J and I talked to each other all day, listened to music at my house, and went to Six Flags. He stole my first kiss in the darkness of Runaway Mountain on a group date—a moment I would relive over and again in giddy anticipation of the next one. Robby's acceptance not only gave me access to Black events I longed to be a part of, but our relationship also increased my confidence among Black people and connected me to others who would embrace me as he did.

I wonder sometimes if Robby J ever knew what his friendship meant to me. He probably doesn't even remember any of it, but I do. I remember staying on the phone with him for hours talking about anything and everything and feeling safe to be transparent with my opinions and experiences. After so many years of being shunned by my own, I remember going with Robby and other friends to Magic Skate—roller rink by day, club at night—and learning how to dance.

Yes, I said learn to dance. If I wasn't playing piano, I had no rhythm. Constance teased me about it all the time. But confidence is a funny and powerful thing. It gives you the strength to do things you once believed you were incapable of doing. And sometimes all it takes to plant the seed of confidence is someone to believe in you . . . even something as small as dancing in front of your peers. When I turned fifteen and had more independence, I stopped being afraid of getting rejected by other Black kids and actively sought them out.

All I needed was one person to be down for me, have my back, let me be who I was. By the time I entered high school, I had gone from lugging around the thick skin I developed from being called a white girl to snuggling comfortably into my own Black skin. I stepped into who I truly was without reservation or apology, regardless of who was around me. I didn't just become cool through my relationship with Robby J; I became real. I always knew who I was, but for the first time, I could truly express it.

Another turning point came at the age of fifteen, when my older sister Constance enrolled in Spelman College—a private liberal arts college for Black women in Atlanta, Georgia. Look, Black excellence was not something new to me. Not only did I grow up around Black people who excelled, I share a bloodline with some of them. However, until I traveled to Spelman for homecoming, I had never seen so much Black excellence on display in one place in my entire life. At fifteen, during my weekend with those Spelman women and Morehouse men, I saw it everywhere—at the parties, the tailgate, the pageants, concerts, fashion shows, Alpha Elixir, and coronation. These Black folks weren't just talented and smart, they were also fun. They not only mesmerized me, they accepted me the way Robby J had. Nobody called me "white girl," judged the way I spoke, or cared about where I went to school. It was a beautiful Black experience. A diverse Black experience that made me realize that I was trying too hard to assimilate with my white classmates and gave me even more courage to be Black in whatever manner I felt was true to me. *Be Rachel. She's Black enough.*

I came back to Dallas from Atlanta with a fuller sense of my authentic self and a new attitude toward friendships. Those weekends instilled in me so much Black pride that I was determined to fearlessly spend more time with other Black people. I stopped hanging out as much with my classmates at First Baptist Academy and began making friends at the neighborhood high school. Now that I had let go of my insecurities, I had a burning desire to find more Black people with whom I could celebrate our Blackness in all its expressions.

In my usual dramatic fashion, I grabbed all my country music albums and made Constance drive me to the used-CD store (yes, I'm dating myself). Goodbye, Tim McGraw, Jo Dee Messina, and Shania Twain. Welcome home, Hot Boys' *Guerrilla Warfare, The Chronic 2001,* and Jay-Z's *Vol. 3 . . . Life and Times of Shawn Carter.* Constance laughed at me, but this was a major symbolic moment for me—the trading of one life for another.

Now, I still do love my nineties country music. I can boot, scoot, and boogie with the best of them, but the makeover in my music collection represented my letting go of conformity, letting go of trying to perform racially to please others, letting go of all that I was not. *You're going to accept me or you're not, but my not being who I really am to make you comfortable is no longer on the table.*

Then came the day I stood up for my neighborhood at First Baptist. A teacher was putting down Oak Cliff, and I got fed up. Fed up with white people assuming the worst about my community and fed up with myself for being afraid to set them straight. I raised my hand. Then, without waiting to be called, I said, "I actually live there."

"No, you don't." I came face-to-face with the very attitude that compelled me to lie for so many years. And not from a student my own age, but from an authority figure. She was so adamant about my own life, as if my living in Oak Cliff disrupted a lie she needed to believe about the Black students who attended First Baptist to justify our presence at the school. "No way you live there. You just couldn't . . ."

"I do. And the way you're painting it is not how it is. Every neighborhood has its bad spots. I've lived in Oak Cliff my whole life, and you shouldn't be generalizing about it or assuming that everyone who lives there is the same." The teacher was far more shocked that I lived in Oak Cliff than the fact that I challenged her. I told my parents about the incident, and my father loved it.

Now, it may surprise you that I ultimately didn't attend a historically Black college, especially after those magical experiences I had at Spelman during my sophomore and senior years of high school. I did apply to Spelman and Howard but decided they weren't the best schools for me. For one thing, Spelman's known to be a tad bougie for my taste. I'll never forget seeing ladies in high heels and full glam heading to an early-morning class. No secret, no shade, and no wonder my sister Constance fit right in. But as an unapologetic tomboy, I fully intended to wear pajamas or sweats and no makeup to class each day. And let's be honest . . . Morehouse—the all-boys college across the street—was a beautiful distraction that I did not need. More important, I didn't want to spend another four years known as Constance Lindsay's little sister. I wanted to walk in my own lane.

But my commitment to immersing myself in all Black everything remained unchanged. If anything, I made up for lost time. I chose to attend college in Austin, better known as the California of Texas. That is, the culture is one of free and diverse thinking. In the red state of Texas, Austin stands alone. After more than thirteen years of attending a small, private Southern Baptist school where students lived in a protective bubble and learned to conform to a particular worldview, I yearned for an educational environment where we would be pushed to think outside of the box. The only teacher who'd encouraged us to think for ourselves at First Baptist—God, I loved Mrs. Hewlett!—happened to be Australian and in an interracial marriage.

At the University of Texas at Austin, I joined the African American Culture Committee (and eventually was the vice president to my cousin and best friend Andrea's president), pledged Delta Sigma Theta, and participated in endless activities that connected me to people from all walks of Black life. After experiencing only one kind of Blackness at First Baptist Academy and Jack and Jill—African American, Southern, Christian, upper-middle-class—the variety excited me. I spent little time with white classmates during college. This wasn't a hostile decision to reject them as much as a loving choice to privilege my own race. After having few Black friends and limited experience of Blackness growing up in Dallas, the diversity I discovered within my own community in Austin was exhilarating. A thirst I didn't even know I had was quenched. I needed it.

After having my racial identity questioned for so long, it became imperative for me to

just

be

Black.

Please don't misconstrue what I'm saying here. I'm not accusing anyone of depriving me of my Blackness, never mind other Black people. That could never happen under my parents' watch. Plus, no amount of teasing was going to make me believe I was a white girl or drive me to try to become one (which was never desirable, never mind possible). But my K–12 schooling kept me in a bubble I was desperate to pop when I went to college.

Law school marked my return to an unavoidably predominately white educational environment. I chose Marquette University Law School in Milwaukee, Wisconsin, because of their nationally renowned sports law program. The program was small, and far from diverse. Out of a class of about three hundred students, fewer than ten were Black. I keenly felt the heartache of their absence on November 4, 2008, during my first semester.

On Election Day I stood on line to vote with a good friend. He was a libertarian intent on voting for John McCain. We spent three hours in that line, each trying to convince the other to vote for our candidate. This was my second national election as a voter, and I could not have been more elated to vote for the potential first Black president, whose family resided only two hours south on the I-94. Beyond his Blackness, Obama as a candidate also appealed to me more than any of the other contenders for the Democratic nomination. After casting our votes, my friend and I headed back to the apartment building (where we both lived) to wait for the results. When Barack Obama was announced as the victor and became the first Black person to be elected the president of the United States, a rush of emotion surged through me as his family walked across that stage. Elation, pride, hope . . .

. . . and then I looked around the room and saw that I was the only Black person there. Everyone was a fellow law student, but they also were all white. Now, being the sole Black person in a room full of white folks was not a new experience for me, but the special circumstances evoked a strong sense of aloneness that caught me off guard. As happy, and even relieved, as my white classmates who may have voted for Obama might have felt, it immediately hit me that his victory could not carry the same weight for them as it did for me as a Black woman. During this historic moment, I was by myself in the emotional depth of my experience.

I had to get out of there.

I rushed back to my room, hoping my roommate was there. She was a Black student at the dental school. I opened the door and gasped in relief at the sight of her. We ran toward each other, threw our arms around each other, and shared a teary and celebratory embrace. The election of the first Black president in the United States was something we never thought we would live to see and knew we would never forget.

One of the simplest yet most powerful things Black people can do to forge greater unity and advance as a community is to stop measuring each other's Blackness. I say this as someone who has been guilty of doing this despite knowing firsthand the hurt of being told I had to sound this way, dress that way, and hang out with those people in order to be Black. I always knew I was Black, and when I encountered people who did not require me to betray myself in order to prove my awareness and pride, I became closer to my people. If I had never discovered this, then I would never have tapped into the greatest version of myself. Instead of imposing narrow and arbitrary definitions of Blackness on one another and alienating those who do not measure up, create spaces that allow people to be Black in their own way so they can contribute to our collective advancement. The diversity that exists among us is an asset. We need all of us if any of us are to be free.

I WANT MY REALITY TV

*The problem isn't Flavor Flav. The problem is Flavor Flav becomes a
stand-in for the one or two black people you see on TV. And a figure like
Flavor Flav takes on more importance than he should.*
— Mark Anthony Neal

After being raised in a home where my television habits were closely
monitored and very restricted, I made up for lost time in college.
In Living Color, Martin, Chappelle's Show, Living Single . . . I was
years behind. But I was most obsessed with reality TV and stayed
on top of that, especially any franchise with a predominantly Black
cast. *Flavor of Love, I Love New York, For the Love of Ray J, America's
Next Top Model.* If there was a reality TV show with Black
people on television, I was watching it. Once I watched all the
available episodes of one show, I was grabbing the remote searching
for my next fix. *That reunion was a hot-ass mess! But now what
am I going to watch? Okay, let me check out this one.*

Despite the label "reality" TV, I saw the casts of these shows as
characters who were there to entertain me no differently than if
they were actors in a movie who had to memorize dialogue. Even
as the cameras presumably followed them as they went about their
lives, I knew that the cast intended to lead those cameras straight
to the drama. I watched incredulously as these people exploited
themselves effortlessly, holding back no emotion or secret. The con-

trast to my restrained way of being was nothing short of fascinating to me. I could never get away with what they did. *Let me have dinner in the private room of an upscale restaurant and fire a wine bottle at someone's head or run across a conference room table in my bare feet to slap my former best friend.* I loved to come home, turn on the TV, and watch these people display such intense feelings—rage, despair, sexual desire—without caring about people judging them.

People who looked like me.

Take *Flavor of Love*. It premiered in January 2006 right about two months before *The Bachelor* launched its eighth season with yet another white male lead. Flavor Flav hit the reality TV scene and claimed to be the first Black Bachelor. Or, more precisely, "the Blackchelor." From the first episode it was evident that *Flavor of Love* not only borrowed heavily from the *Bachelor* formula, it outright parodied it. Flavor brought onto the show women from all walks of life only to dispense with learning their names. Instead he gave them nicknames that he purposefully misspelled for laughs—like Toastee (because she got drunk the first night of taping) and Bootz (because he wanted to knock them). No wonder in the spinoff *Flavor of Love Girls: Charm School,* when host Mo'Nique told the contestants, "Now, before we go any further with this process, there's something all of you ladies need to lose, and that is those disgusting nicknames," every woman in that room exhaled, and one even yelled, "Hallelujah!" And yet for three seasons, not only did the former member of one of the most respected and militant rap groups in hip-hop history reduce the women to singular characteristics, these women *let* him.

A hot mess . . . but I couldn't turn away from it. The so-called reality on TV was an escape from the reality of my academic grind. At times that sharp contrast between the two was comforting.

When I was not studying, I was working, and when I was not working, I was preparing for law school, all the while minding my p's and q's like the respectable Black Southern Baptist I was raised to be. (Except when I was partying. I mean, this was college.) On a particularly bad day, I could switch on the television, watch their dramas, and think, *Whatever I got going on, at least that's not happening to me.*

As time went on, however, I began to feel unsettled with how Tiffany Pollard and later NeNe Leakes were seemingly playing up specific aspects of their personalities to the point of caricature. The breakout contender of *Flavor of Love,* who leveraged her appearance into leading roles on multiple spinoffs, Tiffany Pollard, aka New York, states that she was the first Black woman to headline a reality TV dating show, and she can make that claim. Even though I suspected that she was purposefully being ridiculous and over-the-top, I still disliked the Black stereotypes that she was perpetuating. When she was on *Flavor of Love,* she played the insatiable Jezebel. (And for the record, there's nothing wrong with her wanting to sneak into Flav's room. When I was on *The Bachelor,* I myself took advantage of the fantasy suites.) When not with Flavor, she became the Sapphire, angrily getting in the other women's faces and posturing about being the HBIC (head bitch in charge). Then her mother would join her onscreen as Sister Patterson, aka the Church Lady—the God-fearing woman who feels entitled to police everyone else's behavior. Just as Flavor Flav had revived the Sambo character—a Black caricature that has been entertaining white audiences for decades with his little jigs and silly phrases—New York's histrionics played into so many negative stereotypes about Black women.

As a Black woman, I can distinguish between Tiffany Pollard

and the character New York. The character of New York was nothing like me or any other Black woman I personally knew. However, not everyone can make the distinction. My Black friends and I were not the only ones watching the show. According to an article from the *Daily Beast*, in a 2017 Reuters poll, 40 percent of white Americans reported not having any non-white friends. To this day, whole sectors of the United States do not know any Black people other than those who cross their television screens or come into their headphones. Some specifically seek out these Black stereotypes for entertainment, knowing—and not caring—that the salacious Jezebel and angry thug are indeed caricatures. They grossly underestimate their impulse to project these depictions onto the Black people they do meet. I knew white people who also watched *I Love New York* and believed that Tiffany's character reflected how Black women truly are. With these shows as their primary reference, everything they learned about Black people was wrong.

My fear was proved justifiable when I went to law school in Milwaukee. At one point in my law school application process, I wrote an essay about the burden of walking into a room—be it a restaurant or place of employment—only to discover you're the only Black person present. Imagine my surprise to move to Milwaukee and discover that so many Black people lived there. Prior to attending Marquette, I had no idea that we made up 40 percent of the city's population. But far more shocking was how highly segregated the city was. (Almost ten years later comedian W. Kamau Bell would expose this on an episode of his show *United Shades of America*.) It didn't take long for me to experience the way pop culture had negatively influenced white folks' perceptions of Black people. Many of the people who attended Marquette University Law School or lived in the surrounding community hailed from very homogenous areas. They came from the segregated Upper Peninsula or small Midwestern towns in Wisconsin, Iowa, Michigan, and Indiana. For such folks I was their first experience of diversity, and my crayon didn't fit their stereotypical coloring box. The white people I encountered constantly gave me backhanded compliments such as "Oh, you're so different. You're not like *that*." They couldn't fathom why I would take offense at these kinds of distinctions. Who are you to determine I'm better than anyone, never mind my own people? In so many words, they would say *Wow, you're kind of like us.*

Even more devastating than experiencing such microaggressions from white people was witnessing how other Black people would run with these "compliments." The opportunities for Black people living in Wisconsin were scant, and it hurt me to observe how infrequently those who succeeded reached back into our community. Believing in survival of the fittest, they uplifted themselves by putting down other Black folks when they could have found ways to create and extend more opportunities. I refuse to roll that way.

The racism crossed into my personal life. Some of the men I met in law school made sure I knew that they had never dated a Black woman before and hoped that I would remedy that. When we went to bars or clubs after studying sessions or a tough exam, they always wanted to dance with me and made comments about my having a big ass . . . and my ass isn't even that big. Just bigger than what they were used to. I could imagine the confusion of my friends back home who joked that I suffered from long-back syndrome. In the Midwest, I was Nicki Minaj. These white men couldn't flirt with me without veering into sexual jokes that fetishized Black women. One particular guy was constantly inappropriate, and I couldn't tell if he was trying (and failing) to be funny or if he truly bought into these stereotypes. One time, another guy got drunk and made a pass at me despite my never having shown him any interest. I came away from that encounter suspecting that he tried it because he thought he could—simply because I was Black. Like, of course I would like it. With stereotypes of the hypersexualized Black women in their heads, white men had a curiosity about me that bordered on fetishism. When wanting to date me, they approached me like an animal in a zoo. *Is it true what they say about Black women . . . ?* "I'm not about to be your Black experience," I found myself saying often. "Go somewhere else to find that." Knowing that they had had little to no experience with Black women, I blamed their stereotypical notions on the spitfires they watched in pop culture. It took these experiences to show me the stark difference between my capacity to watch this genre as pure entertainment and the way others perceived it as art imitating life.

Despite my love for reality TV, the last thing I ever wanted was to appear on it. As a Lindsay, professional success could look like only four things: medicine, business, education, or law. Except for playing piano at church, the arts were not encouraged in my home—not that reality television would qualify as art in my household.

Now that I *have* appeared on several reality TV shows, however, I recognize other reasons why I would criticize Black people on reality TV while still tuning in to their antics. After a day of constant studying, analyzing, thinking, and otherwise being in my head, I desperately needed (or so I believed) the mindless entertainment. Despite elitist concerns I had over stereotypes, hour after hour I gave in to the cathartic effect of watching emotional outbursts I was not allowed to have. Furthermore, lurking beneath my superiority complex was a resentment toward these women. They expressed the full range of their emotions without a care as to how others might judge them. *They were even paid for it.*

Finally, the jealousy. Many of the women on these shows dated professional athletes, which sadly was one of my biggest and most childish fantasies (which did end up happening, but that is a story for another chapter). Until that happened, I had to work for the lifestyle these women paraded so effortlessly onscreen—the beautiful homes, the upscale cars, the exotic trips. Now, I love to work and take great pride in the fruits of my labor, but sometimes the grass is greener and more attractive on the other side.

Judging these women became a part of the enjoyment of watching them. Or more like hate-watching. Their carrying on and constant fighting, their willingness to destroy friendships and endure their partners' repeated betrayals while relentlessly chasing money and fame, often with minimal talent and embarrassing results, made me feel superior about my own struggles, which paled in comparison. These are not easy things to admit, but I do so because I suspect I'm not alone.

The day would come when I would empathize with these women I judged. Several years later and after considerable heartbreak, I would follow a whim and audition for a popular reality TV show I'd never watched. When I sat in the bed in my dorm room to get my reality TV fix and *The Bachelor* came across my screen, I rolled my eyes and changed the channel because I already knew:

No fairy tale for us.

RACHEL'S IDEAL MAN (AGE 18)

- **AN OMEGA**—For those of you unversed in Black Greek life, Professor Frank Coleman was one of the founders of the Omega Psi Phi fraternity at Howard University in 1911. Two years later, his classmate Mary Edna Brown was one of the founders of Delta Sigma Theta Sorority, Inc. In 1918 the first lieutenant of the 368th U.S. Infantry and physics instructor married the class president and valedictorian in a ceremony officiated by her father, the Reverend Sterling N. Brown. This is the beginning of the long tradition of Delta and Que romances known as Coleman Love. If you didn't know, I am a proud member of Delta Sigma Theta Sorority, Inc. As I was always destined to be, since some of the most influential women in my life are members of this respected sorority.

  A Delta is what an AKA ain't,

  What a Zeta wanna be, what a Sigma can't

  What a Kappa like, what an Alpha love,

  What a Que Psi Phi can't get enough of.

  They call them nasty Que dogs—a compliment of the highest order. Yes, sometimes they bark and wear collars around their necks, which now when I reflect on this I realize how problematic this is and the deeply rooted attachment to racism it portrays with the collars and chains, but at that time in my life I just wanted to party, and the Ques epitomized that lifestyle. They're rough, they're hard, they're fun, but they're also studious, hardworking, and loyal. As boisterous as they are industrious, Ques know when it's time to work and when it's time to play and approach both with equal fervor.

The Kappas may be pretty, and the Alphas may be smart, but when you marry an Omega, you marry Dark Kent. The best of both worlds. "In the beginning, there were only two; Eve was a Delta, and Adam was a Que."

I want to strut with an Omega man and have him hoist me on his broad shoulders. First across the yard and then one day down the aisle. Give me that Coleman Love!

- **FUNNY**–Everyone says they want someone who makes them laugh, but that means different things to different people. Not everyone wants to be with the life of the party. Send him my way. The more sarcastic, the better.

- **BLACK**–Obviously. Preferably dark-skinned. One of my home-boys said to me, "Light-skin dudes have no game because all the women are going to go after them. They never have to try. It just happens for them, but for dark-skinned brothers like me? We got to have a personality. To stand a chance of getting you, we've got to have game." I don't know how true this is, but I'm definitely Team Dark Skin. Speaking of teams . . .

- **AN ATHLETE**–I need the hookup to *all* the games. That's how much I love sports. And I specifically want a football player. No other athletes have the swag of a football player.

- **A CHRISTIAN**–He doesn't have to be a Baptist, but he should at least be a Protestant. And I don't want somebody who's afraid to say that they're a Christian. Do you need to walk around with a WHAT WOULD JESUS DO? bracelet or anything like that? No. (I mean, I haven't worn one of those since elementary school.) And you don't always have to walk a straight line. You can love Jesus and still curse, because God literally knows that I do.

But if I ask you, "Are you a Christian?" the answer must be unequivocally, "Yes, I am." No hemming and hawing allowed. I want to be able to take you home and say, "Mom, Dad, this is ___, and he's a Christian, too." When Sunday comes, it's a given that we're going to church without any arguments. My husband is not a closet Christian.

- **TALL**—Ideally minimum height six-two, but since I'm only five-four, there is some wiggle room here. As long as I never have to worry about what shoes to wear, we're good to go.

- **FAMILY-ORIENTED**—It'd be great if he came from a tight-knit family. Bonus points if his parents are still together. And of course he must want kids.

- **INTELLECTUAL**—As a sapiosexual, I need to be able to have in-depth conversations about worldviews, politics, and current affairs. If you knew what a sapiosexual was without having to look it up, you're probably okay.

- **LOVE LANGUAGE**—He must be fluent in both physical touch and quality time, because I'm bilingual.

Oh my God . . .

. . . I just looked at how I described my ideal man at the age of eighteen and . . .

. . . Did I just describe myself or did I just create the most shallow list ever while wrapping it up with "He loves his family and Christ"?

Okay, I'm not tall, but I *am* the life of the party.

Is it because I was the one I was looking for all along?

It's because apparently you think and do dumb shit in your twenties. And life eventually taught me that just because I was wading in shallow waters did not mean I couldn't drown. This list reflects just how much I had to grow and mature.

It was a mighty long road, so let's get started.

THE SEXUAL (MIS)EDUCATION OF RACHEL LINDSAY

Women will only be truly sexually liberated when we arrive at a place where we can see ourselves as having sexual value and agency irrespective of whether or not we were the objects of male desire.

—bell hooks

My sexual education took under a minute.

Fourteen-year-old Rachel was sitting in her bedroom chatting on the phone with a friend, when Mom entered the room. She carried a large white piece of paper, a piece of tape already affixed in each corner. She pressed the eleven-by-four sheet against my wall, slapped each corner—one, two, three, four—then walked out of the room. No words were spoken. In all caps and bold print at the top was one word: abstinence. All through high school that poster hung by the light switch, where I saw it every time I left my room. When friends visited, they would point at it and laugh: "What is this?" And when I left for college, the poster made its way downstairs to Heather's room. I never bothered to read the smaller print. I already knew what it said.

The Baptist Church taught me to abstain from sex until marriage, and I fully bought into that belief. I headed to Austin for college a proud virgin. A family friend introduced me to a current student named Mike over the phone so he could show me the ropes, look out for me, and otherwise help me acclimate to college. When Mike and I saw each other, all those wholesome intentions flew out the window, and we began dating.

We may not admit it, but we all have The List—a catalogue of qualities that our ideal partner has. I had a mental list, and Mike checked off everything on it. He came from a good and affluent family. His mother was a doctor and his father was a successful businessman. Mike graduated at the top of his class in high school, played football, and was a Christian. And then I saw him—this attractive young man rolling up to the campus in an Escalade with rims. (No car on the mental checklist, but when you're eighteen, a fly ride racks up bonus points.)

In addition to the superficial things that grabbed my attention, Mike also had other wonderful qualities. He was understanding, caring, and sincere. He had great values and wanted the same things I did—namely, a family and children. Most of all, when I looked at us, I saw my parents. Mike's demeanor reminded me of my father's. My parents met in college, and Mom had been a virgin when she met Dad. I thought, *I can't believe I met Mr. Perfect on day two of college.*

But I initially gave Mike a hard time. Before I started college, my then boyfriend, who was attending Howard, had blindsided me with a breakup. "I wouldn't be doing right by you if I let you go into college with a boyfriend," he said. "You need the full college experience. If we're meant to be, you'll come back to me." And he meant it. (I have yet to solve the mystery of how the boyfriend I had at eighteen had more emotional maturity than so many men who followed him, or maybe he just wanted to have his own fun without being tied down to a girlfriend. I will never know, but I digress.) He had the unconditional love to let me fly.

And fly I did. Following his advice, I played the field during the first couple of months of college. My interest in athletes piquing, I briefly dated several guys who played a variety of sports—football, track, basketball. But my enthusiasm for casual dating quickly waned. I wanted a steady boyfriend, so two months into my first year of college, I chose Mike. Who does that?

A young woman who grew up in a strict household finally enjoying her first experience of independence, that's who. Mike allowed me to be an eighteen-year-old college freshman away from home and on her own for the first time in her life. He never pressed me if I went to a party or hung out with other guys. I'd even brag to my friends about having the best of both worlds—the comfort of a steady boyfriend and the freedom to socialize like a single gal. "Yeah, Mike doesn't mind if I go to the club," I'd say. "In fact, he'll drop us off in his Escalade and pick us up whenever we're done." If he joined us at a party, he leaned against the wall and watched my purse while I drank, mingled, and danced, no questions asked. Never a bad attitude. He even gave me a beautiful necklace. A dainty thing with a small diamond pendant. I never took it off.

Eighteen-year-old Rachel took great care not to take Mike's trust for granted. After all, this perfect relationship happened too easily. *Can I really come to college, meet my husband, and live happily ever after like Mom did?* And my parents took to Mike, too. (To this day, Dad asks about him.) No one is perfect, but he was as perfect as they come. In fact, I would tell my cousin Andrea, "If Mike and I were to ever break up, it's going to be because of something that I did." I put him on a pedestal and was determined not to mess this up. *This is it. He's the one for me. We're going to get married. We're going to have children. We're going to have an amazing life.*

Only now, as a married woman in my thirties, can I consider how Mike must have felt while dating me. Although I never flirted, danced inappropriately, or in any way betrayed him with other men, it must have bothered Mike when his teammates teased him about my partying ways. *Damn, your girl was wasted onstage at that party last night!* Not the best look, even if I never crossed a line. But Mike never confronted me about it, and I took his silence for acceptance instead of tolerance.

Add to this that his party girl was not having sex with him. Somehow everybody knew I was a virgin—perhaps from those previous athletes I briefly dated and rebuffed. Mike was not the stereotypical football player bragging in the locker room about all the women he slept with—another reason why I believed he could do no wrong. Meanwhile, teammates, fraternity brothers, everyone teased him for not getting any. Whenever Mike's skin broke out, they would call them "sex pimples" and say he got them because he wasn't having sex. Despite all the ridicule, he never pressured me to have sex, and his respect for my decision to wait only elevated him in my eyes. What a sharp contrast to my puppy love with Karim, who took someone else to prom because taking me would have ended in a sexless night. I loved Mike for being able to love me for more than my body.

So you're probably thinking, *What happened?* The final straw: I pledged Delta Sigma Theta. The process consumed so much of my attention. The Big Sisters directed my circle of pledges to prioritize learning the ideals, values, and history of the sorority. With a schedule already busy with work and school, learning what it meant to be a Delta left me no time for Mike.

The Big Sisters were the first to tell me about rumors of his flirting with other women on and off campus. At first, I thought they were testing my ability to ignore gossip and remain focused on the pledging process. I downplayed the rumors, but they lingered in the back of my mind. That is, until the girlfriend of Mike's roommate told me that women were coming over to their place. The demand for unity from the sisters on our line meant I couldn't stay over at Mike's place, and I started questioning how my absence was affecting him and what he was doing because of it.

I was overseeing a meeting of the African American Cultural Committee when she called me. "A girl is here right now," she said. I drove in rush-hour traffic to Mike's apartment. I let myself in with the key he gave me, and no one was there.

Still: Where there was smoke, there was fire. Later I gave in to an impulse to go through his phone and found a contact called "Frat." He had many fraternity brothers—none whom he referred to by that nickname. I called the number, and it led to a woman's voicemail. Why was Mike masking this woman's identity on his own phone?

I held my tongue, vacillating between suspecting Mike's behavior and questioning if I were paranoid, until the dean of my line pulled me to the side. The dean was the mother of the line and so I trusted this was not a test. "I don't know if they're actually true," she said. "But I'm hearing things about Mike." I admitted to her that I'd also heard rumors about him cheating on me and about the mysterious girl hiding in plain sight on his phone.

After two years with no concerns, these fresh but persistent misgivings proved to be too much. With no hard proof, I confronted Mike. He confessed to flirting with other women but insisted he had not slept with any of them. I just could not believe him. Since I never cared if he had female friends, he had no reason to hide them from me unless he was crossing the line.

After all, Mike was *not* a virgin.

He had presented himself to me as the dutiful boyfriend who respected my decision to wait, yet behind my back he behaved like any other athlete seeking to put notches on his bedpost. I told Mike I refused to waste any more of my college years in such a relationship where I had to worry every time his phone rang, and I broke up with him. But inside I felt betrayed, disrespected, and embarrassed—especially when I'd never given him reason to question me.

Mike was devastated and begged me to reconsider. For the next two years, he tried to win me back, but I was too heartbroken. From that place of brokenness, I questioned so many things about sex, relationships, and my ability to have the kind of partner I desired. *If the "perfect" guy that I thought could never hurt me can fuck me over, then what can I expect from the rest of these men?* I even began to question God. *Why would You bring this person into my life only for him to break me like this, especially when the only thing I did "wrong" was wait for marriage like the Church taught me?*

Young Rachel could not grasp how much of her self-worth she latched on to her relationship with Mike and being a virgin. So he cheated on me and hurt me deeply. But why didn't I think, *Okay, so he's not so perfect. Or the one for you, so you were right not to give in. Keep the faith and continue to wait for the man who shares your values.* Instead I concluded that being a virgin didn't make me special or worthy of any man's loyalty. In fact, Mike's betrayal left me feeling naive, even foolish. It so punctured my self-confidence that I stopped caring about waiting until marriage to have sex. If the best man I could ever hope to meet could deceive and embarrass me, why save my virginity for anyone? The wait no longer made sense to me.

Plus I still loved Mike. Greek life kept us in the same circles, and I wanted to remain friends. We often crossed paths at events, and Mike took every opportunity to convey how sorry he was that he'd hurt me. In my presence, he remained the perfect gentleman, and time made it harder, rather than easier, to resist him. Hope that the relationship in which I had invested two years was salvageable began to chip away at my pride—a pattern I would come to repeat even when I graduated from puppy love to a mature relationship. But this hope, too, remained rooted in a belief that Mike's desire for me counted more than my own values. Beneath the pride over resisting his overtures lurked a burgeoning need for assurance. *They don't come better than him. And on the off chance that they do, am I worthy? I wasn't enough to keep him faithful, and he's one of the few good ones.* I thought that if I couldn't make it work with him, I might never have a lasting marriage with anyone.

We were still broken up when I had sex for the first time—with Mike, in May 2005. One day, I visited him at his parents' house. I did not go there to sleep with him, and as usual, he didn't put any pressure on me. But somehow things just started, and I remember lying in the bed and thinking, *I don't even care anymore.* That's how broken and vulnerable I was. Everything I had hung my hat on, believed in, put my faith into, was just taken. Despite all my wishful thinking that sex would repair and solidify our bond, I went through with it from a state of unworthiness. More like got it over with. There was nothing romantic about my first time. The magical experience that I had built up in my head—of giving myself to this man whom I loved so much—never transpired. I just stared at the ceiling and thought, *Okay . . . it happened . . . after holding on to it for twenty years.*

After breaking the Rule, I struggled with the emotional aftermath. Growing up I only received a singular message about sex from my parents, church, and school: It is precious . . . but only if you wait for marriage to have it. I had idealized it for years. With my fantasy of the idyllic first time destroyed, I didn't know how to value sex in any other way. I didn't know where to go or whom to talk to or what to believe in. My sexually active friends didn't regard sex with the same reverence I had, so I felt too embarrassed and even intimidated to confide in them. This far surpassed an abstinence poster on my wall. I was experiencing a profound sense of grief that I didn't think they could understand, never mind empathize with. *Girl, just get back on the horse* or *Rach, relax, it really isn't that big of a deal,* I expected them to say. Even if done in the spirit of sisterly teasing or with the intention to lighten my self-judgment, I knew such responses would make me feel worse. And talking to either of my parents? I couldn't imagine going to my mother, who was a virgin herself when she married my father, and saying, "But, Mom, what if I didn't wait like I was supposed to?" The last thing I wanted to do was admit that I had given away my virginity and disappoint them. The lingering emptiness I experienced felt like the punishment I deserved for disobeying the Church.

And then there was my shame. I didn't just have premarital sex. I had given away my virginity to the guy who cheated on me, was no longer my boyfriend, and probably had sex with Frat and God knows how many others.

Having an emotionally disappointing first sexual experience with my ex-boyfriend set me down a different path. My attitude toward sex went from reverential to cavalier. *Whatever.* Not only did I continue to have sex with Mike without becoming a recommitted couple, a month after losing my virginity to him, I met another guy named Rick who lived eight hours away and began a relationship with him. For a while I went back and forth between the two of them, not sexually but emotionally. Mike continued his full-court press, telling me he was focused on church, working on himself, and otherwise saying all the right things. I almost fell for it until I found out he was getting head from the cousin of a girl I was mentoring. (And because the brother just couldn't help himself from being too messy, her name was Rachel, too.) Of course, I recognized that we weren't a couple, and we were both free to do our own thing—I sure was!—but this was more of the unnecessarily deceptive behavior that had hurt me two years earlier. It affirmed my decision to break up with Mike and focus on bad boy Rick. (Who was so bad, he gets his own chapter.)

I began to use sex to fill my physical needs and forwent any desire for emotional connection. There was no love between my sexual partners and me, and that might not have been an issue if I wasn't still craving intimacy and desiring monogamy. And not because any person or institution instilled that yearning in me. Even as I came to understand that my physical need for intercourse was natural, I also knew that my longing for sex to be emotionally fulfilling was just as normal. At times, the chasm between the availability of casual sex and elusiveness of emotional connection caused me so much despair. It wasn't until 2011—six years after my first time—that I first experienced sex that lived up to its promise.

Our society continues to glorify a girl's virginity, despite a growing movement that calls out virginity as a patriarchal concept based on the belief that women's bodies belong to men. This glorification holds true especially in Christian households. Perhaps in response to the racist legacy of U.S. slavery that labeled our girls and women as sexually insatiable and "unrapable," Black Christians participate in this exaltation from a protective stance. The idealization of virginity depends on the repetition of certain myths, such as *If you save it for marriage, your first time will be magical.*

You already know what I'm going to say, and if your first time—whether or not you waited until marriage—was anything but magical, say it with me.

Miss. Me. With. That.

Nobody has an amazing experience the first time. After having sex with Mike, I lay there recounting all the things I was expecting sex to be that it was not. It wasn't magical. It wasn't beautiful. It wasn't euphoric. And not understanding how normal my first experience was—one that I most likely would have had even if I had been married—I beat myself up for a long time wondering, *If I had only waited . . .*

Mighty is the fall from virginity. When you crash-land into reality, no one is there to pick you up. No one helped me gather the broken pieces and put them back together. I had no one to assure me that my choice to have premarital sex did not irrevocably render me damaged goods and incapable of having a great marriage (or that I wasn't going to be struck by lightning). As a young person raised in a strict, religious home, this very human choice left me feeling like the dirtiest person on earth without refuge.

The irony is that no one judged me more harshly than I judged myself. After all, I told almost no one that I had had premarital sex. My family never discusses sex so I never told my mother or my sisters. (Just like you, they're going to find all this out by reading this book. Please pray for me.) The silence around sexuality is so profound that to this day I feel uncomfortable talking about sex as a married woman in her thirties. Having forsaken abstinence after having it drilled into me that it was the *only* way, I managed the disappointment, guilt, and self-imposed shame alone. I dealt with the painful emotions by turning to that bad boy. I turned to partying. I turned to drinking.

I turned every other way instead of back to myself.

Meanwhile, the choice I made to have premarital sex is the common one, so to the folks who still insist that we should promote abstinence among youth, can we make virginity counseling a thing? The way we talk about it is detrimental. If we continue to teach young people to wait until marriage to have sex, we must accept two things. One, many still won't wait, and like me they'll need support in working through the complex emotions that arise once they act upon that decision. Two, some will wait until marriage, but the mere act of waiting has little bearing on the quality of their experience. Not emotionally or physically. Few, if any, will have the idyllic experience on their honeymoon they're being sold, and that, too, results in some difficult feelings. They just might think that something is wrong with them or their partner or their relationship, creating problems early in the marriage that could be avoided. And what's good for the goose is good for the gander. If we truly value the construct of virginity, we must counsel boys and men in equal measure. And until we eradicate sexual violence, we have a responsibility to provide comfort and healing to all the survivors who are robbed of their choice to wait. I am particularly concerned for the one out of four Black girls who will experience sexual assault before the age of eighteen. Regardless of gender, sexual orientation, or circumstances, a young person needs and deserves guidance in navigating this new aspect of their sexuality and finding the way home to themselves.

Sometimes you learn things the hard way, and I'm glad I did, because now I have this story to tell and lesson to share. We talk about sex as if it were a drug. *Stay away . . . you just might like it.* We underestimate that by building up virginity, especially for girls and women, we're encouraging them to idolize both the act of sex and the person with whom they first experience it. I could not prepare for, never mind process, the emotional consequences of losing my virginity in a healthy manner because I never considered any possibilities other than the one scenario I had been taught.

If I do "lose" it before marriage, what happens?
If he isn't perfect, what happens?
If he hurts me or it doesn't work out, what happens?

We *think* we're teaching young people to value their bodies when we instruct them to wait until marriage, when what we're actually doing is reinforcing the belief that other people's opinions about what they do with their bodies should outweigh their own moral compass. They will face a multitude of contradictory messages about whether or not to have sex. Some will call them promiscuous for indulging, while others will label them prudish for abstaining. Such pressures are a projection of those people's beliefs about their own bodies and sexuality.

Therefore, to make decisions based on fear of how others might judge them is neither healthy nor empowering. Whether or not a young person waits, their sexual choices should reflect their own spiritual values and life goals.

It took some time to reframe my decision to have sex as a natural, even understandable, choice. Today I give myself credit for waiting until I was twenty years old. I made the decision with no pressure from anyone else. Being in an emotionally troubled place, I could have chosen to lose my virginity in a way that was random and reckless, but I did not. Perhaps if I had the opportunity to decide again, I would make a different choice, but as far as choices go, I made a very human and adult decision.

Truth be told, despite the dictates of Christianity, I honestly don't believe I made a mistake. Certainly not one worthy of guilt or shame. Humans, not God, impose these judgments on one another. If I did make a mistake, my God forgives me, and if I want to repent, that's another choice I can make.

In fact, after college I spoke to a group of girls at church in a class called Return to Purity (miss me with that title). Upon completing the class, the girls received promise rings and vowed to wait until marriage to have sex. Far more than rings, they needed education, and I volunteered to give them honest answers to their questions about sex the way I wish someone had done for me when I was their age. I admitted to the girls that I was not a virgin, and that *I was okay*. I advised them to do the best they could, understanding that perfection was impossible, and *that was okay*. I went so far as to tell them that there was no correlation between purity and perfection, so if by any chance they did stumble and have premarital sex, *that was okay*. They could always get back on track.

To this day I recognize the continued repercussions of my relationship with Mike and my first sexual experience. This is the only time in my life I recall having such high expectations and being so deeply let down. For better or worse, it has stayed with me and influences my approach to all areas of my life. As a result, I never count my eggs before they hatch. I see multiple possibilities in any situation. I am always preparing for the worst while praying for the best. Because of this, some people describe me as negative.

I call it being realistic.

What I want for you—or any daughter you might have—to learn from my experience is this: Never place so much of your value into anyone or anything outside of yourself. Not a love interest. Not an idea. Certainly not a fantasy. My self-worth was wrapped up with "saving myself" for marriage, and I became so lost when things didn't happen the way I was told they should. Don't do this to yourself, and don't do this to your daughter. Even as you communicate your values to her and point her in a certain direction, also tell her this truth: She *does* have choices.

This is what I intend to do with mine.

GIVING UP THE GHOST

I hate how much I love you but I just can't let you go.
—from "Hate That I Love You,"
sung by Rihanna, lyrics by Ne-Yo and Stargate

Most women have a story about getting caught up with someone who ghosts them. Often the person of interest disappears before the enthusiastic text exchanges can lead to a date or after a night of passion they never intended to be a one-night stand. In other words, the period of interaction tends to be short-lived, but who gets ghosted after four years of dating someone in another state?

I do, and that's not even the twist to this story.

Why not just give in to temptation and get with the bad boy? That was my twenty-year-old logic after breaking up with Mike. I'd lost my virginity to him in May and met Rick through my friend Twin that June. I went from infatuation to obsession. Like Mike, Rick played football and was an Omega, but the similarities ended there. He was a star player with all the special treatment that entails. No responsibilities except to train and play, any questionable behavior swept under the rug. Rick's magnetism existed in the stratosphere. He was good-looking and funny, and every Delta across the land knew who Rick was: that big, fine yellow Omega!

Rick attended college in another state, but his family was from Dallas, where I usually saw him. However, I crisscrossed the state for that man—Austin, Houston, Waco. I went to his football games in Texas, and together we attended Black Greek events and other parties where professional players made appearances and sports agents courted him. Rick and I spent the Christmas holidays and spring breaks together. Although popular in my own right, being on Rick's arm elevated my social status in Dallas to new heights. We drove up to events in his Crown Victoria like royalty.

And not once did Rick ever ask me to be his girlfriend. Still, out of naivete or ego, I convinced myself that we were exclusive. Twin never told me Rick cheated on me. He may have warned me to watch my back or guard my heart. You know the meme that goes *Yeah, he's a player, but I want to be the girl that makes him hang up his jersey and quit the game*? That was me. I couldn't get enough of him.

Maybe I underestimated my obsession with Rick because I was still communicating with Mike. I didn't intend to be messy, but with these men being callous with your girl's feelings, I quickly became comfortable with allowing my "boyfriends" to overlap. Big Rach preferred to have one man in her back pocket before letting the previous one go, and the breaks were rarely clean. To quote Jay-Z, "They say you can't turn a bad girl good but once a good girl's gone bad, she's gone forever." I probably believed that not being a one-guy gal would keep my feelings for any single man in check.

During one of Rick's trips to visit his family, Mike also happened to be in Dallas. I kept dodging Mike's attempts to see me. After all, we were no longer together, and before making the four-hour trip back to school, Rick was swinging by my friend Brooke's place to say goodbye to me. (See . . . sometimes your girl does make a genuine effort to avoid the messiness, but then all I had to do was stop taking Mike's calls and giving him my whereabouts.) No sooner had Rick kissed me and driven off did I get a call from Mike.

He announced he was on his way to Brooke's because he needed to get something. With Rick gone, I was eager to get this over with. I hung up and waited outside for Mike.

He drove up to Brooke's home and barreled out of his car. As he trudged up the driveway, his eyes were fixed on the necklace that he gave me while we were dating. Obviously, I never returned it and continued to wear it. I mean, it wasn't an engagement ring.

"I saw you kiss him," Mike said. Then he reached out, grabbed the necklace, and ripped it off me. I stood there shaking in disbelief as I watched Mike storm off, the necklace dangling in his grip. I ran back into Brooke's home to tell her and her mother what had just happened.

They were alarmed. "Do we need to do something about this?" Brooke's mom said. With that simple question, she was asking if Mike had ever done anything like this before and if I feared that his behavior might escalate.

Even as I share this story, I feel a resistance to call it what it was: violence. But my reluctance only confirms why I must tell you about it. Especially given how I handled it. Because Mike had never put his hands on me before that moment, I convinced myself that he would never do it again. In fact, I rationalized what he did. "No, he's just upset," I said. This shocking behavior left me feeling both violated and culpable. On the one hand, how dare Mike act so aggressively toward me? On the other hand, did I provoke him out of his sweet character? I begged Brooke's mom not to tell my parents. I needed to forget the incident ever occurred and protect their image of Mike, whom they liked so much. And siccing the authorities on a Black man was unthinkable to me.

Meanwhile, my parents never liked Rick. I thought, *Parents just don't understand,* but, oh, they understood exactly who ol'

Rick was. Knowing me and learning from my relationship with Karim, they never prohibited me from dating Rick. That would just inspire me to double down, make it work, and prove them wrong about us. Instead Mom and Dad left me to make my own bed once they made it clear that they did not trust whoever might be in it.

The next flag appeared about a year into our relationship. That April Rick became preoccupied with my birth control. Despite feeling annoyed and suspicious, I never questioned his fixation and assured him I was on top of contraception. My feminine intuition said, *Girl, he had a pregnancy scare with someone else. Or an STD. Or both.*

And my infatuation said, *You hush now.*

Then his usually warm parents turned cold on me. That November I approached Rick's family after one of his games in Austin, and instead of hugging me, his mom could barely spare a hello. *Is she . . . giving me the side-eye?*

The truth came out as some friends and I planned our first New Year's Eve party. Before we party, we must church, so I went to pray for anticipatory forgiveness for the debauchery ahead. (Just kidding. I always attend church on December 31 to get my mind and spirit right for the New Year.) In the church balcony, I caught up with Twin about friends who were home for the holidays.

"Man, everybody has a baby now," he said.

"Not everybody, Twin. You don't have any kids," I said. "And Rick doesn't have any kids."

He blinked at me then chuckled in disbelief. "Are you crazy?"

The revelation did not click. "You're kidding." Twin's a jokester. He had to be playing with me. "Rick doesn't have any kids," I said. I could begrudgingly imagine Rick having another girlfriend, but a baby? No way he would father a child while we were together, never mind not tell me.

Girl, you already know . . .

Twin sighed and motioned for me to follow him into the church foyer. Once out of earshot from our fellow congregants, he called Rick and put him on speakerphone. "Hey, what are you doing?"

"Oh, I'm just at the mall," said Rick, nonchalant AF. "You know, with my baby and my baby mama."

Don't ask me how I held it together; hold it together is what I always did. At least, long enough to drive home, run upstairs, and fling myself on my bed. I cried as if I intended to flood the house. I felt so gutted, I lost track of time. Then I sat up and wiped the tears off my cheeks. I had to pull myself together. Not only did I not want my parents to know, I had to show up for our New Year's Eve party at the Fairmont Hotel.

It was epic. We'd expected forty guests when hundreds filed into the lobby. The hotel shut it down but not before Big Rach got drunk, roaming the suite with red cup in hand, pretending to be unbothered while dying inside.

When I finally confronted Rick, he confessed. His skittish behavior in April was on the heels of learning that his ex-girlfriend Goldie was pregnant. He rushed to remind me that he slept with her during a six-week break we had. His daughter was born two days before his mother snubbed me after his game. Meanwhile, I had stayed with Rick at his hotel the previous night and attributed the fact that we didn't have sex to pregame superstition!

The math added up but provided little consolation. Bottom line, Rick had no excuse whatsoever for hiding the pregnancy and his daughter for almost a year. "I was going to tell you, but I didn't know how," said Rick. He claimed to have written me a letter he could never bring himself to give me out of fear of losing me. He promised he'd slept with Goldie only once. And like the Black Ross Geller, he reminded me, *We were on a break!*

So what did Rachel do?

She took Rick back.

I know what you guys are thinking. *Not Big Rach!* But when I say I was obsessed with this guy, I am not exaggerating. I was so *Rickmatized* I chided myself for being angry with him for getting it in with his ex-girlfriend when we were technically not together. *How could this dog keep this pregnancy from you* became *Wow, Rick cares for you so much, imagine how hard it was for him to not tell you the truth! He figured it'd be so much easier to keep it a secret and didn't realize how problematic that was. Rick loves you so much he didn't want to tell you the truth and hurt you.*

I'm telling you . . . *Rickmatized!*

All I demanded from Rick was that he no longer be with Goldie. And of course he assured me that being a good father to his daughter did not entail being a partner to her mother. *All right. If there's nothing going on, fine.* I even respected Rick for stepping up to his responsibilities as a parent.

For a spell I withheld the news of Rick's child from my parents, who made it easy by never asking about him. At some point, however, I dropped the fact that he had a daughter in a casual conversation with my parents. The response was *Hmmm . . . okay . . . noted.* I continued to see him, and they continued to wait for me to accept he was a dog and be done with him. And prayed. They probably prayed a lot.

Rick's parents were another story. He had begun playing professional football, and one time at his agent's house, Rick's father confronted me. The irony is that we were watching *The Maury Povich*

Show just as he was informing an anxious guest, "You ARE the father!" Maury just might have inspired Rick's father. Or maybe he was just waiting to be alone with me to tell me how he felt about my continuing to date his son. No sooner had Rick disappeared to take a shower did he turn to me and say, "You know a family should be together, right? That's what I did for his mom. I didn't love her when I got her pregnant, but I stayed with her because it was the right thing to do."

He basically told me to get the fuck out of his son's life. At the time, I was so hurt because I felt close to Rick's father, but today? He should have missed me with his attempts to shame me as if Rick was not an adult making the choice to have a relationship with me. But younger Rachel just fidgeted on the sofa and held her tongue because she was raised to respect her elders. "He needs to be with his baby mama like I did, and you're a distraction."

Then my hurt was compounded by confusion. Why would his father say this to me if Rick was no longer involved with Goldie? Later when I told Rick about his father's lashing, he waved it off. "I can't believe he said that to you! He's trippin'." In the moment, I found his comfort validating, especially when I was planning to leave for law school soon. There's this saying about law school—the first year they scare you to death, the second year they work you to death, and in the last year they bore you to death. Some even say the first year is designed to make students drop out. Between moving to a new city where I had no friends or family and facing the most challenging academic experience of my life, I could not stomach the idea of also going through a breakup (if that's even the right word for ending whatever it was that we had). "You don't worry about that," he said. "That's not how I feel." So I continued to see Rick through my first year of law school. (In hindsight, I realize he gave me nothing, which pretty much defined our entire four on-and-off years together.)

God made another attempt to stage an intervention during the holiday season like He was intent on preventing me from carrying this futile relationship into another New Year. I started getting calls from unknown numbers. Finally, a woman called me and asked for someone with a different name. "You have the wrong number," I said. I lingered, sensing that the conversation was only beginning.

Eventually the woman revealed herself, and yes, it was Goldie. "Are you dating Rick? Like, are y'all boyfriend and girlfriend? Or are y'all just fucking?"

I was livid. One, she had my number. Two, she had the audacity to call me. Three, clearly there was something going on between Goldie and Rick if she even would want to call me. She admitted to waiting for Rick to fall asleep to go through his phone. Then she waited until he actually left her to call me.

"All of the above," I said hotly. "All. Of the. Above." *If you're bold enough to call me, then I'm bold enough to hit you with this truth for the one time.* "Any further questions?" I snapped. We went back and forth on the phone about whom Rick was seeing as if he weren't playing us both. In the moment, I thought, *The audacity!* But in hindsight, I recognize Goldie's vulnerability. What my younger self read as brazen, my older self understands as desperate. Goldie was fighting for her family. The family Rick convinced her he also wanted while assuring me that he loved me and could not bear to lose me. For a year he swore to each of us that he was done with the other.

Rick got upset when I told him about my argument with Goldie . . . *with me!* She was threatening to put him on child support. Now that Goldie knew Rick was still seeing me, she would make him pay. Literally.

Rick and I were never the same after I discovered he was carrying on with Goldie, but I wouldn't move on and give a serious relationship with someone else a chance. I'd date other people but missed the high I had with Rick. One time I abandoned a sweetheart of a guy in the middle of a date when Rick called me to hang out. That was the life I was living. I could date someone else—someone great—but if Rick called, I was out. I'd stop seeing him for spells only to resume (albeit with my guard up), hoping that the dog would change his coat.

Rick once drove me to a park, where I read him a letter. I had to work through my feelings and desires in writing first because I knew once I was in front of him, my emotions would swallow my words. Sure enough, I began to cry. "I need to know if this is real and how you feel about me," I sobbed as I read. "If you want me the same way I want you, can we just put a title on this? I have to know where this is going." Rick sat emotionless. Then he did what he always had throughout our relationship through my graduating college, doing a summer internship with the NBA in NYC, and even starting law school in Wisconsin in 2008. Rick said he cared for me. Even that he loved me. But he refused to assure me that we were in a monogamous relationship, never mind had a future together.

After a near-death experience in 2009, Rick ghosted me. While he was driving under the influence, his prized Crown Victoria slid under an eighteen-wheeler. The truck ripped off the roof of his car. If Rick had not grabbed his sleeping passenger and thrown him to the floor seconds before the shred, his passenger would not have survived. I have never had a near-death experience, but I can imagine that it changes you. You reevaluate your life, recognize what is important, and change your priorities. That summer I finished my first year of law school and stayed with my grandmother in Houston while completing a sports law internship at a local university. I called Rick, but his number had changed. At first, I thought I had made a mistake. After fifteen attempts (a conservative estimate), reality sank in.

Rick had ghosted me.

Rick ghosted me before it even had a name! That made his disappearance that much more humiliating. To be such an integral part of my life only to vanish like Casper the Friendly Ghost. I felt a mixture of rage and relief. How could he date me for four years then disappear on me the way dudes creep out after love-bombing their way into a one-night stand or go silent after a few text messages on a dating app? As if I meant nothing to him. But beneath the anger was the relief. We were wrong for each other, and he had the courage to do what I could not. Had I run into Rick a week after he ghosted me, we would have gotten back together. Neither one of us could let a breakup stand.

I started a relationship with a guy I met during my internship but could not escape the gnaw of my unfinished business with Rick. Uncertainty can hinder your growth as a person, and in this particular situation, the lack of closure held me captive. Not understanding why the relationship ended, I remained trapped in the past and unable to move forward.

I was still Rickmatized by his ghost!

Ghosting is not a new phenomenon, and people who do it may not intend to cause harm, but social psychologists now confirm how it negatively impacts the other person's well-being. "Ghosting is the ultimate use of the silent treatment, a tactic that has often been viewed by mental health professionals as a form of emotional cruelty," wrote Dr. Jennice Vilhauer for *Psychology Today*. "It essentially renders you powerless and leaves you with no opportunity to ask questions or be provided with information that would help you emotionally process the experience. It silences you and prevents you from expressing your emotions and being heard, which is important for maintaining your self-esteem."

Two years after Rick's disappearance, someone told me that they saw him working at a club as a bouncer. I gathered a couple of girlfriends whom he also knew, and we headed to the club. And when Rick and I saw each other, we did the reunion bop. You know . . . that dance you do when you run into an old friend and you're excited to see each other. You gasp in surprise, covering your mouth with one hand and pointing with the other. Then you run circles around each other like happy puppies. Finally, you embrace, and as you squeeze each other, you realize, man, you've missed this person! Not the relationship you had but who they are.

"Listen. We've got to talk," I said. "It's been two years."

"When I get off, I'm going to hit y'all up," he said.

I let him know where I was staying with my friend, never expecting him to follow through. To my surprise, he showed. I got into his car, and we talked. Rick admitted that he came to agree with his father. While he knew ghosting was a terrible thing to do to me, he also knew that if he faced me, he would not follow through on the commitment he made to create a family with Goldie and his daughter. Disappearing was far from ideal, but anything but a clean break between us would be far more painful for everyone involved.

And Rick was right. We were addicted to each other and trapped in a toxic cycle. Deceiving me about his daughter's conception and birth, getting the cold shoulder from his mother, and being confronted by both his father and Goldie . . . none of it shamed me. That night in the park several years prior, I'd delivered an ultimatum, threatening to walk if he didn't commit to me. He balked, and I settled. After all my doubling down on our relationship, he disappeared, and I made no attempt to chase him. Ghosting proved to be the final humiliation, and I finally forced myself to move on.

With that matter resolved, Rick and I caught each other up on our lives. He told me about Goldie and his daughter, and I mentioned that I was seeing someone. We talked until the sun came up, letting our past fade into the night. No sparks flew or lines were crossed, but I remembered why I fell for him. Still, time had passed, and I was no longer that infatuated girl. And yet I so appreciated that conversation. Part of why I felt so embarrassed and bereft when Rick disappeared was that ghosting had yet to be recognized widely as a common, albeit dysfunctional, phenomenon. I took his evaporation from my life very personally. After dating for quite some time, Rick's lack of commitment did not render our relationship casual. But when I learned he was working at that club, pride almost squashed the impulse to go see him. It told me, *Fuck him. You don't need that.* But I did need something. To know what happened and why. The passage of time and the maturity that came with it gave me the courage to know, and I was able to receive the closure that few people who are ghosted get.

My attraction to Rick was based on superficial things. I would brag about being with him, and I spent far more time describing how our relationship appeared than any depth we had between us. *That Coleman Love. Campus couple. Prom king and queen.* Even though Rick never defined our relationship, I was hooked on the way it defined me. Instead of directing the relationship, I let the relationship direct me, making reckless decisions and doing things outside of my character (like sass the mother of his child and abandon a guy who was nothing but kind to me). My involvement with Rick epitomized the difference between obsession and love. Obsession fills you with anxiety—each person relying on the other person's presence to feel grounded. Love, however, keeps you centered in your partner's absence. You miss them because you want to be with them, not because you cannot stand being without them.

Rick and I never dated again, but we remained in communication and occasionally hung out with mutual friends. When he proposed to Goldie, he showed me the ring. They now have three daughters, and Rick has sent me their pictures. (*Three daughters.* This always makes me laugh. They call that karma, homeboy.)

The full-circle moment came when I told this story at an audition. The gig was to cohost an MTV show called *Ghosted.* When I landed the job, I called Rick. "All things happen for a reason," I said. "Thanks for doing me dirty. It got me this show."

If a conversation is a safe possibility (and by safe, I don't mean to your ego, because that's not how love works), you should always have one. However, I empathize with how challenging it can be to communicate when your heart is on the line. It already requires time and effort to cultivate a self-awareness that allows you to be honest with yourself about what you need and desire in an intimate partnership. And then it takes both courage and practice to communicate those wants and needs to the person you're dating, who has wants and needs of their own.

So, miss me with that ghosting. In fact, let it miss you. Ghosting is the easy way out, and if the person you're interested in prefers emotional shortcuts, the best thing to do when they take the one closest to the door is to thank them. When the ghost gets going, let the ghost stay gone.

RATIO DECIDENDI

Success is only meaningful and enjoyable if it feels like your own.
—Michelle Obama

Growing up, I was a goody two-shoes, toeing the line yet looking forward to having more autonomy once I graduated from high school. I applied to only four colleges, each for a different reason. As you know, I applied to Spelman but ultimately chose to attend UT Austin like my parents. (Have we noticed the pattern?) However, I also applied to Howard University and NYU. My boyfriend at the time was attending Howard, but I promise you puppy love was just a bonus and not my main reason for applying. In addition to being a historically Black college, Howard is in Washington, D.C.—a Black metropolis. Of course, my parents thought I wanted to follow my boyfriend, and since they were footing the bill, they nixed that idea. However, I took their decision in stride because my heart was set on going to college in the Big Apple.

After spending twelve years in a privileged, parochial Christian bubble, I was yearning to experience more of the world, and what better place to do that than NYC? When I fantasized about attending college there, I always saw myself thriving. During my senior year, my mom and I took a trip to New York City, and I immediately fell in love with everything about it. The things that often intimidate people—the pace, the noise, the smell—hooked me. Mom and I went to all the touristy locations like Times Square and the Empire State Building, but even the smallest things fascinated me, from eating a Sabrett hot dog from a street vendor to taking in the massive billboards. I even tried to pretend that I was from New York, and you couldn't tell Big Rach she didn't blend in with the native New Yorkers with her denim fit, Chucks, and pageboy hat. (Somehow the foam Statue of Liberty crown and Texas accent kept giving me away.) Every minute in Manhattan, including my visit to NYU to meet with a professor, deepened my craving for the concrete jungle. When I found out that NYU had accepted me, I was ecstatic.

"That's great, Rachel, but who do you know in New York City?" Mom said. "Because we're not sending you there by yourself. Not two years after 9/11." Attending NYU and living in New York City was prohibitively expensive without a scholarship, but I now understand how fearful my parents must have been about my leaving the only home I had ever known to live in a huge city where I had no family. At the time, however, I cried for weeks over my parents' refusal to allow me to attend the school of my first choice. It might as well have been the end of the world. I had gotten a taste of a new reality only for it to evaporate in a few sentences. However, I have no regrets over attending UT Austin; those four years proved to be among the best of my life.

When I enrolled at UT Austin, however, I didn't know what I wanted to do other than practice law. I didn't even know what kind of law, so I chose to major in government. It bored me to tears. And once I became old enough to take the steps toward becoming an attorney, I learned what it truly entailed. While in college I spent my summer interning at a law firm as a receptionist. It involved a lot of paperwork. A lot of research. A lot of plant watering. Not what they did on *Matlock*.

One of my dad's good friends was the Honorable Ron Kirk—attorney-at-law, mayor of Dallas, the first African American to serve as the U.S. Trade Representative, under the Obama administration. "You don't want to be a lawyer, Rachel," Ron once said to me. "You can make way more money as a businesswoman."

I was already grappling with doubts, and Ron's advice raised more questions for me. At one time, I found the courage to broach the topic with my father. "Daddy, Ron Kirk says I shouldn't go to law school," I said.

"Ron's an attorney," my father said. "Don't listen to him."

And rather than ask Dad why Ron would say that, I retreated back into that little girl who wants to please her father. *Don't push. Just do what Daddy says.*

As college exposed me to new people and fields, my genuine interests became evident. The most profound eye-opener came when I was having a conversation with another student after my government class. We were walking through campus and he began telling me about a class he was taking. This class made me realize it was possible to combine my favorite pastime with my career goals. Between my love of sports and knack for communication, I decided to switch to sports management. It encompassed business, public relations, finance, all with sports as the foundation. I ate up the variety this major had to offer.

For most college students, changing their major is nothing more than a trip to the bursar's office. Rachel Lindsay had to get her parents' permission. When I drummed up the courage to tell my father that I wanted to change my major, he directed me to make my case. And like a teenage attorney, I spent hours preparing, which included meeting with an adviser in the sports management program and designing a PowerPoint presentation. (I see what you did there, Dad.) I delivered it after dinner at the kitchen table as my father sat in his chair, arms folded across his chest. I clicked through slides outlining the benefits of the program and opportunities in the field. I described the core classes and internship requirements. With Dad footing the bill for college, however, there was no way I could tell him that I was not going to follow in his footsteps and become a practicing attorney. Law school does not require specific majors—you can get accepted with a degree in any field—but that was not enough of an argument for my father. Therefore, the key point of my presentation was to convince Dad that a sports management major would still allow me to pursue a legal career.

My presentation was successful, my father gave me his blessing to change my major, and I threw myself into the sports management program at my college. I especially enjoyed working for the University of Texas athletics department because the gig involved writing. I interviewed athletes across gender and sports, like the women's basketball and track teams. I also kept and compiled stats for players on the baseball, rowing, and soccer teams. Whether in my university's athletics department or a company off campus, I hustled for one sports-related job after the next to build my résumé. I found a website that listed openings in the industry and submitted dozens of applications.

The sports management program also required an internship for graduation, and after applying for hundreds of positions, I scored the one of my dreams. A program called NBA University called me for an interview. One of my interviewers was a woman who said, "Your résumé stood out to me for many reasons. One is that you're a Delta. So am I." Although I had heard about the power of networking, it still floored me how that affiliation could help me land a job. Four years after having my New York City dreams dashed, I was going to spend the summer in the Big Apple working for the National Basketball Association. And this time not only did my parents approve, they told me to go for it!

So I flew to New York City by myself and found a place to stay on—of all places—Craigslist. The place was a three-story house in North Bergen, New Jersey. I shared the first floor with my roommate Karen, and she was nothing like the Karens we love to hate these days. She was dynamic, talented, and so welcoming. She babysat during the day and starred in off-Broadway shows at night. Our schedules didn't match, but sometimes our paths crossed on the weekends, when we would catch up over breakfast and dinner. I loved my summer home. It had a view of the New York City skyline, and I could hop on a shuttle that took me straight to the Port Authority terminal. For the most part, I worked from the Secaucus office in New Jersey, but sometimes work brought me to Madison Avenue in the Big City.

Between the work and my community, the summer of 2007 was one of the best in my life. At the NBA league office, I worked in the sports and attractions unit, where we handled community relations and organized NBA events up and down the northeastern corridor. One day we might bring in players to run drills and contests at South Street Seaport in Manhattan, and the following weekend we'd head to Washington, D.C., to promote the WNBA All-Star Game. We once traveled to Philly to set up the NBA All-

Star Experience. I enjoyed every minute of it. The icing on the cake was that so many of my good friends from Texas also moved to the New York City area. That summer I had two homies drafted to play professionally in New York City—one to the New York Liberty and the other to the New York Giants. Another homeboy had an internship at Sony. Between sporting and music events, my social card was full. I'd have a blast with my coworkers during the day (as the intern they called me the Rook) and then meet my friends for a night on the town.

My colleagues at NBA University liked me so much, they offered me a job. I did the math and was crushed. At the salary offered, living in New York City would have been a major struggle. I loved my work with the league, and the offer was a dream come true. But I worried about how little the job paid . . . and what my father would think. And I felt that if I did not get a legal education, I would regret it—as a potential employee and as a daughter. I made a vow to myself a long time ago to not live a life of what-ifs.

When I worked for a marketing firm in Austin, I discovered how much I enjoyed talking with people. Whether marketing or public relations, communications lit me up. While working at the firm, I met a UT alum whom I still consider a mentor. He told me about the sports law program at Marquette University in Milwaukee. I had never heard of it before and researched it. Marquette boasted the best sports law program in the country. Students had access to internships with organizations such as the NCAA and the U.S. Olympic Committee and corporations like Nike. Alumni landed positions in major sports leagues and conferences as well as specific teams, from the Oakland Raiders to the Orlando Magic. Best of all, I would not have to submit an additional application to enroll in the sports law program. If I gained acceptance into the law school, the program would be available to me.

For some reason, when the time came for me to take the Law School Admission Test, it wasn't being offered in Dallas. Instead I registered for it in the closest city—San Antonio—which would also give me the opportunity to spend the weekend with my uncle Larry and my aunt Gloria (of whom I'm the spitting image, may God rest her soul). I packed up all my test materials and planned it all out.

Or so I thought.

Nervous and early, I arrived at the test center. The proctor asked for identification, and I handed her my college ID. She inspected it. "What's this?" she scoffed.

"My student ID." I didn't see the problem.

She smirked at me. "It doesn't have a signature on the back." The proctor flipped the card over and slapped it on the table like a blackjack dealer.

"Okay . . ." I still didn't see the issue. I opened my pocketbook to find a pen. "I'll sign it now."

She shook her head and shoved the card toward me. "No, you need a government ID with a current photo and a signature on the back."

In other words, something like a driver's license. The one in my wallet had expired. Meanwhile, I had lent my valid license to a friend so she could drink and had forgotten to get it back from her before I left Austin for San Antonio.

What an auspicious start to my legal career.

I usually can talk my way into anything. Not this time. In short order, the proctor expelled me from the test center. After studying for two months (when Rick wasn't a distraction) and traveling one hundred miles to take the LSAT, I was blocked because of an impulsive decision that thousands of American young adults make every day.

I was so upset, I could barely walk. I don't know how I made it back to my uncle and aunt's house. Surprised to see me, my uncle met me in the driveway. "How are you home already?"

I burst into tears then confessed. "How am I going to tell my parents that I couldn't take the LSAT?"

I ultimately lied. *I had to!* (Well, they know the truth now . . . by reading this book.) I told them that I could not find my license and that they would not accept my student ID. My father was livid, but not with me. He couldn't believe they wouldn't let me take the test. Dad's support, encouragement, and righteous anger just added to my guilt.

I got off the phone, ran to my guest room, and cried all day. Knowing that I could reregister to take the LSAT a few months later did nothing to soothe my guilt and embarrassment since everyone knew I was taking the test. Later that evening my uncle knocked on the door. I sat up from my tear-soaked pillow ready to pass on dinner, and not because, just like me, Aunt Gloria couldn't care less about cooking.

"Freshen up because we have to leave soon."

"Leave?" While I didn't want to disrespect my family's hospitality, the last thing I wanted to do was go anywhere or see anyone. "Where are we going?"

"We've got tickets to the Spurs game tonight," said my uncle, "and we're going to use 'em."

Knowing how much I loved sports, Aunt Gloria and Uncle Larry had cooked up tickets in advance of my trip. They genuinely felt no need to punish me for lending my friend my driver's license. According to my uncle, my aunt and he were satisfied that being unable to take the LSAT was a sufficient consequence for my youthful mistake.

And just like that, my endless tears evaporated. The moral of this story is clear. Be prepared, don't take shortcuts, and if things still don't work out as you planned, the world doesn't end. You might even get to go to the Spurs game. Just kidding. Sort of.

My challenges in applying to law school, however, were not over. I have only shared with a few people that I took the LSAT twice. The first time I received a low score and failed to get into my top-choice law schools. Not enthusiastic about my options, when I returned to Texas after my NYC internship, I chose to take a year off to focus on studying for the LSAT and improving my score.

That year I worked as a substitute teacher in the Duncanville Independent School District. They initially placed me in a high school algebra class, and I was so excited because I love math. Upon my entering the building, however, a school officer mistook me for a student and tried to ship me to the principal's office for being out of uniform. I told him, "Oh, I'll go to the principal because I'm actually here to teach." Think about it. I was only twenty-two, and some of these kids were seventeen, eighteen. The students also thought I was one of them, and the boys hit on me. *Yo, who's that? Ms. Jackson's substitute?!? She fine!* I was done when one kid tried to give me his number. That lasted one day.

Middle school was even worse. Remember that scene in *Sister Act 2* when Whoopi Goldberg is excited for the first day of music class only for the kids to act out? They're yelling that they don't have to listen to her, throwing things at her, drumming beats on the table. That was me. When people ask me what subject I was supposed to be teaching, I can't remember because I quit so quickly. "I wasn't teaching anything," I say, "but the subject was disrespect." My middle school teaching career lasted forty-five minutes.

Grades K through four proved to be my sweet spot. Sadly, I was filling in for the students' PE teacher, who needed someone to take over her third grade class because she was fighting cancer. The kids and I hit it off, and I ended up staying with them for the entire year, helping them pass their annual physical tests. I became their teacher, with all that entailed—parent–teacher meetings, mentoring moments, trips to the principal's office. But they liked me and gave me the honor of getting to know them. While I remained committed to becoming an attorney, I experienced firsthand what teachers mean when they claim that their students changed their lives. I came to their school under the pretense of changing *their* lives, but through their innocence, light, and resilience, they changed mine. So much so that my students became the subject of one of my law school application essays.

The work experience helped my law school application, as did the additional test preparation. With my better test score, I changed my admission strategy. I applied to a new round of schools based specifically on my interest in sports and entertainment, although Marquette remained my top choice. I also applied for scholarships. Not only was I admitted into Marquette, the school offered me a small scholarship. So off I went to Milwaukee, Wisconsin—a place I never thought I would be.

I liked almost nothing about the first year of law school, including Milwaukee. The stark contrast with everything I knew overwhelmed me. At law school, they overwork you, and much of the work lacks a distinct purpose. And it engulfs you, because you're inundated with your studies and yet no one teaches you *how* to study. In fact, you're bombarded with a lot of conflicting information. Meanwhile, your classes have no bearing on your specific interests in the law or your goals as an attorney, because you have no choice. The classes, the exams, the Socratic method—they could have missed me with all of it.

In the second year of law school, you can choose your coursework, exploring various things and choosing a specialization. The third year can be a waste of time unless you're smart about it. I chose to be strategic, working for the public defender's office in Milwaukee County, spending time in jails, participating in revocation and bail hearings. With my legal career foremost in my mind, I was always thinking a step ahead. *Which class should I take to prepare for the Texas bar exam? What work will help me land that internship? Who should I be sending my résumé to?*

While in law school, I wanted to work for a law firm that represented players or teams where I could focus on marketing or sponsorships. (I ultimately worked at a municipal firm, which I will explain shortly.) As a law student, I interned at the National Sports Law Institute. On the first day of law school, I walked right up to the associate director of NSLI, Paul Anderson, and told him that he needed to know me, and I had to work for him. After all, I did not move all the way to Milwaukee to waste time or play games. To this day, Professor Anderson loves to tell that story when I return to speak to law students. We remain close friends, and I am grateful to him for hiring me and giving me so many opportunities. Based on my work with the NSLI and my grades, I eventually landed a dream legal internship with the Milwaukee Bucks. My responsibilities included working on sponsorship agreements, endorsement deals, intellectual property, and even labor relations, and I loved it all. I would have jumped at the opportunity to work for them, but with only two attorneys in the entire group, there was no job to be had.

Having a clear idea of what kind of work to pursue, I found a directory of agencies and firms at the NSLI and sent my cover letter and résumé everywhere I could. I'm talking printed documents tucked into manila envelopes, each individually addressed to every place of business. I must have sent at least a hundred packages.

I had no idea how hard it would be to break in. Not one responded. Not once. Not even a perfunctory *We'll keep your résumé on file should an opportunity arise . . .*

The following summer I lived with my parents in Dallas and worked at Brown & Hofmeister, LLP. The firm specialized in municipal law and mostly represented government entities outside of the city of Dallas. Upon my graduation from law school, they offered me my first job as a lawyer even as I awaited my results from the Texas bar exam. I was on track to having the career my parents hoped for me.

In retrospect I recognize that although my parents had these expectations, much of the pressure I felt was self-imposed. My father genuinely believed following in his footsteps was in my best interest and would make me happy, and I wanted to make *him* happy. Yet working in sports made *me* happy. It would take several jobs throughout my twenties—and a volunteer stint as a reality TV show contestant in my early thirties—to figure out what I wanted and follow my heart.

In other words, creating a fulfilling career is a lot like finding a life partner.

YOU SAY HE'S JUST
A FRIEND

Men and women can absolutely be friends, and that's what we need to be.
Part of the problem is that we aren't friends enough. Our relationships are
negotiations, and that is not friendship.

—Hill Harper

I wasn't going to write about the boyfriend I had throughout law school. *That wasn't a significant relationship,* I tried to convince myself. But then I remembered the price I paid to maintain this seemingly insignificant relationship, and it's one I never want you to pay.

My first semester of law school was very difficult for me. It began with a culture shock that spiraled into depression (although at the time I did not know it). Moving from Texas to Wisconsin was like living on a different planet. The weather was overcast and cold. I left my car at home because I was too afraid to drive amid the black ice, and public transportation proved to be as gloomy as the weather. We lost daylight much too early. The food was bland, and I didn't know how to cook, so I ate the same thing every day. I gained weight. I'd go to class, return to my tiny room, and sit alone for hours, doing my work and watching TV. Whether to study or socialize, I had to force myself to go out with my classmates. That first semester I became a shell of myself.

Worst of all, I suffered in silence. When I called home, I would tell my mother that I didn't enjoy law school and didn't see myself practicing law forever. But unaware of my own anguish, I never conveyed how miserable I was. While I knew I was unhappy, I chalked it up to not having adjusted to a radically different environment or finding my tribe. I was spending the bulk of my days doing things I disliked.

Every student in a new academic environment must find their way, and this takes time, but I had some additional hurdles. In addition to moving to a new city where I knew no one, my class had fewer than ten Black people, and only one of them was a man. The first woman I gravitated toward hailed from Milwaukee, and she took me under her wing. But then we had a falling-out at a New Year's Eve party in New York City, and I was back at square one.

I made a concerted effort to bond with my white classmates. I found the first group I rolled with because we would study together and go out, but I didn't feel like a peer. Their conversations with me rarely referenced our legal studies or our experience of law school. Instead many of them viewed me purely in a social context, and I often stomached some problematic behavior. Few had Black friends, and they acted as if they became cool by being adjacent to me. They were impressed that many of my friends from Texas were professional athletes. And then there were the men I mentioned earlier who were interested in dating me for the wrong reason.

And because Rach is gonna Rach, I found my footing in the second semester by wilding out. In the few free hours I had, I went to extremes to find any joy off campus. A friend from Houston introduced me to an older man in Milwaukee because his daughter was interested in law school. This gentleman owned a dealership and, I soon suspected, some other "enterprises," because he had the keys to the city. When I hung out with his daughter, no facet of Milwaukee's nightlife was off-limits. If she and I went into a club, we cut the long lines, got free drinks, and sat in the VIP section.

That second term I went from hanging out in bars with my white classmates to entrenching myself in Milwaukee's urban life with the locals. Concerts, parties, strip clubs. I was hanging with the who's who of Milwaukee—businessmen, D-Boys, pimps, and athletes—and even had a fling with an R&B artist who spotted me from the stage and had his bodyguard get at me. By day I was an assiduous law student and by night I was diligently working the scene. (Funny: I chose Marquette University Law School over the University of Miami School of Law because I was afraid of having too many distractions. I guess if you want them bad enough, the distractions you're avoiding somehow find you.) As I have done since college, I managed my workload by placing myself on a reward system. If I completed my work for the week and studied during the day on Saturday, I gave myself permission to party that night and take off on Sunday.

It worked until two things happened.

One, I tired of the lifestyle. In the beginning, it excited me because it was so far off my beaten path. I was always out. At this nightclub, at that strip joint. It became the same thing night after night, going to the same venues with the same people. The lifestyle lost its allure, and I grew bored.

Two, I had a couple of revelations. While the nightlife made for a good time, it would not take me where I wanted to go in life. Not personally or professionally. And while nothing terrible had happened to me, it occurred to me that this lifestyle carried a certain amount of risk. I had something to lose yet had surrounded myself with folks who didn't. *Let me get over this before it gets over me.* Spending the summer in Houston with my grandma helped me find myself. Between my time with her and tiring of nightlife, I returned to Milwaukee for my second year renewed and committed to getting back on the straight and narrow. That included finding a steady boyfriend so that I would not be running the streets seeking attention.

I met Jeff the summer after my first year of law school. While staying with my grandmother in Houston, I had an internship at the athletics department at the college he attended. Come to think of it, our relationship was probably against the rules because I worked in compliance, and he was a student athlete. In the beginning, Jeff was the perfect antidote to the emotional tailspin I was in due to Rick's ghosting, and my Milwaukee vices.

We had our first date on June 25, 2009—the day Michael Jackson died. The shocking news of his sudden death knocked me out. (Meanwhile, my cousin locked herself in a bathroom and demanded that her coworkers call me. She did not feel like anyone could understand her sadness and emotion regarding Michael Jackson like me. We always promised one another that if this day came to not look for us because we would be on the first thing smoking to Neverland with a lighted candle and a picture of MJ in our hands. Obviously, that did not happen, so we resorted to the next best thing—consoling each other and crying in a way only we could understand. I don't know which one of us is more dramatic, but this is probably why we are best friends.) I awoke to my grandmother peeling me off the floor. "We all have to go sometime, baby," she said.

I had been crying all day and wanted to cancel the date, but Jeff promised that he could make me feel better. I finally agreed to go—in sweats and no makeup—and true to his word, Jeff made me laugh. I was hooked. To this day, I'm unsure how or why our relationship developed so quickly. While Jeff was a kind soul and had a beautiful heart, I honestly believe it was because he was the exact opposite of what I had become accustomed to—he was an upstanding guy from the Louisiana countryside. In other words, what I selfishly needed most then. Over time I decided it couldn't hurt to continue a long-distance relationship with him to keep from running the streets of Milwaukee after lectures in torts and contracts. *Why not? When you're not studying, you have someone to come home to even if it's only via phone. It's all you need.* Sweet and solid, Jeff seemed like a good dude to ease my way back into monogamy even though I knew from the start I would never marry him.

We remained a couple through my final two years at Marquette, and I never meant for Jeff to become more than my law school pastime. As planned, I went home after class, completed my schoolwork, and spoke to Jeff on the phone. Being committed to someone in another state offered me a balance of emotional stability and freedom. I enjoyed Jeff's companionship and appreciated him as the right guy at the right time even as I fully intended our time to be limited. Which is why to this day I harbor so much regret for sacrificing my longtime friendship with Isaiah to appease Jeff's jealousy.

Isaiah came into my life toward the end of high school. His

friend was dating mine, and I agreed to be his senior prom date. I knew he liked me, but I didn't want to give him the wrong impression, so I kept my distance until we eased into a solid friendship. My homeboys and I separated when each of us chose to attend different colleges in the Big 12 Conference. Twin went to Oklahoma, Mark enrolled in Kansas. We remained close throughout college, but I grew especially tight with Isaiah because he chose Baylor, just down the freeway from me in Austin. The irony is that Isaiah played football and pledged Omega; i.e., the kind of guy I wanted to date at the time. But Isaiah was a terrific friend.

Throughout college Andrea and I would make the ninety-minute drive to hang out with Isaiah and his friends (she even started dating one of his friends and heading to Baylor without me). Some of my best memories of college star Isaiah and his friends. In addition to being cool and funny, I trusted him to have my back.

One time Andrea and I drove down for Baylor's homecoming. We took some shots (our first time) and got so drunk, and we never made it to the party. We were on a bench outside with a bunch of people when I got sick. I had my head back and was gurgling, and Isaiah had the presence of mind to push my head forward so I wouldn't choke on my own vomit.

I have no recollection of this. My only memory of that night is that Andrea and I could not stop laughing. Isaiah made sure we remained safe. At a moment when anybody could have taken advantage of us, he took us home, put us to bed, and stayed with us until we were okay. Who knows what might have happened to us had Isaiah not been there? Always drink around someone you trust.

Now . . . was Isaiah also a dirty dog? Absolutely. Dude made the worst boyfriend, and I braced myself for drama whenever he got involved with any woman I considered a friend. But when it came to our relationship, I trusted Isaiah without reservation. Even my family loved him.

Not only should every woman have male friends in her inner circle, she needs both a Stanford Blatch (RIP Willie Garson) and a Jack Berger. For those of you who never watched *Sex and the City* (and please know that the last thing that this reality TV consumer, personality, and critic is ever going to do is judge your viewing habits), in addition to Charlotte, Miranda, and Samantha, Stanford is one of Carrie Bradshaw's closest friends. A talent agent who has known Carrie since they were barhopping in the eighties, Stanford is as vulnerable as he is wise. In this fictional universe and in real life, many women forge satisfying friendships with gay men whom they can trust to keep their secrets and call them out as needed.

And Berger? He often tops the list of worst men Carrie Bradshaw ever dated, and with good reason. (Spoiler alert: He broke up with her with a Post-it Note.) But in the fourth episode of the sixth season of *Sex and the City,* Berger demonstrated that there are valuable things that a woman can learn by hanging out with straight men. This is the famous "He's just not that into you" episode that later inspired a *New York Times* bestseller of the same title.

Carrie and Berger are hanging out with Charlotte and Miranda. Miranda is trying to figure out why a man who kissed her after a promising date declined her invitation to come upstairs. As your best girlfriends are wont to do, Carrie and Charlotte fixate on positive explanations for why Miranda's date has yet to call her.

"He likes you but wants to take it slow," says hopeless romantic Charlotte. "That's nice."

Berger listens to the women and fidgets as they reach for one optimistic excuse after the other. But then Miranda turns to him for the proverbial man's opinion. After asking her if she really wants to know the truth, Berger says, "I'm not gonna sugarcoat it for you . . . He's just not that into you." Carrie and Charlotte gasp, stunned that Berger could say something so harsh.

Not me. Thanks to my guy friends, I long ago picked up what Berger was putting down. No matter what else he may have going on in his life, when a man is interested in a woman, not only is he accepting any and all invitations she may have, he's extending some of his own. As Berger broke it down for Miranda and her girlfriends, I nodded. *This is why you can't just hang out with women all the time,* I thought. *You've got to be friends with men, too.* If you believe men are from Mars and women are from Venus, then recruit a few translators. Even when we were teenagers, Mark and Twin were helpful with boys. I bounced things off them, and they would give it to me straight, no chaser.

I have been arguing since the beginning of time that men and women *can* be friends. From a young age my male friendships helped shape me into the person I am today. I may not have been the prettiest or smartest girl on the scene, but I always felt like the coolest, and I attribute that to having a diverse network of friends. Since coming into my own, I've always maintained a tight-knit circle of girlfriends and a large crew of homeboys.

Having a lot of male friends growing up helped me when I began to date. For one, it made meeting men easier. Some of my earliest boyfriends were friends of my male friends. Also, meeting men through the homies sometimes served to vet the pool. Granted, these introductions don't guarantee a great experience, and at times they created friction in my friendships. Twin introduced me to Rick knowing he was a dirty dog, but he also knew that Big Rach had her sights set on dating that Omega regardless of his reputation as a player. But we were all adults (albeit inexperienced, gullible, and, yes, lusty ones) responsible for our own choices.

Girl, you need to know how these men are out here, and your male friends' honest takes will save you a lot of tears and heartaches. At a young age, I got hip to the dating games that men play simply by hanging out with my boys. Men often talk freely with one another about the women they're seeing—from the naive ones whom they will play to the hilt to the potential girlfriends for whom they are on their best behavior. Regardless of whether you're dating for fun or seeking a committed partner, you never want to be the woman whom men are making fun of, dissecting sexually, or otherwise discussing disrespectfully, if you have a choice in the matter. Promiscuous or prude or someplace between those two extremes, no one wants to be treated like an insentient object. Until we topple the patriarchy— And actually, maybe one way to do that is by having a front-row seat to such conversations among your boys at the club, learning the signs, and making empowered choices about how you interact with the men you're dating.

But you must be willing to heed them the way Miranda did Berger. Regardless of why you're dating, it should be fun, and it's empowering to know what's up. Except for Rick, I reached my thirties having dated many men while avoiding Miranda's situation, because Mark taught me how to know when a guy was just not into me. Thanks to my male friends, I recognized the games that men played and avoided many pitfalls that easily caught up too many of my girlfriends. Of course, I still experienced challenges in my serious relationships because I had so much to learn about myself. But when I didn't want or have a serious boyfriend, the insight of my male friends enabled me to enjoy dating by protecting my dignity.

And should you meet a man who you hope has relationship potential, having a male confidant who can decode his behavior in the way Berger did for Miranda is priceless. Again, Mark was that tried-and-true confidant for me when I was single. He answered any questions I had honestly. *What does it mean when he does this? How should I respond? What should I do?* He taught me how to talk—and text!—the lingo. There's a reason why Steve Harvey sold more than two million copies of *Act Like a Lady, Think Like a Man,* and if you're going to maximize his advice, you must spend time with men. The only man in your life can't be your significant other, and no better man to trust for guidance on dating and relationships than one who has invested time and energy to get to know and love you for who you are. Let a man who genuinely cares about you burst your bubble so you can avoid the one with dishonest intentions breaking your heart. Get you a Mark who will spare your feelings and tell it like it is! This is not to devalue all the wonderful advice Dad has given me, but sometimes I needed a good word from my male peers. There is a difference between the counsel from the Marks of the world and that of an overprotective father.

A word of warning here: Don't let the gift of male friendship turn into a curse. Just as the romantic Carries and Charlottes in your life might encourage you to don rose-colored glasses when you most need to see a romantic scenario for what it is, take care to not let the cynical Bergers scare you into putting up walls around your heart. I have always been proud of the ways I behave that are problematically deemed traditionally masculine, such as cherishing my ambition, reveling in competition, and safeguarding my independence. Never have I been the clingy or jealous girlfriend who cannot go a day without seeing her man. But after witnessing guys saying things like *I can make her do this because she needs me* and *Watch when I pick up the phone what this girl does,* I inadvertently built defense mechanisms to protect myself from men who might attempt to play me in the same way. At some point, I decided I'd rather hurt a man before he hurt me, and this cynicism proved detrimental to my desire for a fulfilling relationship. To assert my independence, for example, I sometimes made the men I dated feel as if I didn't need anything from them but space. On the inside, I yearned for a heartfelt connection, but on the outside I appeared detached. It took me until the age of thirty-one to develop the courage to be completely vulnerable with a man and trust him with my feelings.

Many of us have a story where we made the mistake of choosing an ill-fated relationship over a true friend, and I want to confess mine. Having straight men for friends was never a problem for my significant others until I got to college, and the issue worsened when I graduated.

My chosen career tracks—law and sports—are very male-dominated fields, and my friendships with men helped me navigate relationships with male athletes, executives, and agents. Their presence in my life, however, sometimes triggered the insecurities of my boyfriends who never had platonic girlfriends. Without that experience, these guys couldn't fathom an abiding friendship with someone of the opposite sex. This ignorance caused me so much trouble, but not until I betrayed Isaiah to placate Jeff did I learn a painful lesson: A true friend, regardless of gender, is someone you take a stand for when confronted with a partner's insecurity.

After eight years of friendship, Isaiah was no longer this cool and funny guy whom I loved to hang out with but a brother figure I trusted implicitly. Under the weight of Jeff's possessiveness, I failed to reciprocate Isaiah's loyalty.

Jeff's first and only trip to Milwaukee to visit me was hectic, because my studies left me with so little free time. We managed to travel to Chicago (where I paid for almost everything) to explore the city and enjoy each other. At one point during our stay, Jeff saw an instant message that Isaiah sent me over the computer. While I can't recall exactly what he wrote, I can assure you that it was nothing more than a cheesy innuendo. But Jeff was prone to overreacting to my interactions—real and imagined—with other men, and this time was no different.

"He shouldn't be talking to you like that," he said. "Not having it. You can't be friends with him anymore." He often complained, but this time he meant it. Jeff not only pressured me to call Isaiah and end our friendship, he insisted that I do it in front of him. We argued and argued until I grew exhausted and caved. I remember throwing up my hands and reaching for my phone, all the while thinking, *Rachel, why are you doing this? This isn't going to work. Instead of breaking off your friendship with Isaiah, you should be breaking up with Jeff!*

Yet with Jeff watching me, I dialed Isaiah and hoped to get voice-mail. But as usual, he picked up and sounded happy to hear from me. I told him I was in Chicago with Jeff, and if my stilted conversation tipped off Isaiah, he didn't let on. Finally, I blurted out my true reason for calling. "I can't hang out with you anymore," I said. "It's disrespectful to my relationship." Isaiah initially thought I was joking. My heart ripping in two, I had to repeat myself a couple of times until he got it. "No, this is a wrap." Isaiah went from hurt to confused to silent, and to this day, I feel embarrassed that I made that call. As Isaiah and I exchanged goodbyes, I vowed to myself to call him back as soon as Jeff left for Houston.

But I never did. Shame wouldn't allow it. I expected that call to be uncomfortable, but I woefully underestimated the grief that would envelop me once the deed was done. The magnitude of this self-precipitated loss hit when Jeff went back to Houston. Instead of missing him, I was steeped in regret over how cavalierly I forsook Isaiah. I called him a brother but treated him like an acquaintance. *Rach, you truly broke up with a friend of eight years for a relationship with a dude you know isn't built to last from day one.* I allowed Jeff's insecurities to dictate my relationship with Isaiah, and our friendship never recovered. We communicated but the closeness was gone. To this day I feel remorse, and it embarrasses me to admit that I behaved that way. I pray Isaiah forgave me, because I struggle to forgive myself.

At least I can confirm that I learned my lesson and now I can pass it on to you. Not only do I encourage you to have male friends, I implore you to nurture and protect them as you would your girlfriends. When a partner is telling you how to navigate your friendships—especially friendships that you've enjoyed for years before you even met—that's a harbinger of issues to come. This would not be the last time Jeff's jealousy would get the best of both of us, and every time he threw a fit of possessiveness, I would remember *I gave up my brother for this.* I had never had somebody demand that of me before, and I have never allowed anyone to demand that of me since.

So how do you maintain friendships with people of the opposite sex while sustaining a romantic partnership? Experience has taught me that the biggest key is keeping the lines of communication open with your partner. Be honest and forthcoming, plain and simple, and I do mean about everything—your sexual history (not the names or number of partners but certainly if you slept with someone they may know), your financial habits, your ethical positions, *everything*.

These friendships are impossible to maintain if you have trust issues with your partner, and mistrust can take root in any facet of your life together. *If you "forgot" to tell me about such-and-such, what else are you hiding from me?* isn't a soap opera cliché. It's the stuff of true life, so instead of waiting until you must explain the nature of your relationship to another person—platonic or not—put it all on the table before circumstances force your hand. The more honest you are with each other before a situation arises, the more capable you'll be of trusting each other to maintain respectful boundaries in your relationships with others. *Don't ask, don't tell* is a horrible policy for intimate relationships of any kind.

Okay, Rach, but what about those guy friends that you kinda sorta know are romantically interested in you?

Yeah, girl, let those men go.

Guys *do* approach friendships with women differently. Perhaps the difference lies in gender socialization, but when a woman starts a friendship with a man, the potential for the relationship to become sexual or romantic is usually not something on her mind. Meanwhile, a man who is drawn to a woman and becomes her friend does entertain this possibility. If he finds her physically attractive and she gives him the opportunity to cross that romantic or sexual boundary, he might take it. In fairness to men, I'm not saying that they become friends only with women that they ultimately want to date or have sex with. What I'm saying is if you offer someone who likes chocolate a Hershey's Kiss, they're going to eat it. I initially tolerated Jeff's jealousy because I sympathized with his fear.

However, I was wrong to capitulate to it. Some men are quite capable of maintaining and enjoying friendships with women they will never have sex with no matter how much the patriarchy tries to dictate what they should value and desire about women. Isaiah had proven to be one of those friends, and when Jeff's insecurities flared up, I should have stood up for our friendship but also for my own trustworthiness.

My male friends are my friends, period. When I've had male friends express a romantic interest in me that I couldn't reciprocate, I've cut them out of my life. Whether or not I had a boyfriend was irrelevant. I had to go my separate way for both our sakes. You think that's cold? Miss me with that. It's far crueler to knowingly orbit around someone who's pining for you when you will never feel the same way. Despite your best intentions, you eventually will be extracting from them validation, support, and other kinds of emotional nourishment you're conserving for the person you *really* want.

But whether you are a man or woman, if our friendship is meaningful, I will fight for it. I'd always say to Mark, "I'll know that you've found the right woman because she'll understand our friendship and won't feel threatened by it." When he decided to propose to his wife, Candace, not only did I help him plan their engagement, at their wedding I stood as a bridesmaid on her side of the altar.

Except for Isaiah (whom I cannot blame), these men remain lifelong friends. All of them are married, and I know if I hit a rough patch in my own marriage, I can confide in Mark. He married Candace five years before I wed, and they have navigated all kinds of terrain—finances, in-laws and parenting, you name it. As important as it is for an individual to have a variety of friends, a couple needs other married friends who champion their union and serve as a model. Except for my husband, Mark is the only other man who knows pretty much everything about me. After putting in the work since we were twelve years old, he's no longer just a friend. He's family.

FROM BOYS TO MEN

A man has always wanted to lay me down but he never wanted to pick me up.

—Eartha Kitt

Two weeks before I turned twenty-six, I connected with an old college acquaintance (who I always thought was cute) and the timing could not have been better. Not only was I about to graduate from law school, I was ready to break up with Jeff. He had exhausted me with his jealousy and insecurities.

Jeff dreamed of playing in the NBA but the league never called. He had two choices: attempt to play overseas or leave the game for another career. Although I never wanted a life with him, I empathized with his desire for a career in sports and offered to introduce him to an agent friend. For this gesture, Jeff called me a groupie and accused me of sleeping with him. Did I mention that this was my *friend*? Yet another demoralizing incident that reinforced what I knew from the start and tolerated for two years for the sake of companionship—my relationship with Jeff had an expiration date.

A month before law school graduation, I headed to my alma mater for the Texas Relays—the Lone Star State's premier track and field competition since 1925. It attracts five thousand athletes and ten times as many spectators, and like Freaknik in Atlanta or Afropunk in Brooklyn, the Relays is a major social event for Black people across ages and professions in Texas. I returned to Austin that April to attend the parties with my sister Heather, who was a graduating senior at UT.

During the Relays I met Ed at a mutual friend's party. I already knew who he was. He was a year ahead of me in college and had always intrigued me from afar. I still had a type, and Ed fit: tall and husky, as football players are. But I was through with athletes and their sense of entitlement, preoccupation with their macho image, and gallivanting ways. So when Ed mentioned he was no longer playing professional football, he got my attention.

Although we had never hung out before that weekend, Ed knew who I was, and we had chemistry from the start. In addition to that fervent Longhorn pride, Ed was so funny, and you know I'm a sucker for a man who can make me laugh. Especially one confident enough to fall out over his own corny jokes while everyone else blinks at him. I made sure to cross paths with Ed and laughed with him every time. In fact, the next day I returned to our friend's home, and long after everyone else had gone to bed, Ed and I stayed up and talked all night. Despite our physical attraction, we never shared a kiss or held hands. And yet our emotional connection deepened as he told me about his current struggles, of which there were many.

Injuries brought Ed's promising NFL career to an abrupt end. The lost income forced him to foreclose on his home. Ed also lost his medical insurance, but his then pregnant ex-fiancée refused to apply for government assistance. Because she didn't want their child to grow up with that stigma, Ed had to pay out of pocket for all medical expenses throughout her entire pregnancy. Just that January he had ended his engagement with the mother of his then almost two-year-old son.

After Rick's dishonesty and Jeff's insecurity, Ed's easy disclosures were refreshing.

Men often dodged, deflected, and deceived to impress me, but he chose to be transparent. Ed spoke with candor about his previous relationship, and that made me feel safe to share my own romantic past. His willingness to be vulnerable about his issues overrode any alarms those struggles should have set off. Then I reasoned that if communication and trust are the bedrocks of a healthy and lasting relationship, Ed and I were off to a good start.

Neither of us was seeking a relationship when we met, and we reveled in how our magnetism had caught us both off guard. More than once that night, Ed said to me, "I lost it all, but I'm intent on getting it back." An enticing contrast to Jeff, who was fresh out of college and licking his wounds over his flailing basketball aspirations. Ed's determination to rebound in all facets of his life matched my own healthy ambition. Black, Christian, family-oriented, *former* athlete . . . I could have sat on that couch talking to him forever. After we exchanged numbers and promised to keep in touch, Ed dropped me off that morning at Heather's dormitory, where I was staying. I returned to Milwaukee to finish law school but couldn't wait to talk to him again.

Ed induced a magical feeling unlike anything I'd experienced before. Not an infatuation like with Mike, an obsession like Rick, or a pastime like Jeff. This was something different. With almost a thousand miles between us, we talked every day without fail for the first month of our relationship. Poised to check law school off my life plan, I was eager to stop playing with boys and find a man to marry and start a family (and I was already behind on my life-plan schedule). Ed had done things that the others could or would not do. He had owned his own home. Unlike Jeff, who had yet to start a viable career, he had played in the NFL but was prepared to move on to something else. Unlike Rick, he told the truth about his son and his mother. Most of all, he assured me that I was the only woman in his life.

Once Ed's ex-fiancée accidentally sent me a blank email while lurking my law firm's website. (And why wouldn't she? I appeared a mere four months after their breakup. Can't say I would not have done the same thing.) "I proposed to her because she got pregnant and that was the next thing to do," Ed said. Echoing Rick's assurance that he no longer wanted Goldie tripped a small alarm inside of me until Ed said, "*I* broke off the engagement. I just knew that things were no longer right between us. Believe me, Rachel, we're done."

And I believed him. Ed's honesty when we first met earned him a chance to win my trust, and through the boundaries he set with his son's mother, Ed sealed it. Any resentment she may have harbored over how quickly Ed had moved on never erupted into drama with me. Not once did I worry about him crossing lines with her the way Rick had with Goldie. *This is a man,* I thought. *Finally a mature relationship.* Ed's early words and deeds kept setting him apart from the men before him, and I convinced myself that all the red flags were go signs.

Before I brought Ed home, I sat my parents down. They braced themselves for bad news. Like I was pregnant. (Or worse . . . that I wanted to quit law.) "I'm dating this guy. You've actually met him." Big Rach had slipped Ed into her sister's college graduation that May, asking him to tag along with a mutual friend. "Ed. He came to Heather's graduation."

My father deadpanned, "I knew it." At the graduation I hadn't introduced Ed as my new boyfriend, but Sam Lindsay's no one's fool.

I had never formally introduced my parents to a boyfriend, and it signaled to them that I wanted a future with this man. Soon Mom and Dad took to Ed for many of the reasons I did. (After all, they heavily influenced some of the qualities I wanted then in a husband.) A solid guy who carried himself without pretense or airs, Ed embodied *What you see is what you get*. With my parents he radiated the same humor, charm, and authenticity that had captivated me and accomplished something no other boyfriend could: He made Dad comfortable.

I also marveled at the profound similarities between Ed's parents and mine. His mother always reminded me of mine, and our dads were both country boys who had done well for themselves. It touched me to watch Dad loosen up with Ed and his dad in a way he rarely did with other men. When the older couples hit it off, we seemed destined to become one family.

After graduating law school that June, I moved back to Dallas, where Ed was playing for the Arena Football League team. We practically lived together, building on that amazing first night in April. The most compelling thing about Ed was his presence. He had a tremendous capacity to focus—on tasks, goals, and, most of all, people. When Ed became clear about what mattered to him, his attentiveness was unrivaled. And addictive.

And sex finally became special. The idyllic experience I had fantasized about for years became a reality with Ed. No matter how much I may have desired a man, sex with previous boyfriends did little to enhance our bond, leaving nothing greater between us once the physical act ended. With Ed I could look past our bodies and envision possibilities for our relationship. *This is what it's supposed to be like.* No matter whom I had crushed on, lusted for, obsessed over before, Ed was the first man I truly loved.

C'mon . . . you know how that is. The Disney fairy tale, waltzing through the field of flowers kind of love. That butterflies in your belly every time you lay eyes on each other kind of love. That *Singin' in the Rain* kind of love and flash mob in a Broadway musical kind of love.

You know . . . that bullshit. Our honeymoon phase expired in ninety days. A week after we exchanged our first *I love you*s and three days before I was scheduled to take the Texas bar exam, Ed lost it.

After months of studying for hours each day, I desperately needed a break. Ed and I attended a dinner party to celebrate my dear friend Jade's birthday at a popular Tex-Mex restaurant called Manny's Uptown in Dallas. Ed's best friend, Corey, whom I had befriended independently years earlier, came as well. (Although I lost him when Ed and I broke up. You know how it is . . . Even if you never married, the end is still a divorce, and you have to split the assets. Ed got Corey in the breakup, but I'm getting ahead of myself.)

We had a fabulous time over dinner and margaritas, then took the celebration to a club. The place was teeming with people rushing the bartenders, and Ed was drunk out of his mind. When Corey placed his arms on either side of me at the bar to block off space for me to order, Ed got in his face. "You're just going to be all up on my girl in front of me like that?" Next thing I knew, Ed and Corey came to blows in the club. I had just professed my love to this man who was charging his best friend over me. Imagine this scene: two three-hundred-pound, six-five Black men squaring up in this Texas bar jammed with white folks.

I mentioned that this was three days before the Texas bar, right?

They kicked us out of the club only for Ed and Corey to square up on the street. We miraculously pulled them apart before somebody got arrested. Corey somehow got Ed into a car and drove off while I rode with the women. When I apologized profusely for ruining Jade's celebration, she reminded me of a previous incident when Ed drank too much, got jealous, and went off. "I think you need to leave him alone," she said.

"No, you don't know him like I do," I said. "I know him."

"Look, I'm not saying Ed's not a good guy . . ."

"He drinks because he's at a crossroads in his life." Yes, I attempted to justify Ed's excessive drinking and the angry outbursts that often followed. Instead of running from this behavior, I excused it. "He's trying to figure things out." Then I called Corey to escape the conversation. "Hey, what's up? How's Ed?"

He echoed Jade. "Rachel, he's a good guy. One of my best friends. But y'all don't need to be together."

"Why?" Despite all that had transpired that night, no one was giving me a good enough reason to mistrust our connection. I look back now and shake my head at the depth of my denial.

Corey said, "Because with all the issues he has right now, he doesn't need to be in a serious relationship!"

"Just tell me where you guys are." Maybe it's because I'm a Taurus or an ENFP. Or a woman. I believed I could fix him. No one could tell me otherwise. *I'm going to get him through this, and we're going to be so great together.*

Corey finally told me that they were headed to where I was staying, so I asked Jade to drop me off. When Ed saw me, he began bawling. "I'm not good enough for you," he sobbed. "Nothing I planned on is happening, and I don't know where my life is going. My son doesn't even know me."

I pulled Ed into me for a hug. And now this giant of a man was sobbing in the arms of a five-foot-four, 125-pound girl in the middle of the street in downtown Dallas. As I held Ed, I forgot that I had just ended a relationship where jealousy was a constant problem. Instead of telling myself, *There are some real issues here. Maybe you can be a much better friend than a lover to him right now,* I thought, *What he needs right now is somebody to support him, stand by him, believe in him. Someone who won't neglect him. What he needs is me.*

Love drowned out so much. The selfishness of Ed's possessive outburst three days before I took the biggest exam of my life. The risk of getting involved with a man whose dream had collapsed, leaving him without direction or purpose just as I was embarking on the legal career for which I had prepared for years. Three months into this relationship, and I was already putting aside my feelings, needs, and goals to rebuild this broken man. I romanticized my savior role in Ed's life, pledging to stand by him through this dark period.

For the next five years, Ed and I would run a relay of our own, circling the track again and again and never getting anywhere. He did take some admirable steps to rebuild his life, including returning to Austin to finish his college degree. And when we were at our best, I never laughed so much or felt so safe in a relationship. But at twenty-six, I could not see that Ed first had to get right with himself before he could do right by me. That our short-lived honeymoon in Dallas would mark the only time in our five-year relationship we would live in the same city. I also could not foresee how far and fast I would fall in the list of things that mattered most to him. That no support from me could be a substitute for the work he needed to do on himself. That *I* had self-work to do.

Would I have placed so much stock in Ed's radical honesty if it hadn't been for Rick's deception? I can't say for sure, but I can tell you this: There's a difference between learning the lessons of a previous relationship and allowing those past experiences to catapult you toward the other extreme. Assess the rightness of a potential partner on his own terms and not just by comparing him to the ones before him—especially if they broke your heart. Girl, that's like moving to the unbearable heat of Death Valley and saying "I can make this work" because you narrowly survived the South Pole.

A year into our relationship, Ed again became drunk and belligerent while we were out with friends. This time he suddenly jumped into his car and drove off, leaving us standing there. I panicked. *What if Ed lost control of the car and hurt himself? What if he hurt someone else? What if the police pulled him over, and they hurt him?* After the most frantic hour of my life, Ed called me. He was lost and could not tell me where to find him. Only by the grace of God did Ed find his way home. When he walked through the door, my terror gave way to rage, and I issued an ultimatum. "If you don't stop feeling sorry for yourself and stop drinking, I'm leaving you," I said. "Tonight you not only put your life in danger, you endangered other people." Shame clouded his eyes, and I softened. "Ed, I'm scared for you, and I wouldn't be doing right by you if I didn't hold you accountable for getting yourself together."

That ultimatum marked a turning point in our tumultuous first year. Ed returned to therapy to stop drinking and strengthen his relationship with his son. His tenacity inspired me as I struggled to find fulfillment in the legal career I was building for myself. As with the start of law school, I disliked my first year as an attorney. I encountered roadblocks in my pursuit of sports law and wound up practicing civil defense litigation. Maybe every new attorney claims to not know what they're doing, but now I realize that my discontent with law ran much deeper than first-year growing pains.

Rather than sort through my professional discontent, I sought fulfillment in supporting Ed through all his challenging transitions. His schedule became my schedule. I bore the burden of traveling to him wherever he might be and dropped everything to make myself available for long phone calls as he wrestled with sobriety, academics, career, parenting. Sometimes Ed welcomed my help, like when I did research for his courses (an improvement from writing papers for Jeff, I guess. You read that right the first time. I had been one of those girlfriends even as I was inundated with my own coursework). Other times he balked at my support. Ed never asked for money, but I would offer it then trivialize his embarrassment about accepting it: "Just take it." I gave so much while patiently waiting for our draining saga to morph into my fantasy where we beat the odds and emerged as a power couple. Ed's positive changes had zero net effect on our relationship, because as much as he worked on himself, he never worked on *us*.

My every action was driven by the need to lift, encourage, and support this man, all while tiptoeing around my need for a commitment. Meanwhile, I forfeited so many other desires to be in this relationship. Between the time and cost it took to constantly travel between Austin and Dallas, Ed and I had little opportunity for romance and adventure. We were constrained by his schedule and finances, so date nights were rare and idyllic getaways were impossible. But because I loved him, I convinced myself to focus on "the bigger picture" and trust that the sacrifice was worth it. I believed that when Ed finished his college education and landed a coaching gig, our relationship would be his next priority.

In fact, Ed and I had agreed that he would seek a coaching job in Dallas, only for him to accept a position in Rockwood, almost two hundred miles away from me. When he told me about the offer, his mind was set. It especially upset me because a viable opportunity had opened in Dallas. Ed's curveball made me begin to doubt his intentions to move our relationship forward. "I thought we were trying to come together."

"No, I'm going to Rockwood," he said. "It's a great move for my career, and it's closer to my son." It floored me that he made this decision without consulting me. I had been navigating this relationship thinking of us, but Ed was only thinking of himself.

Ed took the job—his first coaching position—and I soon questioned whether the lifestyle was for me. I had no idea how selfless the significant other of a coach must be. Ed and I barely spoke during the week because he worked from seven in the morning until nine at night. Every other Friday night after work, I drove two and a half hours to Rockwood, but once I arrived, we had no time together because Saturday was game day. At most I had a few hours with him on Sunday before I had to return to Dallas for work. To cope with Ed's move to Rockwood, I convinced myself that I was the kind of woman who thrived off the distance between us— *Yeah, I don't need you around me all the time.*

The truth is I was much needier than I realized. To this day I maintain that Ed was my first true and mature love. And falling in love with a man—as opposed to being infatuated with a boy— made the emotional stakes so much higher.

THE COACH'S GIRLFRIEND

You've got to learn to leave the table when love's no longer being served.
—Nina Simone

After two years of wrapping my entire life around Ed's needs, I discovered that he had been texting other women. One day while Ed was visiting me in Dallas, he took a shower while I was in the bedroom. His phone lit up as it sat in the charger. This was nothing unusual except for the overwhelming compulsion I had to look at his phone. You guys, I cannot explain it. Before that moment I had never gone through Ed's phone. It was as if I had no control over my actions. I scrolled through his phone log and text messages to discover he had been having inappropriate communications with not one but two women. One had sent pictures of herself and Ed invited her and her friends to Vegas with his group of guy friends on a pre-planned trip. *Hey, we're going to Vegas, and you should come, too.* Then, there was the second woman. No stranger to the strip club, I couldn't care less if Ed visited them to blow off steam. I cared a lot, however, that he had asked a woman he met there for her number.

I confronted Ed, who assured me that the woman was a waitress, not a dancer—as if her job had any relevance. Since I had no hard proof against him, he never admitted to cheating. Still I packed up his shit, threw it outside, and told him to leave. I was too devastated to even cry! Seething with rage, I called his sister.

After all I had sacrificed for this man, he cheated on me . . . with a bop *and* a stripper. However, I did allow Ed to come back in and sleep on the couch, and eventually did my best to forgive his "flirtations." (And if you're frustrated to read about this pattern once again, imagine how I feel writing about it!) But my dissatisfaction with Ed mounted as he held on to me while refusing to meet me halfway. This just didn't feel like a partnership. I depleted myself to make him better, but he did not replenish me. My growing resentment, however, was no match for the potent combination of three other emotions—the continuing love I felt for Ed, the entitlement I felt to a happy ending given all the sacrifices I'd made to be with him, and the hope that Ed would reward my devotion with a marriage proposal.

As I lost confidence in the relationship, the trust issues worsened. Valuing my friendships with men, I had never been the jealous type. Now I began to question Ed's female friends, our limited conversations ending with tense interrogations.

I tried and failed to hide my misery from my own friends. In addition to being a cocky bitch who thought I could fix a broken man, I wanted to protect Ed from their judgments and safeguard his secrets. Despite avoiding confiding in them—or maybe even because of it—Andrea and another girlfriend saw right through it. Once they accused me of not being myself, and I put up my guard, played tough, and insisted I was great. They noted how I was losing my spirit. That my light was dimming. I got lawyerly and demanded examples they could not provide. Still they refused to back down: "You're a shadow of yourself." Because she and Andrea knew me so well, they could pick up on the subtlest change in my energy, and no matter how much I pretended, they knew something was off with their girl Big Rach. And not once did my girlfriends refer to Ed. They didn't have to. As I remember that dinner, I recognize that my pushback came not from anger but fear; it frightened me that my anguish had become too big to hide.

Even my usually incurious father attempted an intervention during our family's annual trip to North Louisiana. As I mentioned earlier, every year we come together to drive to Homer for a big trail ride on horseback through the family property. This has become a yearly adventure for Dad and me. Traveling for hours on the road to Louisiana, riding horses on our family's land there, dancing and laughing with our relatives, made for some quality father-daughter time. True to his stoic nature, our conversations during the ride usually remained light, but I still learned things about Dad and cherish those five hours I had him to myself. On this particular drive three years into my relationship, my father turned to me and asked, "What's up with you and Ed?"

Wow. His question shocked me. My father rarely gets personal, and both my parents loved Ed and fully supported our relationship. In fact, their approval was a factor in my persistence. Our families had become so enmeshed—Ed visited my parents' church whenever he came to Dallas, and I had grown close to his sister and nieces—and I didn't want to lose his family any more than I wanted to break up Ed with mine!

"Whoa, whoa, whoa!" I said. How concerned my father must have been to press me about my intimate relationship. Once I recovered from that bombshell of a question, I said, "I want to take it to the next level. You know . . . get married . . . have kids . . ."

Without missing a beat, Dad said, "Then he needs to step up. You guys have been dating for a while now." Then my father really unloaded. "You know, Ed's the youngest, the baby . . . a star football player in high school and college . . . Everyone is always catering to him. I know he's a good man, but I feel like he moves in a selfish way. Doing things for himself and not really for you both. Especially considering how long you've been together. Y'all need to have a serious conversation about where this relationship is going, Rachel."

That conversation had to be extremely uncomfortable for my father. Whether Mom put him up to it or he took it upon himself to confront me, Dad had observed things in my relationship that concerned him so much he had to speak out. The Judge had spoken. He called out what I was too afraid to admit and accept: I was not a priority in Ed's life at all. His main goal was to recoup what he had lost when injuries forced him out of the NFL. Through coaching he wanted to chase the same money, status, and notoriety promised by the league. After his career, Ed cared most about his son, and then there was me in a distant third living across the state.

But he took steps only to advance his career and never our relationship. "I just want to get to a certain place in my coaching career first," Ed would say. "And if I were to get offered a job in Montana, Rachel, I'm going to take it."

"And I'm supposed to move to Montana to be with you for what? For you to leave yet again for another opportunity somewhere else, expecting me to follow you when you won't even put a ring on my finger? How am I supposed to commit to you, Ed, when you're not committing to me?" This bickering over our future dragged on even as I searched for coaching opportunities for Ed in Dallas.

My single-handed fight for our relationship finally wore me down. Reflecting on my girlfriends' observations, I said, "We either take a break or break up, because I'm not myself right now." Ed and I did break up but continued to talk all the time. (To quote Vivian Ward in *Pretty Woman,* "Big mistake. Big! HUGE!") I tried to date but remained stuck on Ed, and by the summer of 2015, our on-again, off-again relationship was on once again.

Women are often told, *How you get him is how you lose him.* That means don't get involved with men who are married or otherwise committed to someone else; even if he eventually leaves that person to be with you, expect him, at some point, to be unfaithful to you as well. After my relationship with Ed, I think this advice needs a corollary: *How you get him is how you keep him.* The things you do to pique a man's interest at the start of your relationship had better be rooted in who you truly are, or at least who you desire to be. Just as in the retail sector, bait and switch is a problematic tactic in the dating marketplace. In a bid to entice a commitment from someone, don't talk yourself into performing behavior he finds attractive that you cannot sustain. For example, if you don't like to cook, have no time to do it, or just plain suck at it, don't stock up on cookbooks and pretend to be the second coming of Carla Hall because his dating profile says the way to his heart is through his stomach. The day you chuck the recipes and order takeout three nights in a row, expect an upheaval in your relationship. So, learn from my mistakes: Don't try to be someone you're not at the beginning of a relationship. Know who you are, accept and love yourself unconditionally—and don't settle for someone who isn't giving as good as he's getting.

Because rather than break up with Ed, I, too, chose selfishness. First, I reclaimed my time. When I cut my trips to visit Ed, he complained that I was not there for him. In hindsight, I take responsibility for cultivating that expectation. For the first two years of our relationship, I gave Ed everything he asked and requested little in return. But my resentment was building.

Then that resentment veered into cheating—both emotionally and physically. I met my refuge—an older man named Daniel—at a legal event. He already had an MBA and worked as a financial adviser when he enrolled in law school on a full scholarship. (My parents would have loved him; he was so Obama-esque.) The night we met, Dan and I kissed, and I immediately backed off. "No, I can't," I said, surprised by what I had done. "I have a boyfriend." But we continued to communicate, and I eventually made trips to Houston to get from him what I desired from Ed. Romantic outings. Verbal affirmation. Great conversation that stimulated my mind and relaxed my emotions. Basically, he was speaking my love language—quality time. Dan often asked me why I stayed with Ed when he could treat me better. And he would have, but I convinced myself Ed's shortcomings were a temporary consequence of his first full-time coaching position in Rockwood. Long distance, packed schedule . . . anything but willful neglect. I made it clear to Daniel that I had no intention of leaving Ed, and when his insistence threatened to expose our relationship, I pulled the plug on our affair.

(Have I mentioned that at one point Dan and Ed lived in Houston at the same time? I told you that I was messy and promised to be honest about it. I have never even admitted to cheating on Ed until now. The problems in our relationship came from both sides. We both made mistakes.)

At the time, I thought I'd cheated on Ed to make him jealous. He had suspicions, questioning my whereabouts and associations, and his audacity triggered my rebellious side.

Now I recognize I also wanted to punish him for taking me for granted. And abandoning me. Yet I clung to the hope that somehow we could revitalize our initial connection. There was no denying we were in love with each other, and Ed had yet to express doubts about a future with me. When you put years of effort into a relationship, you're loath to start over, no matter how difficult it becomes. This is especially true if, like me, you take too much pride in not quitting.

> *If I truly want this, then I have to fight for it.*
> *I can't let this end.*
> *Start another relationship???*
> *I'm almost thirty now.*
> *According to my life plan, I should already be on Kid Number*
> *   One!*

After my hundredth complaint about the lack of time we spent together, Ed asked me, "Do you truly want to be a coach's wife, Rachel? My mother told me to ask you that. Because this is the life."

Mother knows best, I thought. And yet I said, "No. I want to be yours."

That's how desperately I wanted him. It takes a certain type of woman, with a particular kind of strength, to handle that lifestyle. Knowing that I was not built for it, I *still* would have committed to those extreme feats of selflessness if Ed married me. To be his wife, I would have given up my job to follow him from city to city and raised our children as a single parent as he put his players first. I convinced myself that I was capable of the sacrifice and that being married to the man I loved would make the sacrifice worthwhile. Even if deep down inside I knew it would not make me happy. Even though I knew the lifestyle was not for me. And even though I knew I was losing myself in this relationship.

The final straw came in the summer of 2015 when Ed accused me of cheating with a deejay—someone I had no romantic interest in and with whom I never crossed any sexual lines. Just after spending most of my waking hours with lawyers, I loved spending time with an artist. Our conversations echoed those scintillating times listening to Maxwell with Robby J or watching Karim onstage. In retrospect, I was emotionally cheating on Ed, who forbade me to speak with this man again. Even as he continued to make selfish decisions that impacted our relationship without regard for my wants and needs, he expected my choices to account for his feelings and desires. Ed wanted to do as he wished in Rockwood yet control how I behaved in Dallas.

So what did Big Rach do? She told her boyfriend she was calling it a night.

Then she headed up the street to listen to her favorite deejay, who just happened to be in town that night.

And *then* she posted videos of the event on Snapchat because Ed was not on that platform, and the post would disappear in twenty-four hours.

The Lord really wanted us to break up, because all of this was very dumb of me. (God is like, *Child, do not put my name in this mess!* But how else to explain how I was sabotaging the relationship I had been pushing so hard toward marriage?)

A friend who saw my post innocently tipped off Ed. He called to confront me, and as usual, his furious attention triggered a mix of excitement and apprehension. *Uh-oh . . . he is so pissed. But, hey, that's because he's jealous. Which means he cares after all!* Then Ed told me we were done and didn't speak to me for a month. Yes, for a month, despite my efforts to contact him. He would send my calls to voicemail and keep my texts on read. As per our dysfunctional pattern, we eventually started talking again, and I even resumed going to his football games. But I must admit that things were never the same between us after that summer.

Then one day in November 2015 at three in the morning, a woman called me from Ed's phone. I jolted up in bed, making out the ebb and flow of rushing cars as if she were calling by the side of the road. The woman ordered me to call a man that Ed coached with.

"Who is this?"

"Rachel, I need you to wake up Kevin." I didn't know whether to be angry that this anonymous female was calling me from Ed's phone or to be worried because Ed had gotten into a wreck and perhaps this Good Samaritan called the first number on his phone. Before I could decide, this girl hung up on me.

So I got mad.

I dialed Ed's number. No answer. I kept calling, getting angrier with every failed attempt. The woman finally picked up, and I went off. "Who the fuck is this? Why are you calling from Ed's phone? Is he okay?"

She finally responded. "It's Cynthia." Like I should know.

"And who are you?" She hung up on me. I scrambled to figure what to do next, desperately making call after call. First, I called Ed's mother, but she did not pick up. Next I called his dad, and he didn't pick up, either. I called his sister, and thank God, she answered. After calling her mother for me, Ed's mom returned my call.

As I cried hysterically, she checked his bank account and confirmed that he had recently been in Houston, which is seventy miles from Rockwood. She calmed me down and promised to call once she had more information. I didn't sleep a wink for three hours until she did, with a shocking update: "Ed's in jail. He got a DUI."

Not this shit again. "So I guess he's okay." But after all that turmoil, the answer to one question remained outstanding. *Who the fuck is Cynthia?*

A few hours later, Ed called me. "Do you want me to come down there?" I immediately asked. The blurry lines in our relationship never mattered. I always responded to Ed's needs like a committed girlfriend.

"I'm okay. Just embarrassed. Now I have to talk to my kids," he said, referring to the players who would inevitably learn about his transgression.

"Ed, I'm an attorney," I said as if he needed reminding. "Let me help you. At least let me see if I can find somebody for you down there."

"You really don't have to."

"Okay . . . well . . . Who's Cynthia?"

"She's the assistant to the head coach. A group of us from the program went to Houston."

That was all he gave me, but when my research confirmed that Ed was telling me the truth, I left it alone. But Ed and I didn't spend Thanksgiving together.

Nor Christmas.

Nor New Year's Eve.

I ignored the writing on the wall. Even through all our turmoil, Ed and I maintained this lovely tradition for Valentine's Day. I'm a huge fan of Disney, and every February the studio opens its infamous vault and releases a classic film for sale on DVD, which Ed would buy for me. This small gesture meant the world to me, because every year he made me look forward to a holiday that I'd previously cared little about. Valentine's Day 2016 came and went. No *Snow White and the Seven Dwarfs* DVD for Rachel. And I *really* wanted that one.

This "oversight" forced me once again to address the obvious. "What are we doing, Ed? Where are we going? What do you want this relationship to be?"

"I don't know what I want to do with this." *This?* After so many years, we had not progressed from *this* to *us.* Yet I convinced myself that *I don't know* was a far cry from *I don't want you.*

"Do you even want me?" Silence. *Oh.* His responses to such questions were never encouraging yet somehow allowed for a sliver of hope. His silence leveled me like none of his three-word answers had. "Well, since you don't know and aren't trying to put in any effort, I'm out." Happy Valentine's Day.

Please learn from me. If you test a man by saying *You don't want me*, and he reacts with silence, then no, he does not want you. If he answers *I want you but* . . . no, he does not want you. If you ask him explicitly if he wants you—and you should—treat any response other than an enthusiastic *Yes, I do* as a *No* and move on. Double negatives do not make a positive, and your heart isn't a logic puzzle in the back of a magazine.

And that was the end of us . . . again. And again I tried to date other men, although this time around I became especially reckless.

It took one dog to rescue me from the rest of 'em.

WOMAN'S BEST FRIEND

*One of my greatest teachers is my dog, Sophie ... And it wasn't until
she passed away that I understood the depth of my love for her because I
learned ... that there are big souls and little souls. Sophie was little but
had a great impact on my life. And when I lost her is when I realized that
nobody on earth had ever loved me like that little dog.*

—Oprah Winfrey

When Ed and I officially broke up on Valentine's Day 2016, he continued to keep tabs on me. As much as I resented Ed's possessive
texts, I also still wanted to reconcile with him so I never insisted he
stop contacting me. My need for attention and validation reached
new lows when I started talking to a guy who Ed knew in the hopes
that word would get back to him. When it did, he would contact
me to read me for filth, and I would revel in it. *You want to text me?
I'll give you a reason to text me!* Petty, I know, but who has not had
a petty moment or two?

To truly hear and heed that inner voice requires stillness and
solitude, but I could not stand to be at home with my feelings.
Instead I would grind for long hours at my firm during the day and
then club-hop on the nights and weekends. Every opportunity I
had, I jumped on a plane to another city to run from myself on
different streets. The only thing waiting for me at home was a half-
empty fridge and the fear of a future without love.

As if the love I sought was in those loud nightclubs and dark restaurants. So desperate to be seen, heard, and appreciated, I went out and put myself at risk emotionally and physically. Any man could come along and give me attention, and if I was slightly attracted to him, was slightly impressed with his status, slightly believed he could do something for me, I was ready to buy whatever he was selling. Once again, my self-worth was wrapped in the wrong thing. Five years in the wrong relationship will do that to you.

That May my sister Constance almost hit a dog with her car. She took him to the vet, where a woman agreed to foster him while my sister found him a home. Constance took a few photos of him, posted them on a website for lost dogs, and sent them to the family, including me, even though I had vowed to never own another pet.

When I was eleven years old, I begged my parents for a Russian Blue cat. Also known as Archangel cats, Russian Blues are a gorgeous but rare breed with black coats that are so diluted they appear blue, especially against their green eyes. Their fur is supple, and when they walk, they seem to tiptoe like the royalty they are. Every morning I would get *The Dallas Morning News* and look at the CATS FOR SALE ads in search of a Russian Blue cat. When we found one, my father drove Heather and me two hours to get him. I named him Smokey, took full responsibility for him, and loved him with all my heart. Then one day he went missing. I waited upstairs at my bedroom window as Dad and Heather searched the unfenced gorge behind our house. Heather ran back to the yard crying uncontrollably behind my dad as he carried my dead Smokey in his arms. Given the puncture wounds in his belly, the vet speculated that a dog had gotten to him. Smokey's death traumatized all of us, and me most of all. I couldn't even bring myself to attend the funeral my family held for him. Instead I watched the service from my bedroom window as my parents buried him in our backyard where he remains buried. From that day forward, pets were for other people.

Until I saw the picture Constance texted me. "Oh my gosh, he's beautiful!" I said. I had no intention of taking him but did want to help my sister find him a home. Whenever I circulated an email, however, I would pause before I hit send, hypnotized by his photograph. Nobody claimed him from the website or offered to take him. "Maybe it's because I'm lonely, but I can't stop thinking about this dog. I feel drawn to him in a way I can't explain," I told Constance. I had already narrowed down two names for him. Either Simba or Copper. "I want to meet him, and if he responds to me, I'll take him."

Constance and I headed over to the couple's home to meet the dog. As they were telling me about him—how sweet he was, that he was already potty-trained, etc.—the dog walked over to me. I looked into his eyes, and he placed his paw on my lap. He imprinted on me.

The dog *chose* me.

Copper chose *me*.

(Unlike somebody we know.)

"That's it," I said. "I'm taking him home."

Copper and I have been inseparable ever since. A DNA test revealed that he is one-half Pomeranian, a quarter German shepherd, an eighth Chow, and an eighth American Eskimo. No wonder he's so beautiful.

I was completely obsessed with Copper when Ed and I started

talking again in June. He was coming to Dallas on a recruiting trip, so I invited him to stay with me. As he was on his way from Rockwood to Dallas, I said, "Oh, by the way, I got a dog."

It was not love at first sight. When Ed saw Copper, he said, "He's looking at me funny."

"Oh, he's never seen a man in the house before," I said. "It's just the two of us." Then Copper started growling. "Copper, stop!" I had never seen him respond to anyone that way. "Just stop."

Copper eventually did stop, but he did hate Ed. He followed him around the house as if to keep an eye on him. I worried that Ed might want to leave. I believe dogs can sense bad spirits or at the very least tell if someone's energy is off, and I couldn't help but wonder if Copper was trying to warn me about Ed. *Mom, this ain't it. This man needs to leave. And I don't want to see him again.*

I thought, *Well, if I ever put myself back out there again, maybe I should let Copper vet these men.*

On the second episode of *The Bachelorette* in May 2017, I had my first one-on-one date with Peter. We arrived at an airport to take a private flight to Palm Springs. Before we boarded, however, I broke some news to him. "One of my best friends was in a really, really bad accident, and I haven't seen him in a really long time," I started. "And if that's okay with you, I'd really, really like him to come with us." Peter was game, and out from the back of the car hopped Copper. With one of his front legs wrapped in a royal blue splint, he ran toward me. "Copper, this is Peter. Say hi to Peter."

While nowhere near as hostile as he was toward Ed, Copper wasn't as intrigued by Peter as I was. At least he was polite, allowing Peter to shake his paw, and he eventually warmed up to him during the flight to Palm Springs. There we went to Barkfest—a huge pool party for dogs and the people who love them. Peter was very attentive to Copper, and that was something I appreciated.

It turns out that my date with Peter and Copper was another historic first on the show. According to entertainment writer Caitlin Gallagher, bringing along my rescue dog on the traditional one-on-one was a first for the franchise. "One of the biggest struggles for *Bachelor* Nation couples once they leave the elaborate world that the ABC reality series creates for them during their whirlwind courtship is integrating into one another's real lives. So making sure whoever she picks gets along with her dog is totally legitimate," she wrote for *Bustle*. "Another reason it's cool that Rachel brought her dog is it confirms how she has her own life outside of the TV show." She was right.

When I appeared on *Jimmy Kimmel Live!* after the premiere of *The Bachelorette*, I said, "That's my dog child and he said whoever's gonna be his newest daddy—if I pick one—he needed to be a part of it." And now that I look back, Copper clearly had his say during the hometowns. In the *Bachelor* franchise, hometown dates are when the lead travels to the hometowns of the final contestants and vice versa, to meet their friends and families and to imagine what their life together might be like after the show. Just like the rest of my family, Copper was around when we were filming the hometown visits. Although they had met before, when I brought Peter home, Copper behaved as if he didn't know him. He had nothing for Peter. Absolutely nothing.

Meanwhile, Copper's first meeting with Bryan was very different. Bryan came into the den and sat down next to me. At one point, Copper came into the room and sat at Bryan's feet. Not my feet. Bryan's feet, even though he had never met him before. I later told Bryan, "That was validation for me." I had come to understand that Copper's desire to protect me included emotional support as well as physical safety.

In fact, there's considerable scientific research on the healing effect of pets, and I now understand how Copper boosted my mental health (and even Smokey, RIP). At a time when I felt emotionally unmoored, his presence gave me what psychologists call ontological security—the ability to manage and be engaged in everyday life. When a person has ontological security, they feel a sense of order and continuity in their life rooted in a positive view of themselves. Simply put, they manage their lives better because the meaning they give to their lives comes from within. According to the Human Animal Bond Research Institute, caring for a pet cultivates ontological security in a variety of ways. Pets do emotional work, knowing when their owners need support (and that's why I believe Copper placed his paw in my lap the day we met and gave my ex-boyfriend the business). The practical work of caring for a pet is a healthy distraction from emotional concerns, provides a person with a sense of control, and even creates a rewarding identity as a "good owner." These benefits are just the tip of the iceberg, and the evidence for "animal medicine" in reducing stress alleviating symptoms of anxiety, depression, and PTSD and even treating some physical conditions is growing in leaps and bounds.

In the past five years, Copper has taught me so much about myself. I wasn't a homebody before I adopted him. Whether or not I was in a relationship, I always felt a need to be out and about, doing things, and keeping busy. But when Copper came into my life, that changed. *This has been great, y'all, but I got to get home to my dog.*

Copper also made me realize that I thrive on routine. As a self-described organized scatterbrain, adopting him made me less selfish and more responsible. Caring properly for Copper requires me to maintain a schedule and keep his things in order. When I travel, he travels with me, so I must think ahead, packing a bag for him so if he has any accidents, I have everything I might need. I've always been a results-oriented and disciplined person, but now I experience deep fulfillment on a daily basis, because the only goal of these consistent tasks is to love on this dog.

And as such an independent person who used to think, *I can't stand needy, dependent people,* Copper has taught me that I *enjoy* having someone dependent on me. Our long walks are extremely therapeutic for both of us. I love making sure Copper's meals are planned, his pills are in order, and his vet appointments are scheduled. And as crazy as this is to some, I even like picking up his poop!

Copper has brought out my motherly side. While I've always wanted kids, his presence affirms that I'll be a great mom and will relish motherhood. If nurturing him satisfies me this much, I cannot wait to experience the fulfillment of raising my children.

Sometimes people describe Copper as a rescue dog, and you can miss me with that. I didn't rescue Copper. He saved me. It's as if God knew how badly I needed a companion to keep me at home, where I could heal instead of chasing Mr. Wrong. When I hit rock bottom, Copper appeared and uplifted me. I shiver to think how my life might have unfolded if I hadn't seen his picture and heeded that magnetic pull. I might have descended into depression or become entangled with the wrong person. Because I had someone who needed me, I wanted to be better. Instead of racing around looking for someone or something outside of myself to fulfill me,

I slowed down my life and began figuring out what Rachel wanted and what Rachel needed. I thank God every single day for bringing Copper into my life.

Obviously, I can't go so far as to say that everyone should have a dog. But I will say this: If you do feel an instant connection to a dog, only allow him into your life if he has four legs.

IN(TO) SANITY

I was always apprehensive of the term "strong Black woman" because it dehumanizes us and makes it seem like we don't hurt.
—Taraji P. Henson

You ever find yourself perpetuating a "positive" stereotype about your community? While there are some negative assumptions that have you side-eyeing someone or shooting an email to HR, there are others that are a source of pride or at least make for a good joke. When you belong to a marginalized group that must fight against a registry of offensive and harmful generalizations, sometimes you cling to that rare stereotype that inherently endows you with some spectacular trait and gives you an edge over others. Who doesn't want other people to presume that we are preternaturally attractive, industrious, or otherwise gifted in some way? You sit with your folks and laugh about *Because you know how we are and how we do.*

Black women can count on one hand the so-called positive stereotypes circulating about us, and at the top of the list is that of the "strong Black woman." On the surface, it seems like an empowering archetype to embrace, especially when you compare it to the others imposed on us, like the sexually insatiable Jezebel or the blissfully domestic mammy. As we move through a world where misogynoir lurks at every corner, of course we want to project images of ourselves as resilient, independent, and most of all, unbothered.

Not me. Not anymore. I'm with Taraji. Miss me with all of the stereotypes, especially the myth of the "strong Black woman," which I lived up to for years . . .

. . . until I went into therapy to impress a man.

It's okay. You can laugh. Girl, I look back at that time and laugh at myself. The reason I *can* laugh at the foolishness that got me on that couch is because I needed it, and it worked. Knowing what it has done for me, I am now a strong champion of therapeutic services for everyone, but especially the Black community, where experiencing mental illness still carries a dangerous stigma.

At the time I began writing this, Earl Simmons, better known as the iconic rapper DMX, died at the tender age of fifty. The autopsy eventually confirmed that the heart attack that killed him was caused by a drug overdose. Earl had a lifelong and public battle struggle with substance abuse, and the heart attack that killed him was induced by cocaine. As DMX lay in a coma on life support, I saw an outpouring of compassionate tributes on social media by devastated fans who hoped and prayed that he would miraculously pull through. I also read, however, an alarming number of posts shaming him for becoming addicted to drugs in response to his childhood trauma. After an unprecedented year of meaningless Black death, the callousness drove home to me what a strong grip misinformation has on a community that is particularly vulnerable to mental illness.

When people listen to me speak in the media, they confuse my outspokenness for imperviousness. The assumption is that because I have strong views on social matters, I somehow lack deep feelings about personal issues. It may surprise you to know that I am actually a sensitive person who feels very deeply. The Strong Black Woman stereotype looms like a shadow over me as people quickly (and conveniently) forget that I was the same woman whom they witnessed having that heart-wrenching breakup with Peter Kraus on *The Bachelorette* (especially when they had such negative reactions to my choosing Bryan over him, but we'll talk about that later). My ability to connect to such vulnerability, never mind express it before millions of strangers, reflects a tremendous victory for me because I had to fight for years to regain that level of sensitivity.

Not only was I a crybaby as a kid, I conveniently forgot that fact when I grew up. Ask my older sister. I did recently, and as big sisters do, Constance was (too) eager to remind me that not a day went by that I did not burst into tears over something.

"No," I said, falling back into defensive little sister mode despite knowing she was right. "Not every day."

"Yes, every day!" she insisted. Constance recalled a slumber party I once threw. "Remember how you couldn't function without sleep? That night you started crying because you got tired and wanted to go to sleep, but all your friends wanted to stay up. Then, when they came into my room to keep the party going, you cried about that!" My sister reminded me that school was no different. "Kids would come up to me and say, 'Your sister's crying on the playground,'" Constance said. Even my dad nicknamed me Bull Baby because I was always crying about something.

At some point in my life, however, I internalized the message that crying signaled vulnerability, and broadcasting such feelings was dangerous. It's difficult to pinpoint exactly when this happened because the message came from multiple sources. The first probably was my family. While my mom's side of the family is expressive and affectionate, my dad's relatives are not ones to dish out hugs or pepper you with *I love you*s. I ultimately was raised a Lindsay, and according to the Lindsays, the world isn't easy or fair or going to cut you any slack. To succeed, you cannot show any signs of weakness. You did not reveal your hardships to anyone, never mind a stranger, let alone a therapist. Although there was one exception.

God.

While I grew up in a small church in Dallas, my family moved to a much larger church when I was in college. There we learned that when we encountered problems during the course of our lives, we were supposed to turn them over to God.

Be careful for nothing; but in every thing by prayer and supplication with thanksgiving let your requests be made known unto God.

Casting all your care upon him; for he careth for you . . .

Cast thy burden upon the LORD, and he shall sustain thee: he shall never suffer the righteous to be moved.

In other words, we were raised to believe that it was possible to pray away our challenges—no worldly interventions required.

Maybe my switch from sensitive to tough began in high school or college. Knowing that I wanted to be an attorney, I became a workhorse. Because I was on a mission to do everything that I set out to do, including follow my father's career path, I turned into a machine. Everything became a hustle—my studies, my internships, my sorority. While each of these things was valuable to me in its own right, the fact is, they were also the building blocks of a strong application for law school.

The emotionless hustle continued as I completed law school, studied for the bar, and became an attorney. People expect lawyers to be logical and dispassionate. You cannot react. You cannot be dramatic. You cannot cry. If you're a female attorney, you have to be especially tough because people will test and try you. Add to this that I was attempting to build a career in sports law. From the college internship required for my major in sports management through my early career as a lawyer, I held a variety of jobs in the sports industry, and when you are in the male-dominated business of sports, you've got to be one of the boys. That means you've got to be hard.

Once Bull Baby reached adulthood, her mindset shifted radically. Big Rach looked at her calendar and said, "Let's see . . . where can I fit in a good cry? This week's gone. Next week's packed, too." She finally closed her planner and decided *I just don't have time for tears.* And what was crying going to do for me? Nothing.

Until I chose to go to therapy to prove to Ed that I was working on myself in a bid to win him back.

One of the wonderful things about Ed was his willingness to seek professional help to overcome his challenges. This is no small thing for a man—especially a Black man—to do. Ed had done therapy before we met when every facet of his life—career, home, and family—crumbled around him in quick succession. Within the first two years of getting together, he returned primarily to improve his relationship with his son and to stop drinking. After two more years in an on-again, off-again long-distance relationship, Ed and I separated, and wanting to still marry him, I began therapy in 2015.

At the age of thirty, I had done everything I set out to do except for one thing. I was an attorney at a great firm, making good money. I was an independent woman who had her own. I was in great health and enjoyed wonderful friendships. I came from and remained close to a loving family. I had it all except the healthy relationship with a man who would be my husband and the father of my children. The man I had my heart set on was in therapy, and in order to solidify his commitment to me, I figured I should secure a therapist for myself. Not that I felt I needed to speak with a mental health professional. After all, despite this one exception, I had figured out life pretty well on my own. *I know myself*, I thought, *but I want to be able to tell Ed that I'm working on myself.*

My therapist Barbara opened our first session by saying, "So, Rachel, what brings you here today?" Out of nowhere, I burst into tears. Uncontrollably crying. I didn't know why. I didn't know this woman. Was she a witch? What did she do to me? I wasn't on that couch two minutes when I lost it. I think I even scared her. "Wait a minute," Barbara said. "What are you about to tell me?" Even when I caught my breath, I still could not answer her question, struggling to point to a specific thing.

Thank you, God, for Barbara. I didn't even know how much I needed her support until that one question—so simple, so succinct, so sympathetic—turned like a spigot and that flood of emotions poured out of me. Over time my work with her revealed that there was no one thing. Crying on that couch was such a release that first session because I was exhausted. Exhausted from always having to keep it together, tired of pretending like everything was okay, and drained by constantly performing the role of Strong Black Woman. I approached my life the way I did track as a child—pushing through the pain to be the best at things I didn't even want to do. A long time ago, someone told me that the toughest people are the ones you need to check on the most. Nobody checks on the strong because we always assume that they're okay. No one was checking on me, and I was not okay. I sobbed that first session with Barbara because, despite being on the brink of having it all, I was lost.

In my attempt to check off that final item on my life list, I was desperately clinging to a relationship that was dying a slow death from the day we met. Nor could I place the blame solely on Ed. His continued ambivalence was mirroring back to me my own uncertainty. I myself wasn't acting right in this relationship that I supposedly wanted so badly, and for the life of me, I could only point to one reason.

When I graduated college without a boyfriend, an influential woman in my life said, "It's going to be really hard for you to find a husband now." I was only twenty-two and remember laughing it off. *Okay, whatever. I'm sure that's not going to be a problem.* With law school next on the list, I was clear that settling down that young wasn't for me. I couldn't even imagine it.

But I never forgot what that relative said, and as I got older and farther away from twenty-two, her words echoed in my mind, growing louder and louder as my relationship with Ed kept flailing. I thought, *If I let this go, I'm starting over at thirty-one. Will I be able to find someone? Oh my God, my biological clock is ticking!* (A pressure that many women and few men have to worry about.) Having put my all into this relationship for almost five years, I had no other potential men to consider if it failed. Despite an inner knowledge that I should not have been holding on to the relationship, I stubbornly rationalized fighting for it.

There's no way you spent this much time—almost five years!— and it's not supposed to work.
I'm invested in his family, he's invested in mine. We're so intertwined.
We've gone through such deep things together.
I've sacrificed so, so much.
I don't want to have another failed relationship.
I don't know how to start over.

*If I let this relationship go, I don't know if marriage will ever
    happen for me.
Where do I go from here?*

My ego sent me to therapy to hold on to Ed, but my subconscious was saying, *No, you need this space. You're not getting this level of support from friends. You're not getting it from your parents. You're not getting it from church. You need to talk to a third party and figure out what Rachel wants.* For the first time I was asking myself whose life I was living, and the answer was *Not mine.* My job at the law firm made my entire family beam because I was following in my father's footsteps. All the things I achieved and acquired pleased my parents, including the man I was dating. My parents saw in Ed a good man for me to settle down with, but he was not a good man for me to settle for. *What did Rachel want?* The only answer I had at the time was *Not this.*

That first session Barbara said, "When you brush so many things under the rug, after a while nothing more can fit. It just starts poking out." She described me as a person who put on my big-girl pants, chose mind over matter, and ordered myself to get over it, applying the valuable lessons I learned running track to other areas of my life to an unhealthy degree. "It's all coming out now because you just can't run away from it anymore." Life literally is not track and field.

Looking back, I had felt a similar despair my first year of law school. To avoid going within myself, I went out with everyone else. I would not reveal my pain, never mind ask for support. I could not recognize the despair when I was in its grip.

And herein lies the danger of submitting to the "positive" stereotype of the Strong Black Woman. A 2019 study of the "superwoman schema" among African American women confirmed what many of us already know to be true: Donning this armor may temporarily protect us from immediate harm but over time is a tremendous liability to our health. In the words of Dr. Amani Allen, who led the study, "What does it mean to continue to have an intense motivation to succeed, while you're also experiencing barriers to success?" For me it meant maintaining a relentless drive to secure specific things without pausing to ask myself if what I wanted reflected my genuine desires for my life or the desires someone else told me I should have.

To my knowledge, I became the first person on either side of my family to go into therapy. (Maybe a Lindsay went, but none of us would ever know.) While I did not hesitate to tell my parents, I handled it the way I did the news of Rick's baby—just dropping it into the conversation—because I knew they would have a strong reaction for two reasons. One, they were not immune to the stigma against therapy that persists in the Black community—a stigma I suspect might be rooted in a rational fear of having white people in your personal affairs and providing them an opportunity to use your vulnerabilities against you. Two, because we tend to associate therapy with extreme mental issues including suicidal ideation, I knew telling them would make them gravely concerned for my well-being. Another persistent myth in our community is that if you need to discuss your life with a licensed stranger, something must be dangerously wrong with you. Unless you're on the brink of harming yourself, the solution is to pray.

Upon hearing that I was seeing a therapist, my parents were shocked and then worried. "Rachel, what's wrong?" my mother said. "Are you okay?"

"Do we need to do something?" asked my father, wondering

if they needed to intervene on my behalf in some way. "And you know you can always come to us."

"And to God. You have to pray, Rachel, and have faith."

"Please don't worry. I'm fine," I said. "I just need someone to talk to." How could I explain this to them without making them think I was losing my religion or that I wasn't confiding in them because *they* were the issue? Neither of those things was true. My family and friends had their thoughts about my life, and the danger came not from their well-intended biases but the inadequate weight that I placed on my own thoughts, concerns, and hopes for myself. "I'm still a believer. I know I can go to God and talk to Him—and I do!—but sometimes I need a physical presence. Someone whom I can see and hear and touch. Mom, Dad, when things are difficult, sometimes I need someone who will respond. An unbiased, professionally trained stranger." And as my parents usually do, they quickly recognized that I was an adult who was making a conscious decision to seek help from a third party, accepted my decision, and trusted that I was not forfeiting my Christianity in doing so.

It helped that at a recent sermon, our pastor preached about mental health. He opened his remarks by breaking a taboo—he revealed that he himself saw a therapist. Our pastor named ten different mental health issues, from general anxiety to more serious conditions such as bipolar disorder and schizophrenia. In talking about his own journey, our pastor normalized therapy. "We shouldn't shame people for seeking help when they're trying to better themselves," he preached. "Mental illness is a real disease, not a scarlet letter."

I am so heartened that more Christian leaders are embracing therapy as a viable tool for achieving and maintaining emotional wellness—and I truly believe that God approves—but we have so much further to go. A 2018 survey conducted by the Substance Abuse and Mental Health Services Administration found that 16 percent of African Americans reported having a mental illness, which translates to 4.8 million people. The SAMHSA survey also revealed that serious mental illness is on the rise among Black people, including suicidal thoughts, plans, and attempts. Also more frequent among African Americans compared with other racial groups is binge drinking, smoking (marijuana and cigarettes), illicit drug use, and prescription drug abuse. When we consider the prevailing barriers to seeking help, I worry that the actual figure is much higher, especially in the wake of the global pandemic and racial unrest. In fact, in June 2020 the Census Bureau reported a spike in anxiety and depression among African Americans (and Asian Americans as well) one week after the murder of George Floyd. While research has shown that African Americans are becoming more willing to seek mental health services, such beliefs and attitudes are not translating into actually seeking treatment. On the contrary, we still believe that mental illnesses will resolve on their own and we often rely on religious coping mechanisms, such as prayer, to deal with depression. And why shouldn't this be the case when so many barriers make getting mental health help inaccessible and risky? As Dana Givens wrote for *The New York Times,* "Our culture has taught us that we do not have the privilege of being vulnerable like other communities; it has taught us to find strength in our faith. Our history has shown us that the medical field cannot be trusted with Black bodies."

Miss me with that, and show me where the doctor's office is.

In fact, I continued therapy religiously and demanded access to it when I went on *The Bachelor* in 2016. Based on the results of a psychological evaluation, the show provides select contestants with access to a mental health professional. She was supposed to be available only to those who require medication or whose assessment revealed that it was necessary that a therapist check in with them on a regular basis. When I discovered the show had a psychiatrist, I insisted on seeing her. "No, I'm in therapy," I said, raising my hand. "I have to talk to her." I spoke to her every week while on the show, and it proved to be key to my survival and success. When we had a break in the shooting schedule, I went back to my own therapist, Barbara. The show doesn't like contestants going to therapy. (Save those emotional outbursts for the camera, please and thank you.) The producers prefer to have complete control over your actions and access to your conversations, but they cannot mic you during a session because they are required to honor privacy. Therapy provides an opportunity to talk freely with someone, and I became so close to the show's psychiatrist that when I became the lead on *The Bachelorette,* I also demanded that I be able to speak with her every week.

Today I do my part to normalize therapy. I suggest it to friends, recommend it on my podcasts, and share freely how it has and continues to help me. I talk about how to get the most out of it. For example, you must be completely honest and not attempt to trick or hide things from your therapist to get the help you need. Also, a great therapist is never going to tell you what you should do. Rather, as you're talking, you're going to come to the answers on your own.

When I got married, it was important to me that Bryan and I did couples counseling. In fact, we sought the guidance of both my pastor at church and an independent third party. Because my husband doesn't see a counselor, I felt we needed someone to push us to explore the uncomfortable questions that we may not have even thought to ask about marriage. *So why are you getting married? What role, if any, do you see religion playing in your marriage? Are you on the same page about having children, and if so, what is your parenting philosophy? What are your financial goals, and how do you manage money? How do you see your relationship with your families impacting your marriage? What are your sexual expectations and how do you communicate about them? What's your approach to conflict?* Therapy and counseling are tools that I attempt to implement in every aspect of my life.

Now going back to 2015–2016, the more I talked with Barbara, the clearer it became that I shouldn't have been in the relationship with Ed at all. Nor did it take long at all for me to grasp that truth. I just did not know how to act on it. I experienced big emotional breakthroughs from that first therapy session because I was ready. I was ready without even knowing I was ready. I had gone to therapy to win back my ex-boyfriend, and it turned out to be the best decision I ever made for myself. I got more out of therapy than I ever did that entire relationship. Yes, I learned many things from my time with Ed, but therapy gave me the mental stability and mindfulness that evaded me even when the relationship was at its best.

Most of all, it gave me the capacity to finally end the five-year relationship that I'd started therapy to save. Therapy helped me gain courage. When Ed's mom asked if I was ready to be a coach's wife, I already knew the truth. The answer was no. And yet out of fear that this was my last chance at marriage and motherhood, I fed myself a different lie: that loving Ed would make worthwhile the sacrifice of everything else I wanted in my life, including a career of my own and a partner to *raise*—not just make—children.

Without the insight and support of therapy, I never would've had the strength to walk away from him. And mind you, I still wanted the relationship even when I finally let it go, because I'm not just a Strong Black Woman; I'm a Real Human Being with strengths and vulnerabilities, hopes and fears, standards and contradictions. Healing isn't linear, and it would take time and practice to dismantle my toxic impulses, but therapy enabled the first few steps: accepting that the relationship wasn't doing anything good for me and recognizing that it could never work because I wasn't even right with myself. Thinking that I knew what I wanted, I was going through the motions and checking things off the list. *Great, I got the job I wanted. Now I've got to get the husband that matches.* What were nowhere on the list were my own desires. My own happiness. My own self-worth. None of it.

The biggest benefit of my first stint in therapy was the reckoning I had with myself. When I chose to go to the event that guy was deejaying near my place, I could have easily told Ed the truth, but I subconsciously ratted on myself with an upload to Snapchat in the hopes of getting attention from the man I truly wanted. Therapy made me realize that he wasn't a man that the cocky bitch could fix. But more than that, therapy made me realize that I myself was not ready for the relationship I claimed to want. *No, Rach, fix yourself.*

When I gave myself the gift of therapy, I gave myself the safety to be honest and the permission to be selfish. With that came an acceptance that the purpose of my relationship with Ed was to prepare me for the next one. A better one. I grew up in that relationship. I went through those things with Ed not because he was my husband but to become a woman ready for the man who was. I entered therapy for the wrong reasons and came out with the right answers. I went to save a relationship with a man and ended up saving myself.

PLAN A

Don't let what he wants eclipse what you need. He's very dreamy, but he's not the sun. You are.

—Shonda Rhimes

Two younger associates at my law firm came into my office once after work hours. In a serious manner, they closed the door behind them, which is why what they said took me off guard. "You know who would be great for *The Bachelor*?" asked Maryssa.

"You," said Lauren.

Although I had never watched the show, I didn't have to ask what they meant when they suggested I'd be great for it even if my colleagues themselves were not consciously aware. After decades of being the only Black person in white spaces, I instinctively knew. If this overwhelmingly white dating show ever cast a Black contestant, they would choose someone like me. Well-spoken. A practicing attorney who attended private schools her entire life. Daughter of a federal judge.

Even as I laughed at the idea, I had this strong urge pushing me in a direction I had never imagined on my own. *I usually make a right here, but if I don't go left today, I'm going to regret it.* When Maryssa and Lauren suggested I audition for the show, something was telling me to go for it. *Why not?* It's difficult to describe that gut feeling that told me I should act on their suggestion, and I have only had it a handful of times. It had happened with the decision to adopt Copper, a choice that since had blessed me every day. Now this.

The *Bachelor* auditions came to Dallas in June 2016 and my coworkers and I planned to make a day of it. Go have lunch, drum up some liquid courage, and then stroll over to the ABC affiliate station next to the American Airlines Center, where the Dallas Mavericks and Stars play, and across from the W Hotel, where I had spent many a night.

At the last moment, however, I got pulled into a case that required me to put in extra hours that weekend. But when I told my coworker, "I'm not going," that inner voice immediately returned.

You gotta go down there.
This is something you've never experienced before.
What's the worst thing that could happen?
An opportunity like this doesn't come along all the time, so just grab it.
It's just an audition.
You'll regret it if you don't.

Yet I went to work the morning of the audition. Then my colleague texted me. *Rachel, you have to come down here. It's not even that crowded.* This was surprising, because Dallas had always been a hotspot for the show. I agreed to meet my coworker and her friend at the station during my lunch break. Since I was working that weekend, I had dressed for a Saturday at the office. Some flowy pants, a man's ribbed undershirt, and flip-flops. I had just had my eyebrows done, and my extensions were cool, but I had to roll into the auditions with a fresh face. No mascara, no pressed powder, nothing.

When I arrived, my coworker and her friend were already there. An assistant handed me thirty pages of paperwork to complete. Scoffing at the stack, I proceeded to give the most sarcastic answers. *Why do you want to be on* The Bachelor? Because I'm thirty-one years old, and nothing else has worked, so why not?

Both men and women were at the audition, and it was very *American Idol.*

"This is my third time auditioning," said one guy.

"I drove down from Oklahoma," said this girl. "And when they're in Austin, I'm going there, too."

That got me thinking. *Jeez, I just rolled in here like, why not?* If the audition didn't work out for me, I wasn't driving three hours on the I-35E for another shot at love. My next stop would be the Internet—i.e., online dating.

"I'm not doing it," my coworker said. After completing mountains of paperwork, she chickened out, but her friend and I moved on to the next step. They snapped a photo of me holding up a card with my name on it, then ushered us toward three lines. I noticed that two were moving very quickly while one remained at a standstill. My coworker's friend and I were placed in separate lines. They placed me behind four other women on the line that was not moving, and I started to panic. The clock was ticking, and I had to get back to work, so I spoke up.

"Hey, this line's not moving," I said. "And I've already been here an hour." I checked out the fast line. That one was packed with girls, each decked out from head to toe. Party outfits complete with their best jewelry and designer bags. They were showing out in their favorites to this audition.

I checked out the girl beside me on the slow line. Just like me she was dressed very casually. I asked her, "Is it me or is this line not moving?"

"Oh, it's moving slow, but you want to stay in this line," she said. "The others are just filming on camera, but this is the line to meet one of the casting producers. Trust me, it's a good thing that you got chosen to be on this line."

"Wow." It never occurred to me that they would be selecting people based on their appearance or how they carried themselves. And all before they ever stepped in front of a camera. I looked at all the hopeful ladies dolled up in the other line. So full of excitement and hope. Poor things never knew they did not have a shot. At least, not at this particular audition.

But it was just taking too long. I found a volunteer and explained my predicament. She directed me to another producer. "You actually want to talk to her," said the volunteer. "She's in charge."

I approached the producer and offered her the dissertation they required me to write about my private life. "Hey, I'd like to turn this in."

This must have been a novel thing to say. "Whoa, really?" she said.

"Yeah, I can't do this. I've got to get back to work."

"Wait five minutes. I'll skip you to the front of the line." True to her word, the producer let me cut the line, and I entered the room. Suddenly, I felt on edge. This was just supposed to be a fun experience—I never thought that I would get this opportunity.

I stood before a casting producer. "Tell me about yourself."

I was so frazzled, I started talking a mile a minute. "Mynameis RachelI'mfromDallasbornandraisedIgraduated . . ." I only spoke for five minutes yet I was rambling so fast I stopped myself. "I'm sorry," I said. "What was the question?"

The casting producer laughed. "I'm sending you to L.A.," she said. "You're going to the next step. Do you have a purse?"

"No, I don't." When you make it to this point in the process, they give you a folder filled with paperwork, but they don't want you to walk out with it in hand. This was so other applicants would not know who had made the cut and to preserve the mystery of the casting.

"I'll email it to you."

I walked out and headed back to the law firm thinking the entire way, *Wow, I made it to the next step.* When the show sends you to Los Angeles to meet the producers, they have whittled the potential contestants down to between fifty and sixty women. With each season's cast numbering about thirty contestants, I had a fifty-fifty chance of making it onto the show.

After that first successful audition, I began to tell my friends whose honest opinions I truly wanted. Looking back I recognize that I was seeking someone who would tell me not to go through with it. I told my childhood friends Erin and Angela because they watched the show, and of course they encouraged me to do it. "Oh my God, you have to!" Same with Premere, Nika, Andrea, and Mark. I even told my sisters. Everyone was excited for me and cheered me on.

I waited until the last minute, however, to tell my parents I had tried out for *The Bachelor.* I just could not imagine getting on a plane from Dallas to Los Angeles for any reason, never mind an audition, without letting them know. Once again, I needed their approval and blessing. But I only told my parents because the opportunity had become real, and I was on the verge of accepting it. If I had to tell my employer, I had to tell my parents.

The L.A. audition was no weekend getaway. Upon my arrival they gave me another massive questionnaire to complete. As I skimmed through the questions, it struck me more as a psychological evaluation than a personality test. I poured myself a glass of wine and dug in. It took me all night to finish it.

Before the audition a casting director arrived at my room to help me choose an outfit. I thought they gave this style assistance to everyone. Much later I discovered that other hopefuls didn't receive this help. Had I not been naive to this world, I might have recognized the signs; the extra attention indicated how far ahead the producers envisioned my participation in the franchise.

The L.A. process began with an on-camera interview. A producer asked me, "What type of guy would your parents want you to be with?"

"Oh my God, that's so easy," I said. "Barack Obama." Barack Obama was shorthand. My parents wanted me to stop dating athletes and choose men with greater substance. Professionals with impeccable résumés and conservative lifestyles. Someone who would make them proud to call him their son-in-law. A Lindsay. But truly, my parents wanted somebody who would respect me, love me, and treat me right. Someone I had yet to meet at the time of my audition.

She cackled out loud. "Okay, you're done. I'm moving you to the next round."

That meant meeting with the producers of the show, Ernie (who I came to grow fond of over time), and Bert. It took place in a different, big room. In the center of the room was a single chair for the applicant. Across from my single chair were two chairs for Bert and Ernie and behind them a sea of people. I didn't know at the time that they were the show's executive producers. As I walked toward my seat, I looked around the room and immediately took note.

There is nobody else in this room who's Black.

Look, I'm used to walking into the room and being the only Black person in it. Having experienced this situation throughout my entire life, I never *not* notice I'm the only Black person in the room and I know how to navigate it. But this was a radically different space from the ones I'd previously encountered at school and work—these white folks were here precisely to look at me—and I felt a little awkward. I took a deep breath and sat down.

The first thing Ernie said to me was that he identified as a Black woman. He meant it to be funny, and the fact that he had no idea how incredibly offensive his comment was floored me. *And you wonder why you have a hard time getting Black people to come on your show.* I laughed uncomfortably, having no energy to educate him in that moment. Instead I allowed him to have the moment he clearly wanted. Our conversation centered on the lack of Black contestants, and the producers were open and defensive in their explanations from the start.

"We've always struggled with getting people of color to be on the show," said Bert. "They don't want to be on the show—they don't think the show is for them."

You don't say? As I said earlier, this is precisely why during my college obsession with reality TV, I skipped the dating shows and had no interest in *The Bachelor*. I still had not seen a single episode despite making it this far in the audition process.

"Yeah, let's talk about it," I said.

Ernie then said, "It's hard to find *quality* people of color to come on the show"—a statement which I later found to be quite interesting as I learned more about this history of the show, particularly the current and former white contestants. What quantifies as "quality" as Ernie put it. Many of these contestants were living at home, jobless, and did not have direction in life past making it far on this very reality show. It made me wonder if the measuring stick for quality was different depending on the color of your skin. I soon discovered this to be the actual reality of this reality television show.

The sarcasm creeped in. "I'm Black obviously." Then I immediately challenged the producers. "How are you going to accommodate me so that I feel comfortable being a part of *The Bachelor* when it doesn't represent people of color?" Despite being on the brink of getting cast, I didn't believe they would actually put me on the show. People of color filled minimal quotas and served as spot fillers. In other words, they had no true shot at love. To me the show was an opportunity to escape my reality and allow me to experience a world I knew nothing about. I merely wanted to see how far I could go in the process without pretending to be someone I was not. I was going through the motions, unsure still if I wanted to do the show.

The producers loved my nonchalance. "We're so glad you auditioned! Why would you want to come on the show?"

"Obviously for love, but the few people of color you put on the show don't go far, never mind succeed. Why should I put my job and career to the side to come on this show? What chance do I truly have?"

We talked about a couple of other things, and they asked me

who I thought was going to be the next Bachelor. In true lawyerly fashion, I did do some research prior to the audition. A season of *The Bachelorette* was underway, so I watched clips of episodes and looked up some of the front-runners. My research was minimal, but it sufficed. When they asked me questions about the show, I dropped some names. Had the producers asked me about the previous season, I would have had nothing for them.

Then Bert asked me, "Have you told your job?"

Ernie nodded. "You need to tell your job."

In that moment it became real. I knew without a doubt that I had been cast for the twenty-first season of *The Bachelor*. A handler escorted me back to my hotel room. Thirty seconds after I closed the door behind him and began to undress, he was banging on it. "The creator of the show wants to meet you. He's coming to your room *now*. Get back in the clothes you were just wearing immediately!"

"Does this usually happen?"

"This has *never* happened."

Since they had already told me to tell my job I had been cast, I didn't think much of it. *Oh, he just wants to meet me.* Mike Fleiss came to my room along with a female casting director and his attorney friend. We started talking about sports, the show, being a lawyer—a very casual back-and-forth conversation. And as I thought, Mike said, "I just wanted to meet you. I heard you gave a good interview." Then he left.

Later during the audition weekend I also met with a medical doctor, a private investigator, and a psychiatrist. The doctor conducts an exam and tests you for STDs. Check. The PI asked me a few questions about my background and reviewed my social media profiles. Check. As for the psychiatrist, Elizabeth, she told me that my questionnaire was the most normal she had ever seen. Gold star.

Only in hindsight can I see all the signs that they were already considering me as the first Black Bachelorette. Despite not fore-seeing the producers' plans for me—I mean, I expected to be eliminated almost as soon as I arrived at the mansion—I began to get excited about appearing on *The Bachelor* for another reason. While at once intrigued, skeptical, and hopeful about the oppor-tunity, what I wanted most was an escape from my current reality. I wanted to fly, and I understood that in order to do so, I had to shut out the world and focus on how to do that. I needed to get rid of Ed. To regroup. To find myself again.

I returned to Dallas and told my job that I was going on *The Bachelor*. Thank goodness my boss had recently become a fan of the show. (Lauren and Maryssa are relentless.) He thought it was the greatest thing in the world. "Are you sure I should be doing this?"

"Oh my God, you're smarter than those other girls on there."

It hit me that my boss thought I was cast as the Bachelorette. "Oh, no, I would go through *The Bachelor* first." This initial accom-plishment was so highly improbable, I couldn't fathom staying with the franchise, never mind becoming a lead.

"Yeah, you'll be fine. How many weeks do you think you'll be gone?"

"Probably only two. Black people don't go far on this show." Ultimately, I was gone for ten.

When I told my parents I was signing up to appear on a real-ity TV dating show, I don't think it registered at first. My father's courthouse was across the street from my law firm, and I some-times picked him up after work. One evening when we were standing in front of his building, Dad said, "Are you really going to do *The Bachelor*?"

"Yes." At first, I wondered why he doubted it. After all, I had made quite a pitch to my parents. I stressed that I wouldn't be the lead but rather one of multiple women. Then I remembered that in my family I have a reputation for saying off-the-wall things. You know . . . my boyfriend had a baby, I'm seeing a therapist, things like that. It wasn't beyond me to say I was going on *The Bachelor* for the shock value.

"Well, as long as you don't do anything to embarrass the family or lose your job or anything like that . . ."

"No, Dad, I'm not going to do anything like that." When I received the contract, I skimmed through it. It contained some language that concerned me. It stated that they could have cameras wherever they wanted and could use any footage they captured in perpetuity. When I inquired about that, the producers assured me that they did not have cameras in the bedrooms or bathrooms. But I also knew that the agreement was nonnegotiable. As a contestant, I had to sign the contract as written or decline the opportunity. Confident that I would do nothing to embarrass my family or employer (I would though), I signed it. (When I became the lead, however, I hired an attorney to review the contract and negotiate my salary.)

"Then I guess this could be a great opportunity for you," said Dad, warming up to the idea. "You can expand your clientele or go into another sector of law . . ." Confident that I was too old to get caught up in any reality TV drama, they gave me their blessing. (Which is why I was floored when they were vocally against my doing *The Bachelorette*, but we'll talk about that later.)

I had one last person to tell and was hoping for a very different reaction from him. "Despite all my anger and resentment toward Ed, I miss him, Barbara," I said to my therapist. "No matter who I'm seeing I keep going back to him. It's about whether I'm making Ed jealous. Whether I'm thinking about Ed. Whether I'm still loving Ed and whether he still loves me."

"Well, maybe you should reach out to him," Barbara said. "Get the closure that you need. Maybe he's in the same place as you." I doubted this. *How many times and ways do I need to hear that the man doesn't want me?* And closure meant finished, and I couldn't bear that either.

Yes, earlier that summer Ed and I had once again rekindled our relationship. After I had reached out to him for closure, we began speaking every day again, and after six months of not seeing each other, Ed came to Dallas on a recruiting trip. Ed even spent the night with me, and the next day we made a run for food. He waited in the car while I went into the restaurant to order the food to go. When I opened the door to the backseat to place the food in the car, I saw him texting Cynthia. *Don't trip, Rachel. After all, you just got him back, and everything's going smoothly, right? He's here on a recruiting trip; it makes sense that he'd be communicating with her. She's the assistant to the head coach.* Although we were still officially broken up, we were talking and laughing for hours as if the clock had turned back to the first night we met. I believed we were finally heading back to normal.

Girl, I know . . .

Football season started, and Ed ghosted me. (Not a Rick-level ghosting but damn near.) We only spoke if I called him. Otherwise, I would not hear from him. I couldn't believe that we were back in this place with my pursuing this shell of a relationship even as I was trying to get back on track with my own life.

After I signed the *Bachelor* contract, I called Ed. (Obviously.) "Hey, I'm going to go do this show called *The Bachelor*."

"Are you serious?"

"Yeah, I think it's a good opportunity for me, and my job's letting me do it."

"Okay," he said.

"I don't think I'm going to fall in love, never mind get married." *I'll turn it down if you tell me you want to give us another try.* The pathetic thing is that I didn't even need Ed to say he wanted to be with me. I was hungry for the tiniest crumb he would throw my way.

He couldn't even give me that. "Okay, don't mention my name." Five years summed up in five words. I had been looking for someone to tell me not to go on the show, and the person I wanted most to say no dispatched me in five words. If the writing on the wall had not already become obvious, those five words made it clear that moving in the right direction in my life meant moving *away* from him.

"I won't mention your name."

However, after being so flippant with me on the phone, Ed texted me that night: *I can't believe you would do something like this.* He was seething, his messages getting increasingly rude and condescending. He accused me of not honoring the sanctity of marriage and acting as if it were a joke . . .

. . . of never being serious about him if I could go on a TV show like that . . .

. . . of selling my soul to the devil . . .

. . . of compromising myself . . .

. . . and, of course, Ed punctuated all this with the proverbial *You're not the woman I thought you were.*

For a second, I got the usual kick out of his reaction. This meant that my going on *The Bachelor* bothered Ed. That meant he cared about me, right?

No.

This time I knew better.

The fact that he cared about my going on the show did not mean he cared about me.

I texted, *You know what . . . You don't want me, so why are you sending messages like this as if you want to get together and work on the relationship? You want me to feel bad about myself about making this decision when you don't actually want me. I'm doing this. For myself. I'm 31 years old and too old to get caught up in all of this or lose myself in the process. I know exactly what I'm doing and why I'm doing it.*

He never responded. That was the last time I ever communicated with Ed, and you want to know what's crazy? After that heated exchange, I actually reconsidered going on *The Bachelor.* Two shows, twenty-four episodes, and a marriage later, I won't lie to you. If in September 2016 Ed had said, *No, let's work this out,* I would not have done the show.

The irony is that I was looking for somebody to tell me no. Everyone I turned to was giving me the green light. My sisters told me I should do the show, as did my friends. Even my parents were on board as long as I resumed my present career path after the show ended. I was waiting for Ed to finally be the one to say, *Don't do it.*

But he didn't.

He said, *Okay.*

And because I was newly sensitive due to the therapy he'd inspired, I was crying in the shower. Like lighting a candle, singing

Adele songs while hugging myself under the stream of water in the shower.

But I should thank Ed. Appearing on *The Bachelor* was my Plan B. From the first phase of the audition process in that Dallas television station until our last conversation on the telephone, marrying him had remained Plan A. It took his indignant texts to drive home the final lesson of our relationship before it finally came to its inevitable end.

Sometimes what you believe to be Plan B is actually Plan A. Even though you might resist the new pathway when God places it before you, you won't be able to shake its calling. One of the hardest yet most powerful things we can do for ourselves is overcome the assumption that everything worth having in life requires a struggle. Instead find the courage to ask yourself if what you previously thought to be Plan A, with all its friction and angst, *should ever have been an option at all.*

This lesson is one from which many blessings continue to flow. Now, does this mean that Plan B doesn't have challenges and lessons of its own? Girl, I done told you.

This is *not* a fairy tale.

LUCKY TWENTY-ONE

Abandon the cultural myth that all female friendships must be toxic, bitchy, or competitive. This myth is like heels and purses—pretty but designed to slow women down.

—Roxane Gay

Between the time Nick Viall was announced as the Bachelor and my arrival at the mansion, three weeks had passed. My colleagues and friends Maryssa and Lauren were thrilled he had been chosen and called me as soon as he was announced. While on the phone with them, I entered his name in Google. "Oh, he's cute!" Then I found some other pictures where he looked totally different. "Wait a minute . . ." I explained my confusion.

"Oh, that's from when he first came on the show."

"So how many times has this guy been on the show?"

"Only twice."

"Well, three times if you include *Bachelor in Paradise*."

Like I said, I thought he was cute. Maryssa and Lauren were especially excited that Nick was the lead, making a point to tell me that he had expressed interest in dating outside his race. This may seem like an unusual thing to highlight, but not in *Bachelor* world, where a white man openly expressing interest in a Black woman is a novelty.

If you watch enough reality TV where the premise involves competition, a contestant is bound to say, "I'm not here to make friends."

This is especially true of dating shows, where that salvo is meant to warn you that they don't care what their rivals—or the audience, for that matter—think of what they say or do in their quest to be the last person standing. I didn't come onto *The Bachelor* to make friends, but my resistance to the other women was not about competition.

After speaking to Ed and signing the contract, I prepared to leave for the show. While packing I bought a couple of episodes of Season 20 with Ben Higgins. I had never watched *The Bachelor,* and I wanted to understand what the show was like and the type of women that I'd be living with. As I watched the show, I started crying. Panic set in, and I began having an anxiety attack. *Oh my gosh, is this what it's like?* The women were bawling at the drop of a hat, running and screaming with excitement, shouting off balconies, and fighting over stupid things. *Why are Ice Cube and Kevin Hart on this date?*

I called Maryssa and Lauren. "I can't do this show," I said. "I'm not going to fit in." But it was too late. I had already signed the contract. However, the producers assured me then (and maintain to this day) that our season of *The Bachelor* featured a different type of contestant from previous casts. Still I remained terrified of the kind of people that I was going to meet. The night before I boarded the plane for Los Angeles, I went over to my parents' home and asked them to pray for me. Not only did I need their blessing before I embarked on this journey, I wanted to assure them that throughout it all I would remember who I was and where I came from. But I also needed it for me. As a person grounded in Christianity, I lean on my faith when times get hard or I feel scared or confused. With all the strong emotions I was experiencing, the only thing I knew to do was pray.

When I landed in Los Angeles to embark on the journey of filming the show, it was the first time I ever had car service. *Oh, so this is how they roll on* The Bachelor? *A girl could get used to this!* My chauffeur helped me with my bags and took me to the hotel where I would spend a few days. (You don't move immediately into the mansion because you just might get sent home after the first night.) Instead of excitement, I felt terribly sad and lonely. I remember being on the phone with my family as we approached the hotel, because I knew they were going to take my phone away. Having never been cut off from my family before, I needed every final second with them. The car pulled up to the entrance, and it all hit me.

I don't know these people . . .
I don't know whom I'm about to meet . . .
I don't know who this man is.
Wow, you're about to be on an island alone.

There was so much unknown awaiting me, and I don't do well when things are outside of my control. I am a Taurus. An Enneagram 8. A trial lawyer. A producer walked into my hotel room with a manila envelope and demanded my phone. As I dropped it into the envelope, I thought, *There's no turning back now.*

Over the next few days, producers came in and out of my room to get acquainted with me. They were the same producers who would be living in the mansion with the contestants who made it onto the show. They advised us to sleep all day before the first night of filming began prior to starting hair and makeup because once we arrived at the mansion, we would be filming all night until the sun came up. When you're done, you go down to the lobby, where your limo awaits to take you and several other ladies to the *Bachelor* mansion.

The limo entrance is the official start of every *Bachelor* journey. The lead stands in front of the mansion on a wet driveway and watches with anticipation as the limo approaches and stops. One by one, each contestant steps out of the limo, hoping to make a positive first impression, and sparks fly. If you watch the show, you know that sometimes people go to extremes to be . . . memorable. Folks have stepped out of the *Bachelor* limo wearing penguin costumes and prosthetic bellies, playing guitars and karaoke machines, and carrying puppets and dildos. Some have forgone the limo altogether to ride in on camels, oxen, and Indy race cars. However, the *Bachelor* journey begins in the hotel lobby, where you meet the girls you're going into the limo with.

When I arrived downstairs, I saw two women standing there. White brunettes who looked just alike to me. *Oh my gosh, I'm never going far on the show if this is what these women look like!* No dig to my confidence to recognize that I just don't fit Hollywood's Eurocentric beauty standards . . . or better yet the *Bachelor* standards of desirability. There were these two beautiful, graceful gazelles standing in that lobby. Those two gazelles—Whitney and Astrid—were the first women I met, and they rode with me in the limo. They remain my two closest friends from the *Bachelor* franchise and were at my wedding to Bryan.

Isn't that crazy?

On the ride I quickly discovered that Astrid and I both had a dry sense of humor and couldn't help the sarcasm. None of us were interested in being celebrities nor were we deer in headlights in front of the cameras. Honestly, Astrid, Whitney, and I all had the same objective—to enjoy the experience and have a good time. We were all open to whatever this experience brought us. Despite noticing how much we had in common in that short trip, I didn't foresee a lasting friendship in that moment.

My mind was focused on other things. In addition to doing their own hair, makeup, and styling, contestants must plan their entrance. Sometimes producers assist because their biggest concern is that contestants do not duplicate one another. (Meanwhile, they had no problem letting half of us wear red dresses, but let it go, Rach.) But for the most part, you're on your own. "What are you going to say?" they prodded before I left the hotel for the mansion.

"I don't know." I knew nothing of this man and was drawing a blank. I almost settled for *Hi, my name is Rachel. It's so nice to meet you. Looking forward to talking more inside.* Then I decided that I wanted Nick to know that I liked sports. "Is he into sports?"

"We can't tell you that," said a producer, "but if that's what you think, you're probably right."

I had my opening line.

Before we reached the mansion, they touched us up one last time, piled us back into the limo, and took us up the driveway. With the cameras in the distance, each of us was to get out of the limo and meet the Bachelor. We had thirty seconds to say our spiel, have him respond, and go into the house.

Oh, that's the mansion.
It's not as big as I thought it would be.
Why is the ground wet?
Did it just rain?
Wow, he's standing right there!

After you have been building up to this moment for weeks—fantasizing how it will play out and concentrating on not tripping over your feet or words—it all happens so fast! The limo pulled up to the mansion, and I insisted on being the first one out of the car. Trust me, I had everyone's best interest at heart. Once the limo arrives, they turn off the ignition and instruct you to crouch down, even though the lead cannot see you through the tinted windows. Ordinarily, the limo is freezing, but with the air off, it got stuffy and warm fast. Because I sweat easily, I had to get out of the car first lest we suffocate. I did everyone a favor.

They wet the driveway to make it glisten on camera, but this is a nightmare for female contestants. Villa de la Vina is perched on the Santa Monica Mountains, where the temperature drops at night. On top of the natural nerves we're all feeling, we have to step out of the hot limo into this cold environment and navigate the wet ground in high heels and a soon-to-be-wet dress.

I would come to hate that nasty mansion where they crammed six or seven of us into each bedroom, but when I stepped out of the limo, the scene took my breath away. I had never seen anything like it. With this Mediterranean-style mansion serving as his backdrop, a handsome man in a debonair suit awaited me at the end of the driveway. It was eerily quiet, and then I looked to my right. There was a sea of cameras and crew dressed in black. It took everything I had not to run back to the limousine. *He's here! This is real! There's cameras and everything. Here we go. No turning back!*

My hands began to shake as I made my way up the driveway. *Wow, he's cuter in person.* When I spoke to Nick my voice was quivering. After we said hello, shared a hug, and complimented each other's appearance, I said, "I just want you to know that before I got here, I made sure to finish setting up my fantasy team." I reached out and gently laid my hand on Nick's chest. "Because the only play I want to make this season is for your heart."

The producers had told me I had to speak generally to avoid

naming the sport or the league. But because it was football season and Nick was a fan, he got it. He smiled and placed his hand over mine. "It's so nice to meet you."

And in a portion of the conversation that was not aired, Nick immediately asked me whom I had picked in my first-round draft. His question threw me, and I became flustered. *But they said I can't mention football.* So I blurted out the first name that came to my mind.

"Tom Brady?" said Nick, looking confused. "He's suspended."

Deflategate! Brady's out for the first four, and nobody drafts a quarterback in the first round in a PPR league no matter how good they are. Rachel, you're an idiot. I knew all of this, but my mind had gone blank. *Now he's going to think I don't know football, and I just made the worst first impression.* I attempted to play it off. "Yes, of course, and I have a backup quarterback, but Brady's coming back with something to prove to make up for lost time."

Thank God for all the speech meets, mock trials, court hearings, and trials. They had trained me to be quick on my feet. I survived and recovered with what they did show on air.

"Let's talk about it more inside."

Our instant rapport enabled me to relax. Then I walked into the mansion, and I got overwhelmed all over again. The house felt like a sorority, and that intimidated me more than meeting Nick. At thirty-one, I was the oldest woman in the cast, and I had no real desire to get to know these women. I started sizing people up the way I would in a courtroom. It's ingrained in me.

Wow, look at these women.
Maybe I'll go home tonight.
Okay, maybe I can beat her out.

I observed these twenty-nine stunning women and listened to them talk. I even overheard someone say, "Okay, she's not competition." Clearly, I wasn't the only one assessing everyone.

Who's more like me? I looked for other women of color, and from what I could tell, there were nine others besides me. *Women of color don't do well on this show, so I'm going up against the others like me.* Because I didn't know Nick, that's how I was thinking. It was survival of the fittest meets *Hunger Games,* and I was not trying to volunteer as tribute.

The women were so excited to be there. When I realized Astrid wasn't so chatty either, I made my way toward her. "Oh, thank God," I joked. "I met somebody who's like me." Feeling inundated by the noise, Astrid and I hid out in the kitchen, choosing to drink coffee over wine. I wanted to maintain control over myself and stay on my toes. I looked around and could not believe I was going to have to live in the same house with these boisterous women.

"This is very sorority house to me," I said to the producer. I may be a proud Delta, but I did *not* mean it as a compliment. "There's a lot of chatter, and it's so loud." Perhaps a few glasses of wine would have washed away my reservations, but I wasn't drinking because I didn't trust anybody. "It's honestly driving me wild!" I also informed the producer that I didn't want to be one of those women who waited all night to never get a chance to speak with Nick.

The producer pulled Astrid and me aside. "Okay, you'll be one of the first people who get to talk to him."

"As long as I get to talk to him, I'll be fine." Despite feeling at a disadvantage, I had opened myself up to this unusual process. The least they could do was give me a fair shot at this improbable chance at love.

Nick and I had an effortless conversation. We talked football, law, and family, the chemistry between us coursing throughout. We made each other laugh, and it felt like time stood still.

Once I spoke with Nick and realized we had an easy rapport, I relaxed. However, I refused to drink hard liquor. I eventually had one glass of wine and then went straight back to coffee. (Oh, how that would change.) I thought the claws might come out when Corinne swiped Nick away from another contestant and planted a kiss on him, but for the most part the other contestants took it in stride. Eventually I joined the other women as we joked about the unwritten dress code that resulted in fifteen red dresses and grudgingly gave Alexis credit for making her entrance as a dolphin/shark. Days later we would bond over King's Cup and Michael Jackson.

Then Chris Harrison came out and placed a single rose on the table without saying a word. He just came and left, and producers started moving some of us to different areas of the mansion. Everyone was so excited, but I was oblivious. Clearly, they knew what was about to occur, but I had no idea. Once someone explained it to me, I immediately thought, *Oh, he's not going to give it to me,* and moved to sit with a group outside by the pool. When Nick walked over to our seating area by the pool with the rose in hand, I saw him look in my direction. Surely he intended to give it to Astrid, who was sitting next to me, so Big Rach scooted over.

"Rachel, can I steal you for a hot minute?"

I was shocked. Me! I stood up, Nick took my hand, and he led me over to the gazebo. We sat down and he said, "Are you aware of what this is?"

"I know it's a rose, but can you tell me what it means?" My question was genuine. I knew roses were a fixture on the show, but I didn't know the significance of this particular rose.

Nick never actually explained the First Impression Rose. But he did tell me that between my aura and our conversation, he felt I was the obvious person to receive it. Then he said, "So with that being said, I think you should leave." Because, of course, Nick had to rag me a bit. Then with sincerity, Nick picked it up and said, "Rachel, will you accept this rose?"

"One hundred percent."

Then we had the first of many great kisses. Here's a little behind-the-scenes: our first kiss was so awkward. Not because there was no chemistry but because I was nervous about kissing on television. Producers saw the awkwardness and asked us to do it again. We were happy to, and this time it was perfect.

I thought his gesture was so sweet, yet I still had not grasped the significance of it all. In fact, my skepticism kicked in. Once Nick left, I asked one of the other Black contestants, Dominique, "Has a Black girl ever received the First Impression Rose?"

"No, girl. You're the first," she said. "That means you're guaranteed to go far. People who get the First Impression Rose always do."

But I still resisted. I confronted the producers. "Did y'all tell him to do this? Why would y'all tell him to give me the rose? Did y'all force him to give it to me?"

"You really need to chill out," said Ernie. "Nobody forced him to do this. Nick was impressed with you and wanted to give you the rose. Stop questioning it. Savor the moment."

Wow. He really liked me. Could a relationship really happen here?

At that point, I allowed myself to just fall and relish the moment. He chose me. How nice it felt to be seen and chosen, especially as a Black woman in this *Bachelor* world. I more than survived the first rose ceremony. And my girls did, too.

Because the first night required us to be up all night, they allowed us to return to the hotel and gave us a day to sleep. I remember walking into my room, throwing myself on the bed, staring at the ceiling, and holding the rose to my chest. Although tired, I was not sleepy. In that moment by myself, I took it all in. I had zero expectations when I went on *The Bachelor*. While I was genuinely open to the experience, I believed I would be in and out. I didn't think "the guy" would like me. And I certainly didn't think I would get along with the other women. As I stared at the ceiling, I thought, *This is real. He likes you, and you need to accept the fact that you like him, too. You just might get engaged. And make some real friends.*

I was beautifully surprised by the friendships I created in the house. When the producers said the women on Season 21 were like no other cast that had come before them, they were right. Regardless of our ages, many of us had had significant life experiences and were cultured. If you watch our season, our rapport with one another shows.

And yet what aired doesn't do our camaraderie justice. The conversations among contestants back at the mansion while the lead goes out on dates are staged to look like occasional, spontaneous chats. The show's editors make it seem as if the camera is the proverbial fly on the wall as we have unprompted talks. The truth is that producers organize these conversations. They choose the topic and "cast" them, gathering particular contestants who they believe will provide the right answers to specific questions to shape their desired narrative.

These "girl chats" were countless. When not out on a date, we ate, drank, tanned, drank, swam, drank, slept, drank, worked out, drank, filmed girl chats and "in the moments" (or ITMs, aka confessionals), and . . . oh . . . drank. While I never refused to participate in these conversations, I sometimes hid to avoid them. I'd dip into the bathroom or pretend to be asleep. Most times I showed up and played the game.

Naturally, high on the producers' agenda is stoking contestants' feelings for the lead and antagonism toward competitors. Prime targets of girl chats would be whoever seemed to be the front-runner for Nick's attention. "So, Rachel, Vanessa's out on a date with Nick right now. Meanwhile, you've yet to get a one-on-one with him. How does that make you feel?" If we veered off topic, got too silly (usually because we had been drinking), or otherwise deviated from their narrative agenda, they were quick to slap us on the wrist. "C'mon, guys, let's stick to the subject. So how do you feel about the way Corinne pulled Nick away from Taylor?" Such conversations rarely took place organically. To authentically confide in one another about how we were feeling about Nick or another person in the house, we had to sneak around—standing on the upstairs balcony in the middle of the night sans mic while the hall monitor slept.

We did get breaks from shooting, providing more opportunities for genuine conversation about something other than the show. When the leads travel, the producers institute what they call dark days. The cameras shut down, and they may take us on an outing. We had a dark day while in New Orleans, and I seized an opportunity to lead a rebellion. We were on Bourbon Street and I told production we were headed to the bathroom. Having been to New Orleans before, I knew where on Bourbon Street we needed to be. On our trip to the bathroom, we snuck away and stole some time for ourselves at my favorite bar, Razzoo, where they were playing the Cowboys game. Fifteen minutes of freedom never felt so good.

Away from the cameras, we spent hours enjoying one another's company—drinking, playing games, and chatting like true girl-friends do. About things other than Nick. When women did go on dates with Nick, we bombarded them with questions like a nosy sister when they returned. "Oh my gosh, tell us all about it. Did you make out? Is he a good kisser? Did you use tongue?" Not the kind of conversation the show prefers to air.

The catalyst for our camaraderie was rather ironic: We all sensed from the start that Nick was going to choose Vanessa. Did I like Nick? Absolutely. I was shocked by how quickly we hit it off. It delighted me that he was as impressed with me as I was taken with him. Deep down inside, however, I, like many of the others, felt that Nick's connection with Vanessa surpassed all others. Making peace with this took the pressure off the competition and allowed us to focus on our friendships with one another. Naturally, the house became divided into smaller clusters of friends, and my circle included Astrid, Whitney, Kristina, Alexis, and Raven.

Astrid is my mirror. Like me, she's a straight shooter with a dry sense of humor who was skeptical of the process. Even when I drank the *Bachelor* Kool-Aid, she continued to embrace me, and I'll always love her for that.

Whitney and I connected so quickly, we chose to be room-mates. My substantive conversations with her shattered the low expectations I had upon entering the house. Whitney opened my eyes to the world of wellness and taught me about self-love and self-care. It turned out I even knew one of her ex-boyfriends in Dallas. Whitney is the salt of the earth, and someone I immediately knew I could trust.

And Kristina. You can't tell from the show just how funny she is. Despite being one of the youngest people in the mansion, she proved to be the most insightful about love and life. Adopted from

Russia at the age of twelve by a couple in Kentucky, she had an emotional intelligence that few her age do. As a *Bachelor* superfan, Kristina's a walking encyclopedia of the show, and she had tremendous insight into the process. Whenever I had questions about it, I asked her. If they referenced something that happened on previous seasons, she filled me in. Thanks to Kristina's tutelage, I became fluent in *Bachelor*. When Nick strayed from the usual format and sent her home hours before a rose ceremony, I was devastated to see her go, and unsettled by his unpredictability.

Alexis is proof of how foolish it is to judge a book by its cover. Or a person by her costume. When Alexis showed up in that shark costume, I rolled my eyes so hard and muttered, "Ugh." And yet in a short period of time, that same authenticity not only won me over, it encouraged me to lower my guard and open my heart to the experience. Alexis is so much fun that I could not help but feel free in her presence. She, too, comes from a family of sisters, and we bonded over our love for the King of Pop.

(As for Raven, wait for it.)

If I could pick three times in my life to return to, being in the mansion with the other women of Season 21 would be one of them. That's how much fun we had together and how profoundly we impacted one another. While I can't argue with the fact that some people eventually dwell in *Bachelor* Nation to an unhealthy extent, people who cast aspersions on the relationships that persist between contestants once the cameras stop rolling and question the sincerity of their friendships fail to understand how weeks in that mansion can bond you. Part of *The Bachelor* is a social experiment where you spend all day, every day with these other women. You're living together in this bubble without the usual distractions—no TV, no music, no Internet, no phone, nothing. With just each other and the art of conversation, you eventually open up to them, sharing your experiences and feelings beyond the *Bachelor* process. In our *organic* girl chats we dove deep, learned one another's stories, and shared who we were before we got on the show. We got to know each other more deeply than the man we were hoping to have a relationship with. Quite frankly, in addition to all the critiques I came to have of the franchise, I wish they showcased the intimacy that develops between the women as much as they capture the catfights over the lead. If you go back and watch the season, you can catch glimpses of that story in the background of some scenes.

The time away from the distractions of modern life was a beautiful thing, and that experience prepared me for the pandemic. In fact, I remember craving solitude when I became the Bachelorette. How I wished then to be shut off from the rest of the world, focusing only on me and how I was feeling and figuring out what I wanted for myself. That was the silver lining in *The Bachelor*. Despite all the drama, if you make it far enough, you start to focus on what you want as a person, and that's a valuable prize even if you don't get the guy.

After that first night, I talked myself into embracing the experience. To make the most of it, I had to put aside my skepticism and completely immerse myself in the journey. I bought into the possibility and became a part of *Bachelor* Nation.

RACHEL'S IDEAL MAN (AGE 31)

- ~~AN OMEGA~~—As much as I love my fraternity brothers, after dating Mike, Rick, and a few other Omega men, this was becoming a dream deferred.

- ~~AN ATHLETE TURNED BUSINESSMAN~~—Tuh.

- **INTELLECTUAL**—Some things will never change.

- **A CHRISTIAN**—Okay, I need to rethink this one . . . Yes, you still want a Christian . . . but not one in name only.

  Because honestly, Rach, as adamant as you have been about dating men who *said* they were Christian, you've been getting into one relationship after the other with men who weren't acting Christ-like, haven't you?

  Like . . . you went to Rick's church. Rick went to church with you. Meanwhile, dude had a baby on the side and lied to you about it for a year . . .

  . . . AND he didn't come clean until you found out about it from someone else . . .

  . . . AND then proceeded to lie to you about the true nature of his relationship with the mother of his child.

  Not exactly what Jesus would do.

Loosen the reins on being so dead set on how someone labels themselves and focus more on how somebody is actually living. Regardless of his religion (or lack thereof), he needs to profess the same values you do and behave accordingly.

- **FAMILY-ORIENTED**—Of course he still must want children, but we must also be on the same page about how to raise them. And ... okay, I won't rule you out if you have kids as long as there's no drama with their mama. *That* is not negotiable.

- **LOVE LANGUAGE**—After almost five years with a man who lived almost three hours away for 90 percent of our relationship, not only do physical affection and quality time still stand, I demand fluency!

MY FAVORITE EX

You know you're ready to be friends with [an ex] when you can genuinely be happy seeing them with someone new.

—Lia Holmgren

I could not have become the Bachelorette if I had not appeared on *The Bachelor*. But winners don't become leads, so I first had to be sent home by (at the time) the franchise's "most controversial bachelor," Nick Viall.

Being an attorney and having had male friends since high school came in handy. Whether or not they intend to play games, women tend to be coy about their interest in a man. Men are obvious about how they feel, communicating less with their words and more with their actions. Whenever we went out on group dates, I observed Nick's behavior. I'd watch what he was doing, how he was interacting with each of us, and—the biggest tell of all—whom he simply could not take his eyes off of.

And he was most into Vanessa. As strong as our physical attraction was, he never looked at me the way he did her. When he and I were together, he gave me his full attention, but anytime Vanessa was present, she had his focus. Even when she herself was looking elsewhere, Nick's gaze was on her, and that was all I needed to know. Had Nick and I met in the ordinary world, we certainly could have dated, but he never made me feel like he wanted to spend the rest of his life with me.

I made the final three and was excited to travel to Finland for the Fantasy Suite date. While I was on *The Bachelor,* Mom followed the blogs. Through them she learned two things. One, that I was a front-runner on Nick's season. Two, that I was in contention for becoming the next Bachelorette. Once she called to update me on my dog, Copper. I had to use my handler's phone, and she made me keep it on speaker. At one point in our conversation, my mother said, "The blogs are saying you're going to be the Bachelorette." She did not sound excited by the prospect.

My handler immediately grabbed the phone from my hand. She took the phone off speaker and put it to her ear. "You cannot talk about that," she told my mom.

Reality snuck into the bubble and slapped me in the face. *Bachelor* Nation was already naming me the Bachelorette. Meanwhile, I was focused on Nick, thinking we still could have a future. Becoming the Bachelorette was the furthest thing from my mind. How could I be thinking about becoming the next lead when I didn't even know if I would accept a proposal? That is, if I received one. Having never watched the show, I was so naive. Only then did it hit me that people used it as an opportunity to become the lead or otherwise manipulate the situation to some advantage. *This is what they mean when people question if someone is here for the right reasons.* Then I became scared. I worried that Nick would get wind of this news and question my sincerity toward him. Even with my doubts, I was there for the right reason.

Traveling with me overseas was a small crew—my producer, a stage director, and his then girlfriend—and we missed our connecting flight in Finland. We landed in a small airport in Helsinki with eight hours to kill. The day before we left for Finland, my producer escorted me to a Victoria's Secret in NYC, waiting for me outside the store as I searched for lingerie to embody a sexy Mrs. Claus to surprise "St. Nick." (See what I did there? Well, tried to do. I'll explain in a minute.) The stage director's now-wife Kate ran around the airport with me trying to find accessories to enhance my fantasy suite outfit. This was my first glimpse at the more intimate side of production, and we had a good time during our layover.

We finally arrived in Lapland. As if the *Bachelor* bubble did not already feel like an alternate universe, Finland was surreal. Not another Black person in sight. I felt like an endangered species.

Just when things could not seem more unreal, the Fantasy Suite shoot landed on the same week as the U.S. presidential election between Donald Trump and Hillary Clinton. Whether we traveled within the United States or overseas, production removed the TVs from our hotel rooms. (There are two exceptions to this rule. Leads get to keep their TVs, although you're too exhausted to watch anything. They also allow the finalists to watch TV during Fantasy Suite Week because they have so much downtime.) Other than the date with the lead, you have nothing else to do but wait.

That time of year Finland only had three hours of daylight and was ten hours ahead of Los Angeles. Between that and jet lag, falling asleep would have been impossible. However, my insomnia also had an emotional cause—the anxiety over all the fantasy suite expectations. Mine, Nick's, and, yes, the producers'. For the first time, I would be able to spend time with this man without cameras documenting our every move. My mind raced with the possible scenarios that could unfold behind that closed door. *Is he going to be as cool off camera as he is on? What if he's, like, not the man he has shown himself to be? Is he going to profess his love for me? Are we going to throw down in that suite? Or talk seriously about getting married?*

The producers wanted me to express my feelings to Nick. I genuinely was falling for him but kept that close to the vest. While I didn't doubt our connection, my skeptical nature still questioned whether Nick was as into me as I was into him. This made me reluctant to lower my walls with him at all, never mind on camera. And yet I felt pressured to give the producers the emotion that they wanted. Their pressures notwithstanding, I also sensed that I had to be vulnerable with Nick for my own sake. Therapy taught me how important it was to express how I was feeling instead of letting the fear of an unpredictable outcome talk me into silencing myself. However, being aware of that and having the guts to act upon it were two different things.

I poured myself a glass of wine and flipped on the TV in my hotel room. The BBC was covering the U.S. election returns, and I watched from start to finish. Even when Trump hit a hundred electoral votes before Clinton, and I knew he had won, I could not stop watching. The night before the most important date of my life, I sat alone on my bed in disbelief and witnessed the demise of the American republic.

I stayed up all night. It took some time for the results to sink in. *Has my country really succumbed to this? Am I watching the right channel? Is this some cruel joke?* I have always been interested in politics and enjoy conversing about current events; being more than five thousand miles away from loved ones over the most shocking election of my lifetime, I *had* to talk to someone. "Don't talk about it," the producers told me when I brought it up the morning of my date. "Everyone's in shock. Nobody believes this is real life."

The Finnish thought it was a hoot; they let me know that they had plenty of seasonal jobs if I wanted to stay. *No, thank you. After three years in the cold and windy winters of Milwaukee, I'm good.*

And I continued to drink. I drank to stay warm in the subarctic weather. I drank for the liquid courage to make it through Fantasy Week, including telling Nick how I felt about him—or at least to lower my inhibitions enough to enable production to manipulate me into it. And I drank because of my upset over the election results back home.

And I drank through my day with Nick. The daytime portion of our date occurred at the Lapland Safari in Saariselkä, a winter wonderland where we went cross-country skiing, fed reindeer, and cuddled on a sleigh ride. As part of our conversation, I attempted to bring up Trump's election. Just when Nick began to acknowledge it, the producers instructed us to continue with the date. I even suspected that he had been told in advance to avoid the matter. This shocking event was important to me and a topic of conversation I naturally would have brought up on a date in the ordinary world. However, the producers immediately sealed the hole I attempted to poke in the *Bachelor* bubble.

I remain astonished by the power of the *Bachelor* bubble. How would that evening have gone if I'd had no idea that Donald Trump had become president? What might have transpired among the contestants if we had been permitted to follow the campaigns while we were shooting? If I could have a fleeting sense of loneliness when Obama won while I was at my predominantly white law school, what would I have experienced in the mansion? (One thing I never could have imagined is four years later, as an *Extra* correspondent, interviewing Donald Trump Jr. on his father's insufficient response to racial violence and the Black Lives Matter movement. Life is wild.)

I had never felt so much pressure before this moment. The producers made it clear to me that I was behind Vanessa and Raven, who already had professed their love to Nick. I don't do well with authority . . . but I also wasn't ready to go home. Despite my skepticism and against my better judgment, I still wanted the courage to say it. To sincerely believe it. Most of all, for Nick to genuinely reciprocate the love.

Like the girl chats, the ITMs were also countless, and the further you go, the higher the emotional stakes. Throughout my time in the mansion, before several ITMs I had drunk so much, I didn't remember recording them. That said, a lifetime of practicing respectability resulted in a superpower. Once I had a camera on me, I had an uncanny ability to sober up. A young blonde might be able to giggle uncontrollably or repeatedly flub her words in an ITM and come off as a likable everywoman. No amount of alcohol could ever make me forget that as a Black woman I had no such luxury.

After our day in Narnia, we returned to our cozy hut. Nick stated that he didn't know where he stood with me and pressed me to articulate my feelings toward him. I struggled to verbalize my feelings—so much for the alcohol lowering my inhibitions. Nick and I circled the matter as he attempted to get me out of my head. He reminded me of the times I was messy and assured me how much he appreciated that. Finally Nick asked, "If you had to check your ego at the door, what would your heart say?"

"That I'm falling in love with you." My sudden vulnerability and his boyish grin made me burst into laughter, and attempt to bury my face in my hands like a schoolgirl.

Nick said, "Rachel, I'm falling for you. One hundred percent. It's easy to say."

"I love it when you say it so much better than me."

We laughed. We exhaled. We kissed. We exhaled again. And then Nick led me upstairs to the fantasy suite. At least, that was how it was edited to look on air. Having completed its mission to make Rachel say the word *love,* production actually stopped shooting. Nick and I played music, drank, danced, drank, ate, and drank as they removed their equipment so we could eventually be alone in the fantasy suite. Once production cleared the suite, Nick and I sat on the couch to talk. Ten minutes later, cue the Sicko Mode because I went out like a light. I remember nothing after that.

I don't know if Nick believed me when I told him I was falling for him. I had no doubt that with more time or under ordinary circumstances, I could have found myself in love with him. But I was not there yet. As someone who has been the lead, however, I can say that you want to believe that the person means it when they say they love you. You have to put yourself out there. You've broken hearts and brought them this far. You're invested in them, and you want to believe they're as equally taken with you. But at that point, no matter how much Nick and I cared for each other, Vanessa had already won his heart.

I have to give it to Vanessa: She was all in from start to finish. It was easy for me to resent her when I had allowed my skepticism to prevent me from doing the same, and perhaps I was a little jealous. I entered Villa de la Vina that first night believing I would be eliminated hours later, only to receive the First Impression Rose. Then, despite receiving roses after every group outing and having multiple one-on-one dates with Nick, I never trusted that my experience had gone from surreal to real. Between my cynicism and need for certainty, I got in my own way. It was hard for me to go from expecting nothing to accepting everything.

On our Fantasy Suite episode, the last thing viewers saw was Nick and I laughing and smooching on the bed. It never went further than that. I passed out and enjoyed the best sleep I'd had during those ten weeks. I never got to play Mrs. Claus, but Nick was a saint. Before I conked out, he gave me some Tylenol and tucked me into bed. My sexy outfit never made it out of my suitcase, and so the only costume Nick got to see was a penguin onesie. (This later became a running joke when I became the Bachelorette, as there was a misconception that I had a fascination with penguins. The truth is I was just trying to stay warm in the frozen tundra.)

I began Fantasy Suite Week confident that I was the runner-up only to ruin the opportunity. That night is special, but not because it's the sex-filled experience the show plays it up to be. It's a chance to connect without any distractions or intrusions. But after passing out that night and waking up nauseous the next morning, I had sabotaged the opportunity for Nick and me to get to know each other more deeply. The fantasy suite was my last chance to make my case as a partner—physically, mentally, emotionally—and I drank too much (due to the election results and nervousness) and failed the final exam. (But some setbacks are setups, although that was the furthest thing from my mind when Nick made me breakfast then left for his date with Vanessa.) Moral of this story: I blame Trump.

Then Nick sent me home, and the bubble popped. I knew it was coming. As the crew set up for the ceremony, I said my goodbyes. "This is it for me, you guys," I said. I hugged everyone from the camera operators to the sound people. Knowing that I would not see her in a long time, I even wrote and slipped Raven a note in which I honored our friendship and wished her all the best.

Anticipating my elimination did nothing to brace me for the devastation. For the first time, millions of viewers watched me cry until my mascara ran down my face. Still, no one can understand the level of despair you feel after such a rejection. I had lived the fantasy. I got a taste of the fairy tale. I saw a glimpse of my life with someone else in it, and it was as extraordinary as I had hoped. Then, under the pretense of ceremony, the bubble popped. Nick called me one of the most incredible women he had ever met. He wanted me to know he thought I was amazing. He expressed hope that I would remain in his life. But he still did not choose me. The relationship pattern I came on the show to interrupt occurred again, and I ended the show worse than I had started it. Single. Lost. Alone. My desire for a lifelong partnership was at a peak high, my hope in its possibility at an all-time low.

To this day, I dislike red roses.

In sharp contrast to the way I handled breakups at home, I couldn't text a suitor and suggest we meet for dinner or call a friend to pour out my soul. Instead I headed back to my hotel room. Whether toxic or healthy, none of my coping mechanisms were available to me.

Then came a knock on my door. The psychiatrist, Elizabeth. I fell into her arms. And just as I had surprised Barbara in our first session, Elizabeth was shocked at the depth of my upset. She held me as I cried and cried over the loss of this magical world, the walls of the reality I had escaped two months earlier crashing in on me. "You're going to be okay, Rachel," she said. "I'm not worried about you. At all." Elizabeth grabbed me by the arms, looked me in the eye, and shook me out of it. Not only did she insist that I would be fine, she assured me that big things were happening for me. Elizabeth saw for me what I'd stopped believing for myself, and I am forever grateful.

She was right.

That night a producer passed me a note. Raven had written a response to me. *It's happening. You're going to be the Bachelorette. You're going to be great.*

She was right, too.

CLARITY AND CLOSURE

Choose something different. Go a different route. And, yes, girl, change up your "type."

—Trey Anthony

Here's some irony for you. I became infatuated with Ed and dove into our relationship after a few hours of conversation on a friend's couch, and you know how that turned out. What did Rachel do next? She ran a "couch" test on thirty-one men in one night on national television.

Except I wasn't the same Rachel I was five years earlier. I'd learned so much—especially about myself—and was intent on bringing those lessons into this process. I agreed to be the Bachelorette with an open heart but a load of skepticism. If I stood any chance of finding a husband on a reality TV show—and I sure doubted it—I had to give the process my all and take it seriously. And yet the only thing I could control was myself.

I also now had another goal for appearing on the show as lead. I may not have been a fan of *The Bachelor* before becoming a part of the franchise, but as a Black woman, I know how painful it is to never see yourself represented. To tune in to a reality TV show and see all the stereotypes of Black women in full effect but never watch us be glorified, honored, and lifted up. Since we don't fit Eurocentric standards of beauty, TV shows rarely showed Black women being courted, loved, and appreciated. No matter how short-lived I anticipated my experience would be, I had a small opportunity to counteract this. Not only for other Black women my same age, but also for the young girls who watched the show with their friends. Maybe there was a girl just like me, attending a majority-white school and constantly trying to fit in instead of feeling comfortable being her true self. Even if I wasn't the last woman standing, I could go on this show for that young girl, modeling for her the possibility of her own love story. That alone would make the experience worthwhile.

I publicly accepted *The Bachelorette* Valentine's Day week in 2017 and had an anxiety attack the day before I was scheduled to appear on *Jimmy Kimmel Live!* to announce my selection. I was with my stylist in the Roosevelt Hotel across the street when he casually mentioned that the story got picked up in *The Hollywood Reporter*. For two months, I had immersed myself in preparation for an upcoming trial and was out of the loop. I even asked, "What's *The Hollywood Reporter*?" Once I became aware that this made national news, the panic started to creep in.

Once he left me alone in my hotel room, the gravity of my decision truly hit. *What are you doing, Rachel? Why are you doing this? You said yes to this too quickly.* My parents had strong misgivings about my continuing with the franchise. They had no faith in the *Bachelor* journey as a path to marriage and feared I eventually might embarrass our family or lose my job. My mother was most worried that I would be "crucified" by the public. (I think we can all agree that Mom was not wrong about that. At least as it pertains to *Bachelor* Nation.) All I wanted was to return to my normal life, but it was too late. I called Raven, who calmed me down by reminding me that I had a purpose in doing this and talking scripture with me. When I hung up with her, I was good and ready. That was how close we were . . . until we weren't. It is funny—you really do not get to know people from the franchise, discover who they are, and learn who your friends are until about a year or two after the show ends.

I knew that as the Bachelorette I had to pick my battles, and I intended to fight for a few specific things. My first decision: I informed the producers that I refused to consider two proposals. Other women may fantasize about having two men get down on bended knee before them with an engagement ring and ask her to marry them. I get it. Nice problem to have, right?

Miss me with that.

I could never have predicted that this life-changing moment would be the result of such an unusual dating experience. If this unlikely thing did transpire—a man was going to propose to me, and I was going to accept, on national TV, no less—then I would have to have fallen in deep, undeniable, and extraordinary love. When I looked back on this momentous occasion, I didn't want any other man associated with it, never mind a man whose proposal I had turned down. This memory in the making had to be preserved for the one who chose me and whom I had chosen.

Due to my newfound *Bachelor* knowledge thanks to my good friend Kristina Shulman, I knew that I could make this demand, and to their credit, the producers never pushed back. They let me know, however, that I would then be obligated to send that man home after our final date and before the proposal. If for any reason I balked at breaking it off with him, they would make me take him into the finale. He would have to propose to me (or not) and I would have to reject him as part of the finale. And on the same day I said yes to the other contender for my heart.

And so I entered the *Bachelor* mansion knowing that to hold fast to that bottom line, I had to roll with certain punches. To the show's creators this process is a game, one that I had agreed to play, no matter the stakes. While the producers never told me whom I had to date, they had cast some men for my season who had agendas beyond finding love.

Take Lee. The moment that man came out of the limo, playing his guitar and singing with his country twang, I knew he wasn't for me. True, he wasn't my type, but I made a commitment not to judge a book by its cover . . .

. . . so instead I judged him for singing out of tune.

The producers knew quite well the kind of man who would interest me, and Lee—a country music singer from Mississippi who had no familiarity with Black people—wasn't it. My instinct told me that Lee had never dated outside of his race, and questioned why he was there. Not until my season wrapped and people revealed themselves once the cameras were gone did I discover why obvious mismatches had been cast.

Now when Lee sat on that couch beside me, he was nothing short of sweet. I liked that he was Christian and wanted a family, but our conversations were brief and superficial. Already knowing we were going nowhere in the real world, I didn't bother to ask Lee any in-depth questions.

Why ask him how he felt about dating a Black woman when I instinctually knew? While Lee seemed like a good person, we didn't have enough in common or any connection to pique my interest, so I gave the signal—a little scratch to my shoulder—and soon the producers sent another Bachelor to interrupt us.

So imagine my surprise when another contestant let me know that the kind singer-songwriter from Nashville who'd chatted with me on the couch was causing drama in the mansion. (And mind you, this is how the producers prefer it. They want the lead to remain in the dark about what's going on in the house unless one of two things happened. I had to find out because either one of the other men told me or I figured it out for myself.) No one provided me with any specifics, although one did say that Lee was complaining that "they" were being loud. As a Black woman, I know a microaggression when I hear one and presumed "they" were Black men. But because I knew so little of Lee's background and hadn't personally observed his interactions with the other men, I merely thought he was racially ignorant.

Not a full-blown racist, which I realized only when I watched the show.

Look, I'm not some babe in the woods. I understand that this show is first and foremost about entertainment, entertainment is a business, and said business requires knowingly casting instigators. But I like to be prepared and stay five steps ahead, especially in such an orchestrated environment. Certain kinds of surprises I do not fucking like, and never in my wildest dreams did I foresee the franchise casting a racist on my season. Of all the narratives they could have engineered, they chose to cast a racist as a contestant for the heart of their first Black lead. And the primary target of Lee's antics was Kenny, who was not only African American but someone I truly liked.

The second Kenny stepped out of the limo, he lightened the mood. He looked me in the eye and held my gaze, and that alone assured me that he was genuinely there for me. When I found out he was an athlete, however, I let the producers have it. *I specifically said NO ATHLETES.* But Kenny soon won me over with his humor and charm. In our conversations, he was always sincere, thoughtful, honest, and unassuming. At the age of thirty-five, he was the second oldest after Bryan, and that initially appealed to me. Not only did I appreciate his honesty about his daughter Mackenzie Rachel (some things never change), I was excited to learn more about him. And Kenny did not disappoint. The love he had for his daughter was undeniable, and I saw the kind of father he would be if we had children. As I got to know the man, I completely forgot about the athlete and never questioned his sincerity.

Then things went off track when Kenny allowed Lee to get under his skin.

One night during an important cocktail party at the mansion, the competition between Lee and Kenny exploded. This party was a pivotal moment in the journey as it took place right before a rose ceremony—my last opportunity to speak to the men before having to decide whom to eliminate that evening. I was having a conversation with one of my suitors, when suddenly I heard yelling, cursing, and arguing. I was so confused as to what was happening, trying to decipher who was upset with whom and why. Then I heard Kenny in the next room yelling, "Don't try me!" He and Lee got into such a bad screaming match that I wanted to confront them and put a stop to it. The producers wouldn't let me, perhaps to protect me. Now they allow the Bachelorettes to have their say in volatile moments like that, but I think they might have been sensitive to my coming off as the angry Black woman if I stormed into the kitchen to put those men in check.

I was so disappointed in Kenny for allowing this pest to get under his skin. As one of the older contestants—five years older than Lee—I expected better from him. Furthermore, he allowed Lee's behavior to overshadow the connection we had. My time with the men was so short—too short for drama—yet Kenny continued to take Lee's bait. *Please, Kenny, be smart. Don't fall for this. Especially in front of these cameras.* Especially when I didn't give a fuck about Lee.

Truth of the matter is that long before I knew about Lee's antagonism toward Kenny, I wanted to send him home, but the producers insisted that he stay. Then later when I realized how bad it had gotten between Kenny and him, I wanted to send *both* men home. As much as I liked Kenny, his inability to rise above Lee's manipulations was a red flag that I could no longer ignore. Meanwhile, with no idea that he was actively race-baiting Kenny, I wanted to eliminate Lee as soon as possible because I had no connection with him whatsoever.

I flagged Ernie. "I'm sending both men home."

"I know you've been wanting to do that, but you can't just yet."

"What do you mean? Why?"

"Because we need Lee to go on the two-on-one." As in a date with me and another man.

"Two-on-one?" I'd wanted Lee gone for weeks but now had to spend more intimate time with him instead of with a man who actually interested me. "With who?"

"With Kenny."

That was when I broke down, crying on camera about the pressure of being in my position and worrying aloud about how people were going to judge my decisions. My on-camera remarks were, in fact, in response to the producers behind the scenes insisting that, as the first Black Bachelorette, I had to do certain things or viewers would judge me. They were holding me to certain expectations that previous Bachelorettes were not held to, and I was frustrated to tears. I was especially upset that they had cast men who were not into me as a Black woman, and I wanted them to recast. Watching this confessional, you might think I'm talking about the choices *I'm* having to make. What I was actually talking about was how, as a Black woman, the *producers'* decisions were impacting my experience and jeopardizing my reputation. It reminded me of the same power dynamics I deal with in real life.

I couldn't say *I wanted to send Lee home from the start, and y'all wouldn't let me.*

Or *You're making me go on a two-on-one date with two men who are butting heads when I already know I'm not going to choose either one for the sake of entertainment.*

Or *Y'all are making me keep Kenny when I know it's best for him to go home to Mackenzie because you didn't cast enough Black men that liked me the way Kenny did.*

I cried because I was imagining how later the Black contestants I sent home early would watch Lee go at it with Eric and Kenny and think to themselves, *Why did Rachel let him stay week after week but eliminate me?* Because *I* didn't keep Lee that long. The producers did. (And for fans who are wondering, yes, they made me keep that contestant whose annoying catchphrase I refuse to repeat.)

The drama with Kenny and Lee was about more than macho competition or even the subtle racism that played out on camera. The racial problem began with casting and continued with the directing that occurs on set to shape the narrative. When either Kenny or Lee was spending time with me, the producers would send the other to interrupt us, rigging their ongoing conflict to inevitably spill into my private time with each of them. To their own detriment, neither could speak to me without bringing up the other. Now, I never gave a fuck about Lee, but I did care for Kenny and so I was upset that he couldn't see how they were fucking with him, rise above it, and stay focused on me. Soon the damage was done; I could not separate the king from the jester.

And that's what I meant about learning to pick my battles. I had to agree to the two-on-one to finally eliminate Lee, but I insisted that they cut my time with him short. But Kenny could not resist one last confrontation with him, and it raised concerns that I could no longer ignore. I climbed into a helicopter chomping at the bit to leave Lee behind in a haze of exhaust and get back to building my relationship with Kenny. Instead of getting into the helicopter beside me, Kenny marched back to Lee. I sat there thinking, *Is this behavior something I need to pay attention to? Is this how Kenny handles conflict and challenges in real life? Does he have the capacity to rise above difficult situations, or does he allow them to deter him from his goals?* In this process, the goal was a relationship with me, and Kenny chose conflict with Lee over love with me, even after I chose him.

I couldn't get past it. Kenny's momentary indignation undermined all our moments of connection. We finally took off in the chopper, leaving Lee in that field. (And once the pariah was out of the house, the whole vibe improved.) Kenny and I spoke privately for hours in my hotel room, but the spell between us had been broken. In the ordinary world, if Kenny and I had had the time to work through the issue, we may have been able to salvage what Lee had sullied. But in the *Bachelor*-verse, where a minute is an hour, an hour a day, a day a week, time worked against us. I became conflicted, and he could tell. Add to that how miserable Kenny was to be away from his daughter, and I realized that we had to part ways.

Saying goodbye to Kenny was one of the hardest farewells, because it was the first one where I had doubts. Still, I could not justify keeping Kenny from Mackenzie a day longer knowing that

I was questioning whether we belonged together. At a crossroads and under a time crunch, I had to trust that I was making the right decision for all involved. I never wanted to have any doubts about sending a man home, but when Kenny King left me for the last time, I wondered, *What if... ?*

Without a doubt, Kenny was one of the realest men on my season of *The Bachelorette*. We used to jokingly sing to each other "Next Lifetime" by Erykah Badu, since our time in this one was cut so short. I have no doubt that in this lifetime, Kenny will meet his queen, and I'm wishing them all the best and happiness.

While I understand that producers have to consider other things than who might be a match for me, a contestant's potential for entertainment should come second to the needs and preferences of the lead. With the show attempting to cast more leads of color, I have to call out the mistakes the show made during my season to increase the likelihood that the people of color who come next get their happy ending, as well. And the most egregious mistake they made in casting my season which set up a domino effect that tumbled into my entire journey was choosing men who did *not* actually date Black women.

You read that correctly. While casting an unprecedented number of men of color on my season, several of these men did *not* date Black women, never had dated a Black woman, or had not dated a Black woman in several years. (I don't want to knock anyone for trying something new, but I find a televised dating competition to be a highly unusual place for a person to date someone of the same race for the first time.) Because of their poor job at casting my season, when I would decide that certain Black contestants were not a fit for me, the producers, in an attempt to cover their failure, forced me to keep them because it would reflect negatively on them.

Take Will, the sales manager from New York. I liked him, but he made it to the top six by default. When we reached that week, Bert, who was very fond of him, lobbied me to give him a one-on-one date.

"I think you should get to know him," he said. "Give him a chance."

"But Will doesn't date Black women." If we had not been more than halfway through the season, I would have given him the benefit of the doubt, but I had done group dates with Will, and he seemed to have more fun with the other guys than with me.

He gave me an incredulous look, and I stood my ground with a shrug. "How do you know that?"

"I can just tell. I don't know how to explain it to you," I said. Still, I tried. "It's the lived experience of Black women. We develop a sixth sense for knowing who won't date us."

At first, I thought he was taken aback because I dared to insist on knowing the unknowable (it's not unknowable, though. As a Black woman in a society that devalues your desirability, surviving the dating game requires you to take note when a brother keeps peeking over your shoulder at the non-Black women). Then Bert said, "It's crazy that you said that. We just found out that Will and Eric were having a conversation, and apparently Eric told Will he hasn't dated a Black woman since he moved to L.A." Will also confirmed my intuition about him because he told Eric he had never dated a Black woman.

"That is fascinating," said Bert. As if I were on display at the National Geographic Museum. "We must do some type of experiment to see this play out in real life."

You mean like put these two beings out in the wild and see how they respond to each other? "Look, I really don't want to . . ."

"This would be such an interesting topic to explore. We've never had something like this on *The Bachelor*." He saw no problem in insisting that I spend the day with a man that I'd made clear to them was uninterested in me.

I found myself getting a little tight. "Because you've never had a lead of color who could break it down for you like this. You've never had a Black man make it this far on your show before. There's a *lot* of conversations you've never had on this show before. This is only one of them." You would think as the lead I could take for granted that the men cast would find me desirable, only to have men casually tell me that as a Black woman they would not consider me. This painful experience is a common one for Black women and not one I needed to endure on national television. Yet another example of how the producers failed to understand the struggles that Black women face when dating, and even worse, they refused to listen to me explain it.

At this point, I knew who my top contenders were, and all of them had already had a one-on-one with me. There was no point in going on a date with Will, but the producers finally wore me down. Remembering I had to pick my battles, I changed my mindset: *Fine. Whatever. I'm going to show you that he has no interest in me.*

Don't get me wrong. Will is a nice guy. He's super sweet, and I never failed to have fun with him. But there was no romantic spark between us. Ever. Even the one time we kissed. We were in a café in Sweden where an older couple told us their love story and punctuated it with a kiss. I looked at Will like *Okay*. He smiled, laughed, and . . . nothing. The couple literally ordered us to kiss.

It got to the point that while we were exploring Sweden, the producers were directing Will. We barely spoke and Will wouldn't even hold my hand. When we came upon a guy playing music in the street, they yelled, "Grab her, dance with her!" We went to the bakery for dessert, and it was, "Feed her!" The man acted like he didn't have the first clue what to do with me.

I decided to tease Will. I took some whipped cream and painted it on his face. Then I said, "You like white cream, don't you?" Will didn't get my joke. He didn't get *me*.

The final lackluster moment occurred in the most beautiful place—a castle with a gorgeous view of Denmark. Imagine it: Here we are in Sweden standing on top of this magnificent castle as the sun is setting in the west and you can see Denmark from across the water. It was devastatingly romantic. The perfect backdrop for the crew to get a wide shot of the couple kissing. Instead, Will and I just . . . stood there. Finally I said, "I got to pee."

The lack of chemistry between Will and me was so bad that the Bert finally pulled me aside to admit defeat. "You were right. There's nothing there. This is so bad, we can't even edit it to make it look like he's into you."

"I tried to tell y'all."

"We just wasted a whole day."

"And somebody else's time." No affection, no romance, no love. Just two Black folks kicking it in Sweden. Move along, people . . . nothing to see here. "I could have had this opportunity to get to know somebody else, but you all just had to see it play out."

On the ferry ride back, Will and I had time off camera, but we didn't talk. Then we met for dinner for the nighttime portion of the date, and I finally confronted him about not dating Black women. He tried to dance around it, using the excuse that he grew up in a predominantly white environment. I told him that I did, too, but somehow managed to date Black men. Then I checked out. If not for the exposure, why would he choose to come on my season of *The Bachelorette*? Because Will had a better shot at being cast if the lead was a woman of color. Had he auditioned for someone like JoJo Fletcher or Becca Kufrin, he might have never made it inside *Bachelor* Nation.

But in fairness to Will, the disinterest was mutual. When we were ordered to kiss in the café, we were just going through the motions. I felt nothing. Great as Will is, my vagina did not dance when he kissed me, to borrow a phrase from *Bachelor* alum and good friend Alexis. Not a shimmy nor a shake. And that was that.

Casting not only undermined my already slim odds of finding true love, but the producers punted the bad look to *me* because I come off on camera as making these questionable decisions. I bore the cost of casting's need to ration Black men in my heart. This was a problem with both quantity and quality, and I never should've been put in that situation. Thankfully, they got it right when they cast Eric.

Despite being another Black man who had clashed with Lee, Eric entered the mansion with a distinct advantage. About a week before my season began shooting, I went to the gym. On my way to the bathroom, I caught the eye of a six-two brother and thought, *Oh, he's cute.* Then, when I came out, I passed him again, but this time he called, "Rachel! Hi!" They had just announced that I was going to be the Bachelorette so I didn't think anything of the fact that he knew my name. When I said hello, he said, "Nice to meet you." Then he added, "See you soon."

See me soon? Wait . . . is he trying to tell me that he's going to be on my season? YES! If this is what the men in my cast are going to look like, I'm sooo about it.

And because I didn't want to ruin Eric's opportunity to be on my season—and my chance to get to know him—I didn't tell a soul that I had already met him.

Since I made the final three on Nick Viall's season of *The Bachelor*, the producers asked me to make an appearance on his finale. The franchise had broken a tradition by announcing the next Bachelorette before Nick's season finished airing. Even though my selection was already public knowledge, I was game. That is, until they were loading up the stage. Just as I was about to walk on, a producer blindsided me by insisting I give her my phone. I was pissed. The show had given me a precise date when I would have to give up my phone, so why the hell did they need it now? Finally, the producer said, "Rachel, we have a surprise for you, and we don't want you to see it on the Internet." I figured there must have been some breaking news regarding one of the men in my cast, and they didn't want me to find out. Only after the producer assured me they would only hold it for the night, I handed over my phone.

After a short interview about my experience on *The Bachelor*, host Chris Harrison said to me, "You know, obviously, you're the Bachelorette?"

"Yes," I said, grinning through my nerves.

"What you don't know," he said, "is *The Bachelorette* starts right now. Guys, come on out!"

Of course, I was stunned. The franchise had never done this before, and I had no idea it was coming. But even more surprising is that one of the men I met onstage that night was the gorgeous guy who'd caught my eye at the gym, Eric. Our connection was so instantaneous, we began dancing onstage. And unlike the dude who bragged about how he already had two tickets to Vegas and a wedding ring and was otherwise doing too much, Eric was so nervous, his lips and hands were shaking. That immediately endeared him to me, and I thought, *I can't wait to see him again at the mansion*. Having only met three of the other men, I already knew Eric was going far.

As I continued to get to know Eric over the season, I was so moved by his story. Growing up in West Baltimore, he was the first man in his family to break the pattern and attend college. Eric also talked proudly about his aunt Verna, who had graduated from Harvard Business School and become a top executive. Eric and I found out later that Aunt Verna was at Harvard at the same time my uncle was at the medical school and that they actually knew each other well! (And I still have her number in my phone.) I was also intrigued that he attended an HBCU and played basketball (preferences, like habits, die hard). Just as with Bryan and Peter later, Eric's energy grabbed my attention.

But Eric's light began to dim. For one thing, he, too, was affected by Lee, with whom he had his own screaming match. Other men told me that Eric himself was a problem because he got riled up too easily. When I heard this, I believed the negativity was getting to him and dimming his light, because he usually brimmed with positive energy. This Eric was so different from the man who made my head turn at the gym, bopped with me onstage, and touched me with his life experiences whenever we talked. Hurricane Lee and that mansion lifestyle were stripping him of his essence. Eventually, our time spent on the couch went from getting to know each other to my questioning his behavior.

As the lead, one of your biggest fears is that the person who's charming you when you're alone is a radically different person with his friends or in real life. In the *Bachelor*-verse they deny you the usual ways you vet potential suitors in the ordinary dating world.

I couldn't research these men or discuss them with my best friend, sisters, or mother. I only had three things with which to evaluate a man: his own word, what his competitors told me, and what I could decipher myself.

So as much as I liked Eric, I had to figure out *Which Eric are you?* Counter to what I was hearing through the grapevine, he was one of the most positive people I had ever met. Annoyingly positive. The opposite of me. Eric always asked me, "How you doing? How you feel? You good?" in such a contagiously upbeat way that when I said, "I'm awesome!" I meant it. I understood his frustration when I would use our time to get to the bottom of some negativity. He may have known the truth, but I didn't know and had little time to find out. I had to ask those nagging questions instead of rationalizing them away on account of chemistry. If I had gotten to the truth of who he was sooner, I would have felt comfortable enough to give Eric a one-on-one date much earlier. I eventually gave him one, but some time had passed by then, and my relationships with other men had progressed. Meanwhile, I was still struggling to know and understand Eric. In *Bachelor* world, where a week can be a lifetime, every moment is precious, and lost time radically alters the course of your journey.

Our one-on-one in Denmark proved to be one of the most magical moments of my *Bachelorette* experience. For each date, the producers created the itineraries, and I would choose which man to take on each outing. Every week I had three one on ones and one group date.

My favorite dates weren't the super fancy or over-the-top romantic outings, but the ones spent exploring a new city. Eric held me as we took a boat ride down the canal in Nyhavn and shared stories from our lives. Copenhagen has public tubs, and Eric and I had a good laugh when the guy in the one next to ours flashed us. In fact, we enjoyed speaking with the locals along the waterfront amid the brightly colored seventeenth-century townhouses. Next we went on an adventure that I wanted specifically to experience with Eric because of his playfulness—a famous theme park in Tivoli that we had all to ourselves. Turns out that Eric was afraid of heights, but we still rode the roller coasters and swings, screaming our heads off like little kids. To see Eric willing to do something terrifying for me was captivating. Our relationship progressed slower than with the other men, but Denmark saved us. It brought back the Eric that had ignited that initial spark in me and put him back near the top of the list. We ended the evening with a beautiful dinner where Eric opened up to me about his family, growing up, the struggles he faced in life, and his hopes and desires.

My last hometown date was with Eric in Baltimore. During a car ride, I told him that I sent Will home because he had never been into Black women. To Eric's credit, he admitted that he had not been with a Black woman since he moved to Los Angeles eight years earlier. You know how I value honesty, and since I felt confident that Eric was not *avoiding* Black women, I let that matter go.

I had mixed feelings about meeting Eric's family in Baltimore. I was excited to meet his parents because he spoke so lovingly of them. However, I was nervous about facing his sisters, whom I fully expected to be in protective mode and come at me (just as Constance would Bryan). They actually were quite open to me, as were his beautiful mother and grandma.

Eric's hometown date began with a meetup on a basketball court with his buddy Ralph. I asked Ralph when the last time was that Eric brought a woman home. My casualness hid the real concern I had about Eric's readiness for marriage. "Prom."

"Prom?!?"

But my heart remained open to Eric when we were alone, and he shared the role he played in his intimate circles. "I was the friend who took care of everybody. I put this cape on, this front on. When I needed that to be done for me, no one showed up." That so resonated with me.

Eric's family cheered the second we walked over the threshold. Within seconds we were chair-dancing on the couch. Just like when Eric officially introduced himself onstage when my season began. I instantly felt at home. And his aunt Verna moved me when she cared enough to ask me how I was doing as the first Black Bachelorette.

The most eye-opening conversation during Eric's hometown was with his mom. She expressed regret about placing so much pressure on him as she was raising him, because it left Eric feeling unloved by her. Determined that he would not turn out like the other men in their family, she had doled out the tough love. While in retrospect she may have thought her tough love was a mistake, I could see that not only did Eric's mother love him, she was also immensely proud of the man he had become. The hometown visit with Eric was a poignant experience.

After visiting four hometowns, I had already made my choice. Bryan was the only one of the final four whom I could see marrying. Meanwhile, as much as I cared for Dean, I couldn't even imagine having a lasting relationship with Dean in the ordinary world, so I sent him home first. That left deciding who should go home next—Peter or Eric. The decision I made is one of my only regrets—I sent home Eric, even though I had the best intentions toward him.

In the privacy of my room, I cried over my decision to send home Eric. He's such a positive person that I didn't want our parting to be heavy. Unlike Peter, Eric had expressed his love to me, and for that I did not want to send him home. However, I already knew my choice was Bryan, and given the depths of Eric's feelings, it felt wrong to have him stay. As much as I cared for him, I did not feel Eric was ready for the kind of relationship I desired. I never doubted the sincerity of his feelings toward me, but I did question his readiness for marriage. After all, Eric had never had a serious relationship, never mind told a woman that he loved her. So I shed my tears while I was alone so I had little left for the camera. I suspected that Eric saw the end coming, and later Bryan would tell me that Eric always told him, "It's you, man. Rachel's going to pick you." (And he was not the only one.)

As I mentioned earlier, you only *think* you want to have multiple proposals until you send home someone who you believed might be the One. Eric, Peter, and Bryan were the only men with whom I could imagine a future, and so once it came down to the three of them, it became incredibly difficult to say goodbye. I had genuine feelings toward Eric and Peter and grieved the end of my relationships with them.

I so wanted Eric to be the first Black Bachelor, but I should have known the franchise was never going to choose him. Not only did he fail to check enough of their boxes, he was too Black for their fragile fandom. The kind of Black man who talks with his hands, uses his outdoor voice inside when telling racists to keep his name out of their mouths, and just might fuck up your franchise by proposing to a Black woman. Overlooking how great Eric is, *The Bachelor* was not going to select a son of Baltimore as its first Black male lead.

This is why I was so hurt when BET.com published an article about Eric that tore me down for not choosing him. Black journalists rightfully complain about the practice of white entertainment companies blocking access to their casts. I would have welcomed any and all opportunities to answer the questions of correspondents in Black media. As far as I can recall, other than announcing my selection as the Bachelorette, BET.com never covered my season until it ran that piece trashing me. Instead of wasting words to drag me, they should have just kept the spotlight on Eric, who deserved all the love they could give him. They did not have to tear me down to build him up.

If I had to do it again, I would have sent Peter home before Eric. The irony is I sent home Eric before Peter because I knew his feelings for me were stronger than Peter's. Having already chosen Bryan, I didn't want to hurt Eric more than necessary, so I left him behind after the fantasy suite to avoid dragging out the inevitable. I sent him home because he *did* love me.

For better or worse, there's a strategic element to the *Bachelor* contests, and as the first Black lead, I had to consider how my decisions might impact future cast members of color. Again, I should have had the privilege of focusing on nothing more than my own search for love, but I accepted this reality and took the responsibility seriously. I kept Eric as long as I did because of our genuine connection, but when I finally sent him home, I definitely hoped that the producers would make him the first Black Bachelor. Given his sincerity and openness to the overall process, Eric deserved that second shot at love.

If I had known, however, how obsessed the fandom was with Peter and how ugly their reactions to my not choosing him would be, I would have sent him home before Eric. Granted, I felt more strongly about Peter than Eric, but Eric felt more strongly about me than Peter did. I could not get Peter over his emotional wall by placing him in the top two, but I knew he would be less hurt than Eric when I ultimately chose Bryan.

When it came down to Bryan and Peter, the lessons I learned from my relationship with Ed came into focus. Many of us have fallen quickly for someone—your guard is down and you're caught by surprise, your breath is taken away and all logic with it.

That's what happened with Peter.

I gave Peter the first one-on-one date because I was very attracted to him, plain and simple, and his couch test took place on the car ride to the airport. Peter and I rode alone for two hours without any mics or cameras, allowing us to have a private and unfiltered conversation. Such conversations—never mind off camera for so long—are unheard of in *Bachelor* Nation. Peter was honest about his reservations about the *Bachelor* process, and it shocked him when I said that I, too, was at once hopeful but doubtful. Our shared skepticism created our initial connection, setting the tone for our first date and paving the way for us to discover what more we had in common. We laughed about the gaps between our front teeth and our decisions not to get rid of them. We admitted to each other that we had gone to therapy, and from what I understand, a frank discussion of mental health had never occurred on camera before Peter and me. And, of course, Peter took to the true love of my life, Copper. At one point, I turned to my producer and asked, "Is this really happening?" Because quite frankly, I gave

Peter the date because he was hot, but after the date, he became a true contender. As I said on camera, I was one smitten kitten. I am not sure if I ever shared this story, but one thing that truly moved me on my one-on-one date with Peter was an off-camera moment. We were riding in separate cars, with his driving directly in front of mine. He was with his producer and I was with mine, and we were eating lunch on our ride to the next location. We were stopped at a red light, and all of a sudden I see Peter jump out of the car. I naturally assume he is coming to say something to me, but he runs past my car. I look out the back window and see he gave his lunch to a homeless man sitting on the sidewalk. I could not believe that he did such a selfless act, and it seemed to come so naturally to him. There was no camera, no microphone, and no audience. He had no idea that I was even watching him. This to me was an insight into his character and loudly spoke to his integrity. I was literally moved to tears. I knew he was a special person in that moment.

Peter remained a front-runner even though we didn't have another date for quite some time. This time apart can be challenging for both the leads and the contestants. They're watching you date other people while you're trying to assure them that they remain contenders. Peter made sure to stay on my radar by surprising me with small gifts. He wrote me letters, gave me a stuffed animal that resembled Copper, and even made me an original painting. According to Bryan, the other guys made fun of him as he spent days mulling over this art project. And as my husband is quick to tease me, I rewarded Peter a rose for his effort.

When the time for the second one-on-one dates came around, I started to see the cracks in the foundation. Despite our connection, I could not shake how familiar Peter felt to me. And not in that enthralling way when you are instantly comfortable with someone and you wonder if you spent a past life together. I kept telling my producer that something was off with Peter that I could not explain. As a lawyer, I question and read people, and as much as I wanted my emotions to guide this process, my previous relationships taught me how my feelings can lead me astray. In determining which of these men could be right for me, I needed three judges on my internal committee—emotion, reason, and intuition—and I had to give each its due weight.

Right before our second one-on-one, Peter's producer told me that he had been crying. "He has so much he wants to say to you," she said. On learning this, I walked into that date with so much hope, expecting Peter to reveal something meaningful that would put my concerns to rest and deepen our connection.

On the date, I asked Peter about his past, and he told me about a relationship he had while he was in Los Angeles pursuing a modeling career. They were involved for two years, and they eventually moved in together. Peter said that when the relationship fell apart, he packed his bags and drove back to Wisconsin. As he recalled looking at her in his rearview mirror as he drove away, his eyes began to tear up.

As I listened to Peter and watched him get choked up, I became uncomfortable. On the surface, his story made sense. Once I digested it, however, it left me feeling empty. He never described the specific issues with his ex-girlfriend, his reason for returning to Wisconsin instead of remaining in Los Angeles, or any insight into himself or other lessons he learned from the relationship. Big Rach is degreed in bullshit and the dissonance between Peter's display of emotion and the gaps in this story did not sit well with me.

You really just told me . . . nothing. And if this was two years ago, why are you still crying? Either you're forcing tears because you think that's what the moment calls for or you're not over your ex. The thing I had the hardest time letting go of was that Peter had moved to Los Angeles—something he claimed had always been a dream— only to pack his bags and leave his two-year relationship without an explanation to this woman. Two years with this woman in the real world with no cameras, and you just bounce? The scene came off dramatic, but there actually had been no drama. We were at the point in the journey where contestants divulge information that goes beneath the surface. Dean revealed that he had a strained relationship with his father and siblings, and Eric described growing up feeling unloved by his mother. Bryan detailed the demise of a four-year relationship and the tense dynamic between his mother and ex-girlfriend. Peter, however, struck me as aloof and even performative. I asked about other relationships, because I had to know if Peter was ready for the ultimate commitment that I was seeking. He fed me similarly vague stories; the relationships just didn't work out.

"I'm getting the feeling from his stories that Peter doesn't know who he is or what he wants," I told my producers. "I've sacrificed too much to come on this show to end up with someone with commitment issues." And those commitment flags extended to his professional ambitions as well. Judging from the little insight Peter gave me, he moved two thousand miles to Los Angeles to become a model, and when that career wasn't panning out as he hoped, he packed his bags and went home. He just quit. That struck me not only as immature but selfish; he'd played house with a woman who probably thought after two years that their relationship was progressing toward marriage. And I wasn't even asking for marriage from Peter. At this point in our *Bachelor* journey, I just needed assurance that he knew what he wanted in life—including me. I knew firsthand what it was like to feel lost, and Peter seemed to be wandering. That unsettled me.

Our trip to Peter's hometown of Madison, Wisconsin, proved very telling. Bringing Nick home was a game-changer for me. It broke through my emotional walls, and I hoped a hometown visit would have the same impact on Peter. The producers contrived an outing with Peter's friends—something they usually avoid because they think contestants take the process less seriously when in the presence of their buddies. Unlike with Nick, who tackled the matter readily and even talked about it openly with my family, Peter and I had never discussed the ramifications of being an interracial couple. Yet there we were in a bar when in came his two Black friends and their white wives. I have interracial couples in my family and friend group yet could not imagine myself as a part of Peter's social circle or constantly talking about the "mixed babies" they kept bragging about like trophies. They surprised me when they described Peter as goofy—I had yet to see that side of him. I would have loved it.

Peter's friends were nice people, so I took great care not to project my anger at production out on them. They routinely gave me advance notice about the dates yet blindsided me with this one, and I felt manipulated. If they thought this outing would heighten the dramatic tension as the process got down to the wire, it backfired. Just as they shut down my attempt to process the election with Nick in 2016, the producers only wanted drama that they could control instead of the real issues that might organically arise between two people making a serious go at love.

I came away from Peter's hometown suspecting that despite his incredible looks, Peter lived in the shadow of his brother—the proverbial smart one—who had built a successful business. His sister-in-law candidly told me that while Peter indeed wanted marriage and children, something was holding him back. And then his mother flat-out let me know where Peter stood. "Have you talked to Peter? Asked the right questions?" she asked. "Like about his past relationships?" *Ma'am ... what do you think I'm doing here? It's not because I love Madison, Wisconsin.* "I'm not sure Peter's ready for the same things you are. I just can't see him getting engaged." Mind you, in his ITM Peter claimed to be sold after our day date because I got along with his friends. "She fits in my life flawlessly," he said. Yet later he would tell his mother, "I have walls up, for sure, with Rachel, and I haven't figured out when those walls will come down." Like my gut told me: This man did not know who he was or what he wanted, but he was a master of telling people exactly what they wanted to hear.

In fact, in almost every one of his ITMs, Peter expressed reservations, while Bryan, Eric, and even Dean were all in. Watching the show later only confirmed my instinct throughout the process. His reticence paralleled my experience of being "behind" Vanessa and Raven in professing love for Nick except for the fact that I was now on the receiving end of the reluctance and therefore it felt much more intense and therefore disconcerting.

Rather than tell him what his mother said, I made a conscientious choice not to discuss this with Peter at the time. Even if theirs is a complicated relationship, a mother knows her child, and I had no reason to doubt Peter's mother when she cautioned me that he was not ready for the kind of commitment I desired. I kept her insight to myself because I feared that if I told Peter, I'd be giving him an opportunity to defend, deflect, or otherwise write off what she said when I most needed to know the truth. I did not want to give him the power to confuse me so I kept this knowledge to myself. If actions truly speak louder than words, then I was going to watch how he moved during the remainder of this journey rather than giving so much weight to what he said.

Then the visit to my own hometown made it clearer, especially my father's succinct impression of each man whom he chose to meet off camera. He joked that Bryan talked a lot. During their conversation, Bryan related that his chiropractic practice had been investigated for insurance fraud. In trying to explain the circumstance—to an actual judge, I might add—Bryan became nervous, and when he's nervous, he rambles a bit. But the case had been dismissed with prejudice. That means it was dismissed permanently. The case really was a non-motherfucking-factor.

If you watched his conversations with my family that did take place on camera, you saw this for yourself (especially when Bryan speaks to Constance because—as I mentioned—Big Sister Energy). Bryan excused himself from the dinner table because my father had walked into the room. Dad set a boundary; he would not wait for filming to end to speak with these three men. When he came home, we stopped filming so that Bryan could talk to him, but production edited that scene to make it look like Bryan needed a reprieve from my uncle's tough questions. The truth was, he left the dinner table to respect my father's time.

You also saw how annoyed I became with my relatives. They had learned things about Bryan they thought I didn't know because of the *Bachelor* bubble. But I did. Something I have never revealed until now is that prior to my hometown with Bryan, I got my hands on a burner phone and looked him up. I found information about the insurance fraud case filed against his chiropractic firm. Knowing my family as I do, I expected them to find out, bring it up during the visit, and question his honesty. I familiarized myself with the case and had no doubts about Bryan's innocence in the matter. Plus I knew that the case had been dismissed. Not settled. Not adjudicated. Permanently dismissed. I was ready to stand up for my man. My family only knew what they read, but I knew *him*.

They interrogated Bryan, and while he held his own, I felt compelled to defend him. But as my brother-in-law later pointed out, my passionate defense of Bryan reflected how much I cared about him. He saw my passion as a good sign. Meanwhile, my mother and sisters could not see past their protective lens. (Once again, the value of additionally getting a male opinion.) Constance especially needed more time than a hometown but eventually came around. And I still heeded my mother's counsel. Before I left for the show, she told me to trust my gut. I did, and it never failed me. My gut told me to trust Bryan.

Dad admired Eric's story but didn't think he and I were on the same page. Although I had had several meaningful relationships and was ready for marriage, Eric had never told a woman he loved her or taken her home to meet his family before me. My father didn't question Eric's sincerity but considered his relationship inexperience a huge flag. "He's still learning" is how he put it.

The rest of my family liked Peter. After their off-camera conversation, however, Dad stated plainly, "The ends don't match up." Unlike Eric, my father *did* question Peter's sincerity and bought nothing he had to say. It amazes me to this day how Mom and my sisters questioned Bryan's intentions because of his eagerness to respond to their concerns but only Dad picked up and called out the same issue with Peter. (I guess Father knows best in this situation.)

I could no longer ignore it. Peter was a man who did not know himself, and if he didn't know himself, how was I supposed to know him, never mind choose him? In the final stretch, I figured out what I had to ask Peter and I had the perfect opportunity to do so.

The fantasy suite.

If I had my way, however, it never would have taken place, because I was so bothered by the things Peter told me during our dates. At the vineyard in Rioja, he admitted that when he spoke to my mother, he said he was uncomfortable asking for permission to propose to me, but that he did ask for permission to continue to date me. He said it like he did something. Like I was sixteen. (How do all the people on Team Peter not see the problem with this? Don't answer that. I already know.) Before I could respond, we were interrupted by an adorable Spanish girl who led us to the vat to stomp grapes for wine.

Later that night we had the evening date that precedes the Fantasy Suite. Over dinner Peter and I had the conversation that served as the prequel to our breakup. We just were not able to break through to an understanding, and based on that impasse, I did not want to invite him to the fantasy suite. I was so frustrated with Peter that I cried on that date. During a break in filming, I told Bert that I wanted to send him home. He reminded me of my ex-boyfriend, I explained, and no amount of connection could override my frustration. I made it clear that I had not come to the show for a boyfriend, and Peter had been the first to say that he saw no common ground. The producers claimed it was too late to call him a car to take him back, and that it might be good for us to have some time together. I finally agreed to use the fantasy suite as an opportunity for Peter and me to learn more about each other.

That night I received the clarity I had been praying for. Peter and I talked a lot that night. Some of it was good. But some of it was bad. This was the second time Peter and I had complete privacy. Without any mics or cameras, I lay on the bed beside Peter and asked him, "So . . . let's say I choose someone else, and they offer to make you the Bachelor," I said as nonchalantly as possible. "Would you do it?"

"I don't know. I don't know if it's for me," he said. I felt a momentary sense of relief because I believed him. Not only had Peter expressed this hesitation from the start, I initially took his consistency to be a reflection of how much he cared for me. After putting his heart on the line only to come in second place, why try again using the same process he never trusted in the first place, right? But then Peter blindsided me with a brutal honesty I didn't see coming. "Like, they'd have to pay me a half-million dollars."

And he was not joking.

My heart sank. Not just because I suddenly saw Peter as someone who was only on the show for material reasons. What I believed was much more painful and personal. Despite our connection, Peter's skepticism still overrode the openness he claimed to have. The time we spent together was not enough for him to take a leap of faith.

But for half a million dollars he would go through this process—one that he still doubted and was reluctant to give his all to—as the lead.

My response was matter-of-fact. "They're not going to pay you that." Peter didn't know who he was yet somehow believed that in ten weeks he had become a reality TV mainstay like Pauly D. "Not even close."

"They won't?"

"No, in my experience, they pay you based on the amount of money you make in real life." Peter told me what he made the previous year—while I can't remember the exact figure, it was rather low—and I had to repeat myself. "They're not paying you a half million."

I did not care to break this down for Peter at the time, but I want you to understand. The reality TV genre is lucrative in part because production costs are far lower than for a scripted series. No need to pay actors, writers, and other talent guild minimums, build sets, or rent extensive equipment. And to keep their profit margins large, they lowball cast members, including me. When they started our negotiation at five figures, I informed them that I was already making six figures and could lose my job after appearing on the show, so they needed to come correct with me.

For all his stated reservations about the process, Peter was definitely entertaining the idea of becoming the next Bachelor. And he had a price in mind. Although I had no access to social media at the time, I presumed he was a fan favorite and said as much. "America's going to be obsessed with you." He matched the prototype the franchise had molded over almost two decades and *seemed* emotionally available and financially successful.

He said, "You think so?" And that was another fundamental difference between Bryan and Peter. Bryan not only knew who he was, he had tremendous confidence in himself. Peter, however, had many insecurities. I had already come from the hometown visits knowing Bryan was my choice, and the fantasy suites confirmed my decision.

And now to the conversation that 7.5 million people and counting have seen—and misunderstood. Knowing that I did not want to receive two proposals and had chosen Bryan, the producers reminded me that I had to send Peter home after our final date. Viewers mistook my strong emotions in that last conversation, thinking Peter was whom I truly wanted and would have chosen had he just agreed to propose to me. Nothing could be further from the truth. That wellspring of emotion came from a powerful realization.

Peter was Ed in the *Bachelor* bubble. He felt familiar to me in a disquieting way because I had been in that emotionally painful place before. Despite how much I cared about Peter, I needed to honor the commitment I had made to myself to never again head down that same road. Going into that conversation with him, I had no questions, doubts, ifs, ands, or buts. Camera or no camera, our breakup was as real as it was inevitable, and I had to grieve it like any other. I had to say everything that needed to be said, cry it all out, and leave behind all the emotions I had for Peter so I could move toward Bryan with a full and ready heart. To come correct to my relationship with Bryan, I had to walk away from Peter with nothing left to give him but the eyelashes on the floor.

When I rewatch that final conversation with Peter, I see the moments when that unsettling familiarity triggered some old habits. I recognized flashes of unhealthy patterns in my own behavior. I caught glimpses of Old Rachel and am so grateful that the work I had done on myself prevented me from going down the wrong path. That became most evident when Peter grudgingly said that he would propose to me after all, and I said, "Stop! You know you don't want to do that." (Funny how the people who call me Ring Lindsay and said I settled for Bryan conveniently forget that their great white hope was willing to give me a proposal, and I rejected it.) Even though I backslid here and there, I ultimately never veered from the future that I wanted and I knew I could have with Bryan.

So miss me with *Oh, you really wanted a proposal from Peter.* I knew what I wanted from the situation and exactly what I was doing, moments of weakness notwithstanding. When Peter capitulated to a proposal, I could have agreed to accept it. But staying true to my intentions, I still said no, and we were done.

I anticipate that those obsessive Peter fans who read this are going to say, "Well, if you weren't that into him and were confident in your choice of Bryan, why were you so emotional about breaking up with Peter?"

Because despite whatever you presume, I'm a complex human being.

Yes, I'm strong, tough, and independent, but why are you expecting me to be all those things all the time? Should I approach matters of the heart as I would a business transaction? Or was I supposed to stride into that suite and tell Peter, "I really need you to get the fuck out," like I did DeMario Jackson? How quickly you forget how I also fought back tears when I told the other men about eliminating DeMario because he had a girlfriend and how I broke down when I sent home Matt Munson, with whom I bonded because he reminded me so much of myself.

Here's the honest truth: Once I had clarity with Bryan, all I wanted from Peter was closure.

THE LAST MAN STANDING

Be sure it's your real self you're showing. Because it's your real self that needs to be loved.

—Daphne Rose Kingma

Obviously, Bryan aced the couch test, and many more to follow.

Of thirty-one men he was the only one who came in hot. Bryan stepped out of the limo, took my hands in his, and addressed me in Spanish (which is when my friends watching at home yelled, "She's done!"). At another point that first night, Bryan steered me away from another cast member and walked me to the front door of the mansion. Despite being surrounded by a camera crew and only a stone's throw away from the other men, it felt like there was no one else there besides the two of us. As we stood alone at the entrance of this iconic place, Bryan told me a little bit about himself. I was thrilled to learn he was a thirty-seven-year-old chiropractor—an older man with an actual career instead of a job. We joked about the fact that he was trouble although he assured me he only meant the best kind.

And if you're a fan of the show, you already know that not only was Bryan the first and only man to kiss me that night, he made me swoon. No small feat when I adamantly told the producers I had no intention of letting any of the men kiss me on that first night. *Plenty of time for all that,* I specifically said. Yet when Bryan leaned in, took my face in his palms, and pressed his lips against mine, I felt the shimmy and shake everyone hopes to feel when kissed.

In addition to being a phenomenal kisser, Bryan's confidence set him apart from the others. Some of the men acted as if they were afraid of or intimidated by me, and as you probably understand by now, I was over entertaining doubts about a man's interest. I never questioned how Bryan felt about me. He always made me feel like I was the only woman in the world. Our interactions flowed so naturally, I would forget that we were in the *Bachelor* bubble and not out in the wild. I savored this instantaneous rapport because it doesn't happen as frequently as you think. This is why I gave the First Impression Rose to Bryan. One thing I had learned by the time I began this journey was not to confuse chemistry with connection, and I took the symbolism of the First Impression Rose seriously. That first night I experienced both with Bryan, and he deserved the rose hands down. I walked into the mansion eager to get to know Eric, whom I was very attracted to and had already met twice. But when the night was over, all I could think about was Bryan.

I liked Bryan so much, he frightened me. Things between us were too easy, and you know I'm not used to easy. When it comes to men, I was accustomed to struggle. I was used to ambivalence, confusion, and discord. I thought, *This guy cannot be real. What's wrong with him? He's an attractive man with a career, living in Miami, so why is he on* The Bachelorette?

"You're too good to be true," I'd say. Repeatedly.

Finally Bryan said, "Why do you keep saying that?"

"You seem so put together that I just don't understand why you're here."

"I could say the same exact thing about you."

And I had to laugh. "You are so right!" In the moment, I said it jokingly, but Bryan made me realize how hypocritical I was being. Behind my repeated question was a judgment about him that could easily be turned on me. For one, I was a little older—at least as far as *Bachelor* cast members go. I had a career. And there I was on a TV show looking for love. I'd had several previous relationships, and if you asked me why, with all I had to offer, I was still single, I'd simply respond that those previous men and I were not right for one another.

Once Bryan said that to me, I shut up and stopped asking him why he was on *The Bachelorette*. Why couldn't he be exactly who he said he was? At that point, I let go of the limiting belief that Bryan was too good to be true and just allowed myself to fall.

Bryan spoke early and frequently of his parents and their relationship. When he described how his mother took care of his father as he battled cancer, I could feel the love his parents had for each other. They modeled the kind of relationship he wanted for himself but had yet to find. Our conversation reminded me of the sacrifices my father was willing to make for my mom and the family they wanted to have together. Unlike Jeff or Ed, Dad not only had a vision for the kind of family he wanted, he also had far more faith than ego and made the sacrifices necessary to bring the vision to life. He trusted their love, and when Bryan spoke of his parents, I saw his capacity to practice the same commitment as my father.

However, I noticed that Bryan and I had not spoken about his past. As important as his intentions and goals for the future were, I needed to hear more about the experiences that had shaped him. What was growing up like for him? What were his previous relationships like? How did he learn and how did he grow from these past experiences? One telling conversation we had that was captured on camera was about how Bryan grew up as the ugly duckling and how that insecurity affected him when he was younger. *Oh my God*, I thought, *me, too!* I lived in the shadow of my older sister, the beauty queen with the coveted height and figure. Bryan and I connected over the awkward experience of coming into our own—the ugly ducklings transforming into beautiful swans—and struggling to handle the newfound attention we received from other people because we still perceived ourselves in old ways. When recording my ITMs after such conversations, I would interrupt myself to look away from the camera and say, "I really, really, really like Bryan."

With every conversation I had with Bryan, the more evident it became that we shared a similar attitude and outlook. *I took a chance and put my life on hold to see if I could make a connection, and if I do, I'm going all in and not looking back.* Some folks worried that Bryan had an answer for everything, but I found his forthrightness refreshing. Bryan never hesitated to tell me what he wanted for his future. Nor did he withhold out of fear of how I might react. And, importantly, Bryan *didn't* invest any time or attention into the drama at the mansion, and that spoke volumes to me, especially when other men could not wait to tattle on one another.

Bryan held my interest while patiently waiting until mid-season to finally have a one-on-one date with me. We were exploring Oslo, Norway, together, which included rappelling down an Olympic ski jump. At first, I was acting hard because I love thrills and am not afraid of heights. Once he got over the shock, Bryan said, "If you're not scared, I'm not scared."

Then I noticed the lift was 187 feet off the ground, and I panicked.

(Cue Dr. Dre and Snoop Dogg.)

"1-8-7?" I said in my ITM. How was this not bothering anyone? I tried to laugh it off, but I was actually shaken. "Is anybody else getting that?"

"What is 187?" asked a producer.

"MURDER!"

With 1-8-7 in my head, I looked over the ramp and almost bailed, but Bryan coaxed me into it. He knew that this was a rare opportunity to have an unforgettable experience. Later I would learn that he's terrified of heights, but you would never know it by the encouraging way he spoke to me as we inched our way toward the ground. Bryan even kissed me on the way down, and I had no idea he was quaking inside. This gave me a glimpse of our future. If we encountered challenges, and I became frightened, I could trust Bryan to be steadfast and get us through them. Most of all, he was a man who was willing to take advantage of every moment life brought his way.

(Although later when I rappelled again off the side of an even taller building in Dallas to raise money for charity, Bryan would not have it. Homeboy was like, *No, I'm good and I already got the girl.* Anyway . . .)

After our date, Bryan surprised me. While I was shooting my ITM about our one-on-one, he broke away from his producer, snuck up behind me, planted a kiss on my cheek, then ran off like a crushing schoolboy. Then came serendipity. A producer I had bonded with while on *The Bachelor* revealed something about Bryan. She'd earned my trust when I was on a date with Nick Viall in New Orleans. She got me to open up because I never felt she was attempting to coax things out of me. On my season of *The Bachelorette,* this producer was assigned to the mansion with the guys.

And yet somehow instead of his usual producer, she accompanied Bryan on our date in Oslo. At one point while I was unmiked, I asked her, "Do you think Bryan is for real?"

"You know, at first I was skeptical about him, too," she said.

"He's just so together."

"Right! But after spending the day with him, Rachel, I can tell you Bryan is so into you. He couldn't stop talking about you and kept asking, *When do I get to see Rachel again?*" Then she added, "And he's really a good guy."

I can't underestimate the power of receiving that inside information. Throughout the process, I consistently followed my heart and trusted my gut. It was exciting to receive that affirmation from a source I valued, because such real-life assurances are rare in the *Bachelor* bubble. But don't think that was the only information I got from the inside. I would later learn that the intentions of some of my other suitors were not genuine. Ladies, I am telling you . . . Always trust your gut.

Even being equipped with all of this information, I still kept looking for cracks in the foundation. Bryan was as solid as they come, but I was intent on finding out why this man who seemed so right for me was still single. *Go deeper, Rachel. Find the catch. Ask him about his past relationships.* Eric's limited experience with women caused me great concern, and he was eight years younger than Bryan. If Bryan had told me that he had never had a serious relationship before coming onto *The Bachelorette,* we would not be married today. No way would I choose a man who had played the field for almost twenty years to decide to score a fiancée on national television. Like me, he had to have been looking for someone to marry and start a family with and had yet to find the right person.

Bryan actually had a four-year, live-in relationship with a woman who wanted marriage. She checked off the proverbial boxes (men have them, too) and got along famously with his mother. And yet Bryan could not shake the feeling that something important was off between them. Like Ed, who got engaged to his high school sweetheart because she became pregnant, it would have been easier for Bryan to propose to his then girlfriend than to break up. They had a house together, and his family approved of her. But Bryan couldn't see forever with her, and so he walked away rather than betray his heart. Hearing this made me think, *Okay, if this man proposes to me, he's serious because it's something he's never done before.*

Bryan also told me about the whirlwind romance he had with a woman who eventually broke up with him when she could not get along with his family. In fact, he likened the intensity of their passion to ours and admitted that the similarity frightened him a little. To me that indicated a willingness to truly learn from past experiences. Since I was making the effort to be a woman who did that, I needed a man who could do the same.

For every question I had, Bryan freely gave me answers, giving me insight into the kind of man he would be in a relationship. The next step was to visit his family in Miami (where we ultimately lived for two years), and I was so nervous about meeting his mother. Before going to Miami, I knew how I felt about Bryan even though he did not know. I understood the stakes of this visit, and Bryan was shocked at how nervous I was, as he had never seen this emotion from me. I was nervous because I knew I could be meeting my potential in-laws. You see, I have a knack for impressing parents, but the stakes were much higher here. Bryan is his mother's only son, and they were quite close. Unlike my own parents, who prefer to refrain from involving themselves in their children's personal affairs, Bryan's mom, Olga—as the Spanish idiom goes—*no tiene pelos en la lengua.* That literally translates to "she has no hair on her tongue," which means that Olga does not mince words about anything, including her child's relationships. Bryan's ex-girlfriend's inability to get along with his mom became an irreparable breaking point in their relationship. Thankfully, we did not have that problem as it was the start to a beautiful relationship with my future mother-in-law.

Not only was our time in Miami magical, Bryan told me on camera that he loved me. And I melted because before I stepped onto the plane, I already knew he was the man I wanted. I knew when he took me to Calle Ocho and introduced me to arepas (without the cheese because he knew I hated it). I knew when we stopped for gelato. I knew when we went dancing at Ball & Chain for my birthday, and Bryan proved to have two left feet (we are about busting stereotypes in this family).

"He's the one," I told Bryan's producer. I was ecstatic. And a little drunk. But I was sober enough not to break one of *The Bachelorette*'s cardinal rules—do not tell any of the men that you are in love with them. But I had to tell someone and chose Bryan's producer, because her confidence in his sincerity toward me made me take a bigger chance on him. "I'm in love with him."

"Wait . . . what?"

"I didn't say that. I'm tipsy."

But I had one more test. Bryan's focus on me was at once gratifying and discomforting. I had never had a man treat me with such healthy regard, and I didn't always know how to handle it. That's why it was easier for me to hold on to Peter. The emotional tug-of-war I had with him was the devil I knew. Without knowing the chaotic details of my previous relationship, people don't understand why choosing Bryan over Peter reflected my growth. The final thing I had to know during our fantasy suite experience (not that, although you already know that I believe sexual compatibility is important) was the same question I had posed to Peter.

"If I don't choose you, will you be the Bachelor?"

"Why are you asking me that question?"

"I think it's a fair question."

"I'm not thinking about that," said Bryan. He assured me that he came onto the show with the intention of no longer being a bachelor, never mind repeating this on-camera search for love as the lead. Then he asked, "Do you love me?"

His question scared me. First rule of *Bachelor* Nation is do not give away your feelings to a contestant. Especially if you've actually fallen for them. "Yes, I'm falling in love with you."

"No, are you *in love* with me?" Bryan was not going to play these semantic games with me. He had been answering all my questions and taking my challenges and tests in stride. Now he was demanding the one answer I was prohibited from giving him. *Do I tell him what the show says he's not supposed to know?*

"Yes, Bryan," I said. "I'm truly in love with you."

And then we stayed up the entire night. After Bryan left the next morning, I was in the suite speaking to my producer, when he returned to get something he had forgotten. When I say I screamed for joy at the sight of him, I kid you not. I even startled my producer. I wasn't expecting to see Bryan again, and there he was! Later, in the ride back to my hotel room where I wasn't miked, I let her know.

"Bryan's the one," I said. "I'm going to say yes to Bryan."

"Oh my gosh, let me tell you . . . I'm so happy you picked him." She paused before continuing. "I don't know if I should . . ."

"What?"

"I didn't want to tell you what you should do or sway your decision, but Bryan is a good guy . . . I know you like Peter, but he has said some things in the house . . ."

"Like?"

Peter's preoccupation with the aftermath of *The Bachelorette* was greater than what he let on in the fantasy suite. In the house, he was asking lots of questions about what happened next. He even asked if the winner got to go on *Ellen*. Peter asked so many questions about the notoriety that came after the show—where the winner would appear and whom he would get to meet—he actually rubbed the producers the wrong way, making them question his intentions for being on *The Bachelorette*. I could have been upset by this revelation, but it confirmed for me that I had made the right choice, and I felt great.

And yet, as much as the *Bachelor* franchise promises the fairy tale, it rarely delivers. This is because the show's primary agenda is to *forestall the fairy tale*. It's less interested in showcasing a happy ending than it is in making the audience fall in love with the *next* potential lead. Regardless of how genuine or even historic, happy endings do not sustain the franchise. The first Black lead chose and ultimately married a Latinx man, but the depiction of our union paled in comparison to the countless white couples that came before us, many of whom did not last. Granted, I personally benefited from this show business rationale, but I resent how the show didn't give my union with Bryan as much screen time as it did my breakup with Peter.

Especially when I woke up the morning after sending him home to fresh tears. Tears of joy, excitement, and disbelief. After all the heartbreaks and doubts that led up to this decision to come on a reality TV show for love, *I actually succeeded.* Having worked on myself, I had become the woman I needed to be to have the kind of relationship I desired. No one gave me the fairy tale ending. I earned it.

I wish you could have seen my confessional where I'm crying, "I can't believe this is happening for me. This is such a beautiful moment. I'm really getting my fairy tale ending." Thinking that eventually this was going to air and wanting Bryan to see how assured and elated I was, I said, "I can't believe this amazing man loves me."

But they showed none of it. As presumptuous and cruel as it is for many *Bachelor* fans to say that I cared more about the ring than the man, that I received Bryan's proposal with a divided heart and settled for him, I understood their initial skepticism to a small degree. Reality TV makes viewers believe they have witnessed all the significant moments necessary to understand the major events that transpire during the course of a show. They don't know what they don't know. (That said, for people who were unaware of all the factors influencing my decision in 2017, y'all still do too much and are toxic as fuck when it comes to defending your mediocre white men.)

The only documentation I have about my excitement over Bryan's impending proposal is footage of me in the elevator with my three producers on my way to meet him. There I was, wearing a full face of makeup and a thirty-pound beaded dress. Every time I stepped on the train, beads popped off, and as I walked I left a trail behind me. Suddenly one of the producers started playing Beyoncé's "Halo," the song Bryan chose as our song because he said it reminded him of me. From the elevator to the car, the four of us were dancing and singing along to "Halo"—a sharp contrast from the dark place the show chose to paint of the previous night. I was thrilled to say yes to the man of my dreams.

Things were perfect until we reached San Vicente de la Sonsierra—a gorgeous fortress in Rioja, Spain. Mother Nature was not on our side that day. It was cold and cloudy. The wind exposed the tracks of my weave, and I started crying because I wanted to be beautiful for Bryan. So silly of me. He's not the kind of man who cares about things like that. When I saw him approaching me, beaming, excited, I checked myself. *Girl, if you don't stop. You could have shown up in a paper bag. All he cares is that you say yes.* All my tears dried up, and I decided to play with him a little bit. At the beginning of the proposal, I pretend to be somber and torn as if I might actually reject his proposal. "Um . . . my heart has never been more confused than it has been this week . . ." That is, until I say, "Right here in this moment standing with you, I see my forever." And then Bryan's face lit up (although he'll claim that he was just squinting because the sun got in his eyes. Roll tape. There was no sun. He truly feared that I was turning him down).

My weave was all over the place, Bryan tried to lift me in this thirty-pound dress, and I was mortified that we might collapse under its weight. But I was also on cloud nine. So was the crew, including the stylist, who normally left before the proposal. Sensing the magic of the moment, not only did he choose to stay, he cried along with the rest of us.

Then came the moment we most desired and feared. After weeks of being kept separate, the producers told Bryan and me that we could ride together back to the hotel. It took a while for our newfound privacy to sink in. No more cameras, no more mics, no more reason to be *on*. Would this be the same person I said yes to now that nobody else was around?

Before we left the proposal site, I promptly changed out of that heavy gown. The symbolism was not lost on me as I shed the title Bachelorette and returned to my full self. I slipped on something far more comfortable. During our Fantasy Suite, Bryan gave me a gift: a University of Texas football jersey. On the back it read "Dr. Abs and Big Rach . . . I will always have your back." And as I put on that jersey and my hand in his, I knew Bryan truly did. We came separately as single individuals but left together as an engaged couple, ready to build a future as one.

Once inside the limousine, we both let out a huge sigh of relief, held hands, and could not stop smiling and laughing with each other. Later, when we closed the door to our hotel room, and it was finally just us, we embraced, made love, fell asleep, woke up, and then had dinner. We ended our day as a newly engaged couple drinking wine in the bathtub so excited about spending the rest of our lives together. At one point, Bryan grew quiet, and I saw that he was crying. When I asked him why he was crying, he expressed the depth of his joy and excitement about us. Then I began to cry, too. He let himself go and so did I and I knew in that moment once again I had made the right choice.

This unseen epilogue to our Bachelorette journey proved to be the most magical of all because in that moment I realized that this was a happy ending for him, too.

LET NO MAN PUT ASUNDER

Oh my God . . .

. . . I just looked at how I described my ideal man at the age of thirty-one and . . .

. . . *I'm NOT describing Bryan!*

And the biggest departure from the checklist of my youth is that my husband does not identify as a Christian. This "requirement" remained a deal-breaker for almost fifteen years. And then I met Bryan, and you already know how that turned out.

There's a frequently quoted Bible verse during sermons—2 Corinthians 6:14—aimed at couples. *Be ye not unequally yoked together with unbelievers: for what fellowship hath righteousness with unrighteousness? And what communion hath light with darkness?* In a nutshell, do not partner with someone who is not also a Christian. The warning is that if you marry someone who does not believe in and follow the example of Jesus Christ—that person is going to do things that are sinful or otherwise go against what the Bible preaches and eventually bring you down with them.

I can clearly remember being at the chapel at First Baptist Academy as a teen when a guest speaker demonstrated the concept of being unequally yoked. He pulled a chair to the front of the room and asked a volunteer to come and stand on it. From where he stood on the ground, he told the volunteer, "Pull me up." Try as he might, the volunteer could not pull him up off the ground. "Okay, hold out your arm," he then said. "I'm going to try to pull you down." And with one swift yank, he was able to pull the volunteer off the chair and beside him on the floor. "You see how much easier it is for someone to drag you down to their level than it is to lift them up to yours?" That was one of the few lessons from all those years in chapel at First Baptist that I remember, and I took its moral to heart.

However, my dating history made me question why this meant my partner and I had to follow the same religion. I was so forgiving of all those Christian boyfriends doing me all kinds of dirt, thinking, *That Christian guilt will get to him soon enough*. I laugh now because the only time that *might* have happened, dude decided that instead of being honest with me, he would ghost. Young and silly Rachel told herself that Christian guilt is what made Rick disappear like Jesus on the third day from the Garden Tomb.

At least Jesus came back. And He was actually resurrected. So not quite the same thing, but you get my point. He was gone.

I was raised in the Missionary Baptist Church from the time I was born until the age of eighteen. When I was in elementary school, a married pastor impregnated one of the congregants. So, is that Christlike? I'm not saying Christians can't mess up. Nor am I diminishing their capacity to repent and atone. Also, I've known couples in the church who weren't equally yoked when they married, and yet through time and experience, they landed on the same page. My point is this: Just because you marry a Christian doesn't mean that you've avoided any possibility that your spouse can hurt you or you can wrong them.

The Church insists that the only way to be "equally yoked" is to marry another Christian, but what if this Christian deeply hurts me? It's easy to preach, "Just forgive them" (the implication being that once you forgive them, the expectation being that once you forgive them, you remain married). But that's just not how we are as humans. I don't know many people who can just forgive, forget, and move on, especially when the damage is deep and the scars are thick. These archaic sermons are black and white when people themselves are gray. We need help in navigating the complexities of our lives, and this starts with showing some grace in the face of our humanity. Only Jesus is Jesus.

And it's just so crazy to interpret 2 Corinthians 6:14 to mean that someone who is not Christian is wicked. The Church preached abstinence and told me not to have sex. Okay, but I did, so now what? I'm wicked now? Miss me with that! Where's the lesson in these archaic sermons? Christ treated all people well. He didn't talk down to people; He lifted them up. And like many people, He never aligned himself with a certain religion. The truth is, you can find a partner who may share your morals and values but not want to follow the same faith.

When I was old enough and experienced enough to recognize this, being a Christian stopped being a nonnegotiable. I didn't believe my loving God would bring such a wonderful man into my life and expect me to walk away from him because he wasn't a Christian. When other people describe Bryan, the first word that often comes to mind is *sincere*. He says what he means, and he means what he says. Knowing firsthand the heartache of a man's ambivalence (most recently in front of millions of people), I must know without a doubt how a man feels about me. With Bryan, I never questioned what kind of husband or father he was going to be.

So can you imagine my telling Bryan, "You show me loyalty, honesty, and respect, but you're not a Christian so I'm sending you home"? I couldn't and I didn't. We did have to come to an understanding on how we would raise our family. Although Bryan isn't a Christian, when I told him how important church was to me, he agreed to attend with me. We further discussed it and decided to raise our children with a certain foundation in church. Therefore, while we may have different religions, we still share the same values, morals, and goals for our life together.

When it came to the physical attributes on my list, I tossed out most of those preferences when I appeared on *The Bachelorette*. It didn't matter to me what race or ethnicity he was. I didn't care about his height or fraternity affiliation. And yet I'm insanely attracted to Bryan and I have been from the moment I met him. But Bryan filled a need deeper than physical attraction. I wanted to be my partner's priority, and Bryan always made me feel I was important to him, and in turn, I make sure he knows that he's important to me.

In his novel *High Fidelity,* Nick Hornby suggests, "[I]t's no good pretending that any relationship has a future if your record collections disagree violently, or if your favorite films wouldn't even speak to each other if they met at a party." And yet these were the questions that I sacrificed on my *Bachelorette* journey. When you are serious about finding love and have to vet more than thirty suitors in ten weeks, you don't ask things like "What's your favorite TV show?" or "What kind of music do you listen to?" Meanwhile, a person's taste in popular culture—and their response to yours, especially if it's very different—can be incredibly telling.

The day after the proposal, Bryan and I traveled to Madrid to our happy-couples house (your hideaway spot until the season airs to keep the outcome a secret). We made a pit stop at a gas station that sold the most random items, and I found this hideous little toy. I picked it up and said to Bryan, "You know what this ugly thing looks like? You ever watch *Martin* when he and Gina take a trip to a tropical island and they get attacked by this thing?"

I had no idea if Bryan was going to know what the hell I was talking about. He's five years older than I am (which would have made a difference when we were growing up), is Colombian, and grew up in Miami. While I knew we both shared a passion for sports, I didn't know many of his other interests in music and pop culture. I know this sounds bizarre, but this is par for the course in the *Bachelor* process. Between having very little opportunity or privacy for conversations, the strongly defended bubble, and the short amount of time you have to make hard decisions about whom to keep and whom to eliminate, the lead feels pressured to dispense with idle chitchat.

In the middle of the gas station, Bryan yelled, "Ginaaah, that ain't no damn dog!" We laughed so hard as if no one else was around. Later we arrived at the house and were in the kitchen listening to my playlist. Bryan knew all the lyrics to my favorite R&B songs of the nineties, belting along with H-Town, Jodeci, and Aaron Hall. Together we watch *Martin* reruns. The icing on the (wedding) cake. One more time, ladies. Trust your gut. This served me well during my *Bachelorette* journey and delivered the best possible outcomes despite the odds.

The second-best thing about finding love on a reality TV series after defying the odds is having our courtship captured for posterity—from the first time we saw each other until he asked me to marry me and I said yes. How many people can say they have video of them at the moment they met their life partner? This is something that Bryan and I can always revisit, and honestly, I do so at least once per month. No matter what is happening in our relationship—triumphs and challenges alike—whenever I need to remember how we began, I can just go to YouTube and watch how he and I became us. It grounds and centers me to remember how we fell in love and why I took that leap of faith to appear on the show.

Speaking of which, the franchise never offered to pay for our wedding or for the rights to televise it. I initially wanted it but that was a fleeting desire. We took seriously the need for a long engagement. Bryan and I had to get off cloud nine and live our relationship in the real world. We needed to see if we could fit into each other's lives and make the sacrifices that that sometimes entails. Besides, I had heard that we would regret the decision to televise our wedding. Imagine walking down the aisle only to have a director stop you, make you turn around and do it all over again so the cameraman can capture it at a different angle. You already know how I am about control. Some things never change.

And some things do. I had no idea that marriage would change my love language. Until recently I was bilingual (albeit not in the way my mother-in-law would like . . . yet!), needing both quality time and physical touch. After being a newlywed in quarantine, however, my love language is now acts of service. See what needs to be done and help me out. That's what makes me feel loved now.

So don't touch me. Just take out the trash, please. And walk the dog.

When I compare the checklist in my twenties to that of my thirties, the biggest difference is me. The twenties were about hustling, which is why the list leaned heavily toward what a man could provide for me. When you're broke, you're impressed with someone who can take care of you. My thirties are also a hustle but of a different kind. Since I could take care of myself, I sought out a man who could fulfill me in ways that I could not. That required looking within first. While I no longer expected someone to take care of me in a material way, I still needed to be taken care of in other ways. Emotionally, mentally, spiritually.

I want to vibe with you. And I'm not talking about the butterflies. That's for teens. And lust is for your twenties. When I entered my thirties, connection became paramount. If you go back and watch the first episode of *The Bachelorette,* the energy between Bryan and me is immediate and palpable. From the moment we met, we were already finishing each other's sentences. Roll tape, and you'll see how we have always been in sync.

So, about that list. Rip it up, rip it up, rip it up now! I had a man who checked almost every box on the list, and our relationship never worked. If I had stuck to that first list—or even the revision!—I would never have dated Bryan, never mind be married to him now.

Or be so incredibly happy.

THE VOW

After a two-year engagement, Bryan and I married in August 2019 in Cancún, Mexico, before our family and friends. Want to know how far I've come from the eighteen-year-old who swore she would marry at city hall because she couldn't stand the thought of getting emotional in front of hundreds of guests? Before our family and friends, I professed my love and commitment to Bryan in vows that I wrote myself.

Bryan, I love the story of us, but I truly love the story of how we began.

I am completely amazed by you and thank God every day for sending you to me, even if it was via a limousine on a reality TV show. Who would have known that we would fall and land together? Who could have foreseen that in you I would find the place I belonged forever? How excited we were to just be open and true to fall for each other. I love how you first said "I love you," the look in your eyes, and the way my heart knew you were the one. I love being with you and I love all that we've become and will continue to be. When I look into your eyes, I see the pathway to my future ending in forever with you.

We've been through so much and the odds have definitely not been in our favor as we met in the most public and unconventional way. We realized quickly in our relationship that the only way we could get through this was by becoming a team and facing every challenge together as one. For love does not consist in gazing at each other but in looking outward together in the same direction. Facing the world hand in hand as one force, as one team. I know with you by my side I am empowered to do anything.

As I stand here today, I want to thank you. I want to thank you for taking a risk to come on national television to meet me. Thank you for the sacrifices you have made. Thank you for your patience and understanding. Thank you for being my rock and my support. Thank you for being my better half. Thank you for allowing this free spirit to fly. Thank you for acceptance. Thank you for allowing me to be myself and never dimming my light. Thank you for loving Copper and thank you for loving me.

And I promise, as I stand here in front of our family, friends, and before God, to support you, to be patient with you, to inspire you, to be your champion. I promise to always be a team, I promise to care for you, I promise to be honest and faithful. I promise to grow with you. I promise to love you with every part of me every single day.

I come from a past that has taught me to love and to hate. But you have lifted me from the pits of despair, shining your light when darkness lived there. You accepted my past and changed my perception. Cleansing me with your water, washing away all past deception. You changed my life for the better. You give my life so much meaning. You give me love. You give me peace. You give me hope. You inspire me. You make me better. You are my best friend. I believe in you and I believe in us; and that is a story that I will never get tired of telling because that is the story of us.

THE COACH'S WIFE

After I finished filming *The Bachelorette*, I learned that Ed had a girlfriend. Whether he cheated on me with her or had kept her on hold as he did me, my gut told me that this woman had been present throughout our relationship. Then, a month before my wedding, Ed married the assistant to the head coach of his program. The same woman who called me the night he got jailed for driving under the influence. The person he was texting when he came to Dallas to recruit and stayed with me. Ed married Cynthia, and they started a family.

He's just not that into you. In retrospect, it made perfect sense. Cynthia was affiliated with football, and every season, like clockwork, Ed would pull away from me. As the assistant to the head coach, she was not only available to Ed, she understood his lifestyle. She herself might have savored it the way I never would.

Learning about Ed and Cynthia's marriage made me look at the Rockwood wives through a different lens. I assumed that one of the reasons they were cold to me was because they looked down on me as "just" a girlfriend. But maybe Ed was involved with Cynthia, whom they knew and liked, and they saw me as the willing other woman. I can imagine that my trips to Rockwood struck them as insolent and triggered their fear that women game to be mistresses hovered around their husbands all the time. And as Rick's mother had shown me years prior, this fear transcends race and profession. Mind you, this was no excuse for these women to shun me, and I still believe there was a racial undercurrent to their iciness. Nothing stopped them from getting to know me. Perhaps if they had given me the benefit of the doubt and extended me the same compassion they did Cynthia, they would have done us both a favor.

Odd as it may sound, I was grateful to know that the coach found his wife. It deepened my appreciation for our relationship journey, including its most painful moments. The heartaches I experienced were detours that kept me from going over an emotional cliff. Out of touch with my true feelings and desires, I had been willing to disavow myself to play a role that was not mine to play. Imagine if Ed had succumbed to my pressure and put a ring on my finger, obligating me to make good on the sacrifices required of a coach's wife. Imagine if he had said what I was desperate to hear when I told him I was cast on *The Bachelor*. *Don't go on that show because I want to make our relationship work.* Imagine if in return for his sometime companionship, I had committed to a life of following Ed from city to city and forgoing a career of my own.

You'd think that, after the experiences I've had dating men who were struggling in their personal and professional lives and marrying a man who had a chiropractic practice when we met, I'd advise against getting involved with someone based on his potential. I actually don't think there's anything wrong with taking a chance on dating someone with potential who hasn't figured out how to realize it. There's one thing, however, he must also have in addition to the potential.

And that's a vision for his life. Without a vision, his potential has no direction. No matter what other amazing qualities he has or great possibilities are available to him, he'll spin his wheels like a truck stuck in mud. A person with no place to direct his potential is a person who is lost. Expect his potential to remain dormant. Expect the inertia in his life to bleed into your relationship. If he cannot move forward for his own sake, he cannot move forward with you, and your own life will stagnate as you wait for him to self-actualize.

Ed was a good man with a big heart. He came from a family that gave him a solid foundation and a strong example. But when I met him, Ed had no vision for his life after the one he'd held for so long disintegrated. So how could I expect him to have a vision for our relationship? I certainly had a vision of our life together, but that was not enough. Without clarity on what he wanted for himself in all areas of his life, he had no idea if and where I would fit into it.

When Ed finally developed a new vision for his life, we began drifting apart. Whether in romance, friendships, or business, this sometimes happens in the best relationships. With no intention but to be happier and feel more fulfilled, people's visions of their best lives will change, and as a result, their relationships will, too. New connections form, old ties fade. Flowing with the changes, some relationships grow stronger as the respective visions of the people involved continue to align despite the shift. That wasn't the case with Ed and me once he decided to become a coach. His decision activated his potential and inspired movement that drew him away from me. As it should have, because in my vision of my best life, I was never a coach's wife.

And unlike Ed, who would not accept a coaching opportunity in the same city where I lived, Bryan first moved to Dallas for me as I continued to practice law. Then when I stopped practicing I moved to Miami for him. Because a marriage is about compromise and give and take. Then he shut down that practice in Miami and moved to Los Angeles because my career had taken off there. Seeing that my success was for the greater good of our future family, he let go of his business to build anew with me in L.A. and to sustain our relationship. In other words, he did for me what my father did for my mom.

And therein lies the paradox. On the one hand, if I had not gotten honest with myself, I would have remained in that relationship and grown increasingly miserable. It had to come to an end for both Ed and me to be happily married now. And yet at the same time, I might not be married now if I had not taken the risk to be with Ed despite all the red flags, and given my all to make the relationship work. Through that effort—and the inevitable failure—I learned important things about myself. Ironically, Ed's example led me to therapy, which brought me back to myself. What I truly wanted, what kind of partner I needed, and who I had to become to attract and sustain the healthy relationship that had eluded me throughout my twenties.

My relationship with Ed was not supposed to last, but it was meant to be for me to know that Bryan was the one.

FROM CHARITY TO CHANGE

The time is always right to do what's right.

—Martin Luther King Jr.

On May 8, 2020, I laced up my sneakers and went for a run for the first time in two decades. When I was a kid and realized I wasn't cut out to be the next Florence "Flo-Jo" Joyner with her fabulous nails and record-breaking speed (a record that still stands almost thirty-five years later), I hung up my track shoes and focused on basketball. Except for the occasional workout, I didn't run until called to do so in memory of a man who was killed while jogging because he was Black.

Most Black people who grow up in the United States can remember when they realized that they were Black. Many can recall the age, if not a particular incident, when they were first made to feel that their Blackness was a problem for white people. For many of us those two days are the same. I became aware of my Blackness as a very young child. At the age of three I went from in-home childcare to a predominantly white preschool. I remained at that school until I graduated and went to college in Austin.

Like many children I wanted to make friends and fit in with the kids who were popular. Where I went to school, those kids were white. And like many Black children, I received the message that white people found the color of our skin—indeed our very presence—a threat to them. We instinctually understand that our access to opportunities, our sense of belonging, and even our physical safety require that we make white people feel comfortable. Whether we submit to it or not, this pressure hovers over Black people our entire lives.

I met my first and oldest friend Erin when we were three, and I remember her telling me that her grandmother asked her why she hung out with so many Black kids. "Where are your white friends?" she said. Since her grandmother didn't prohibit Erin from hanging out with me, Erin laughed her off. I, on the other hand, recognized that our friendship was an issue for Grandma. Because I was Black, I was a problem. As far as she was concerned, there were too many of me and not enough of *her* around her granddaughter. I didn't find it funny but I didn't feel empowered to speak to anyone about it.

At the age of seven, Dr. Martin Luther King Jr. became my idol, and I memorized a portion of his "I Have a Dream" speech for an oratory competition. I must have practiced that speech three hundred times, intent on getting everything right: the cadence, the emphases, the pace, the pauses for effect. I won first place, and what made me happier than the win was making my parents proud, especially my father because he reminded me of Dr. King. Years later when other ten-year-olds were into *Sweet Valley High,* I had a poster of the slain civil rights leader on my wall. To this day, I can still deliver his most famous speech.

That said, recognizing how I was different from my white peers and learning to celebrate that difference didn't preclude me from compartmentalizing myself. Still feeling the need to make everyone—Black or white—comfortable around me, I would conform to the crowd I was with rather than be my full self in all spaces. Sometime in my tweens, I developed a crush on a white boy named Preston who liked me, too. Junior high love. A classmate came up to me and said, "My parents told me that the Bible says light and dark are not supposed to mix." Yes, a white Christian girl quoted the Bible in her effort to inform me that white and Black people could not be together. Whatever happened to *Jesus loves the little children, all the children of the world, red and yellow, black and white, they are precious in His sight?* At twelve years old it occurred to me for the first time that people manipulate the scripture and wield it as a weapon to harm others. But again, I said nothing.

As I learned more about African American history and built stronger relationships with a broader range of Black people, my involvement in my community increased. Most of my contributions were through church initiatives and were focused on charity. Following my parents' example, I had a heart for service. As a young person, however, I had yet to grasp the difference between charity and change. Between living in my bubble and being a self-absorbed teenager, I failed to recognize the larger forces affecting the Black community that required more than nursing home visits, youth mentoring, and holiday soup kitchens. When I enrolled at UT Austin and pledged Delta Sigma Theta, the scope of my community awareness and involvement expanded to political causes as my sorority sisters and I implemented public awareness campaigns, mentored young people, and participated in marches and rallies. However, protests were not in my toolbox. I was too young to have experienced the savage beating of Rodney King, the acquittal of the white cops despite video evidence, and the protests and riots that exploded over Los Angeles in 1992, and without such a visceral call to action, as an agent of change, I remained in my comfort zone.

All that changed in the summer of 2013 when, for the first time, I became so incensed at racial injustice, I broke out of my bubble and took to the streets by myself. On July 13, 2013, a Florida jury acquitted George Zimmerman on all counts for the killing of Trayvon Martin. Despite being instructed by a police dispatcher not to follow him, Zimmerman profiled, stalked, and killed a seventeen-year-old Black boy for the crime of trying to get home.

I was living with my parents in Dallas at the time and asked to borrow their car to go protest the verdict at city hall. My father was concerned, warning me that sometimes people attended such demonstrations with the intention to be disruptive. "I don't care," I said. "Give me the car. I'm going down there, and I'm marching." I created my own poster with a Sharpie, slipped on my backpack, and drove to city hall. There I purchased a T-shirt emblazoned with Trayvon's face, raised my poster in the air, and joined the calls for justice. Michael Eric Dyson gave a powerful speech that brought me to tears. I know I was not the only one who left that day thinking, *We've got to make a change, but how?*

As I marched for Trayvon, I noticed that my fellow protesters looked like me. Everybody was Black. Everybody was young. Everybody was angry.

By this time, I was a lawyer, and I gave serious consideration to changing the type of law I was practicing. *I'm over here doing municipal law when there's so much more that needs to be done for racial justice.* I considered switching to civil rights law and even joining the Innocence Project—the nonprofit organization founded to fight for the exoneration of people wrongly convicted, using DNA testing. As I mulled this change, I began looking for opportunities—no matter how small—to make a difference where I already was.

Even traffic court.

Since I worked for the municipalities, I was litigating traffic stops and speeding tickets. When I say litigate, I mean that someone accused of running a red light would invoke their Sixth Amendment right to a speedy and public trial by a jury of their peers, and I had to prepare to prosecute them. Yes, people would demand a trial to fight a traffic ticket. Ladies and gentlemen, your tax dollars at work.

I joke now but as a young prosecutor, I did appreciate the opportunity to practice litigation while the stakes were so low. And I seized even the smallest moments to make whatever difference I could. In one case an African American man had been ticketed for disturbing the peace. He asked me, "Have you looked at the tape?"

"No, I haven't looked at the tape yet."

"Ms. Lindsay, please watch the tape. I didn't do anything wrong."

When I reviewed the tape, what I saw infuriated but did not shock me. Not only was the gentleman telling the truth, I could hear police officers saying derogatory things, including calling him a nigger. Seeing all I needed, I hit eject and yanked the CD from the player. I turned to the gentleman and said, "Thank you, sir. Your case is dismissed. And on behalf of the police force, I apologize." When court was adjourned, I marched the CD over to those officers' supervisor, played it for him, and demanded that something be done.

I don't mean to say that these were grand acts of advocacy. Just that the killing of Trayvon Martin and the acquittal of George Zimmerman captured my attention and compelled me to keep my eye out for injustices that were happening everywhere. For as long as I held that position, this heightened awareness got me in the practice of asking myself how I could use my influence—no matter how small—in moments where I held any amount of power. When you are Black in the United States, there are no small encounters. Small encounters with the police have too great a potential to result in fatal tragedies.

All Eric Garner was doing was selling loose cigarettes on a sidewalk in Staten Island, New York City.

All twelve-year-old Tamir Rice was doing was playing in a playground in Cleveland, Ohio.

All seven-year-old Aiyana Stanley-Jones was doing was sleeping on her nana's couch in Detroit, Michigan.

All Philando Castile was doing was reaching for the license and registration that the police officer who pulled him over asked for in a suburb of St. Paul, Minnesota.

And all Botham Jean was doing was sitting in his own apartment enjoying ice cream in my hometown of Dallas, Texas.

And countless more, both known and unknown.

Although the killing of Trayvon Martin shook me out of my complacency, the continued attacks on Black people eventually lost their shock value. While I still struggled with rage, grief, and hopelessness, the senseless killing of unarmed Black people—and the subsequent failure of our legal system to hold their killers accountable—no longer landed on me like bombshells. By early 2020 they were too frequent an occurrence, being reported almost daily in the news like the weather forecast and sports outcomes. I became numb in order to make it through the day.

Then Travis McMichael shot and killed Ahmaud Arbery.

I was quarantined in my apartment in Miami when the news

came over the television in May 2020. I watched the video of three men confronting, then shooting, this twenty-five-year-old Black man wearing red shorts, a white shirt, and running shoes. The image of their savagery gutted me in the same way the Zimmerman verdict had eight years earlier. I started bawling. I couldn't believe they hunted this man in broad daylight because he was running while Black. As if this were not devastating enough, the actual murder had taken place back in February and only made news once the video footage of this modern-day lynching by Travis McMichael, Gregory McMichael, and William Bryan was released.

I picked up my phone to post on social media, my finger shaking over the record button as I attempted to pull myself together. I almost talked myself out of doing it. And then I thought *No*. Why was I trying to wrangle my tears? *You talk on social media about all kinds of insipid things. You shouldn't hide your feelings about something as serious as this. Let your followers see how upset you are and why they should be, too.* I knew I had to model the appropriate rage about what happened to Ahmaud Arbery, because most of my followers do not look like me.

With my hair knotted in a bun atop my head and my cheek still glossy from my tears, I pressed play and recorded from my couch. "You need to be just as upset and as angry as I am right now. To the point that you want this to stop and you want to do something about it," I said. "I'm making phone calls today, and I'm not going to stop until the people who gunned him down are arrested." My Instagram story included the hashtag #ahmaudarbery. The longer I spoke, the less I questioned the righteousness of what I was doing. What did I have to lose when this man lost his life?

And just when I thought I could break no further, we learned that police in Louisville, Kentucky, shot Breonna Taylor to death in her own home. To execute a questionable search warrant, they used a battering ram to shred the door off the hinges to Breonna's apartment. Fearing that her ex-boyfriend was attempting to break in, her current boyfriend Kenneth Walker fired his licensed gun. The police returned fire, shooting Breonna six times where she stood in her hallway. Although she was still alive, no one attempted to treat her, and the twenty-six-year-old medical technician succumbed to her injuries and died.

In addition to the heinous acts of violence committed against Ahmaud and Breonna, I was hit hard by the fact that the public did not become aware of their killings until months after they were committed. It took two months of persistence by Ahmaud's mother, Wanda Cooper-Jones, and the leaking of a thirty-six-second video of her son being stalked, cornered, and shot for the Georgia Bureau of Investigation to arrest the three men who killed him. If not for video-recorded evidence, the tireless fight by their surviving family members and friends, and the support of everyday people committed to spreading the word and organizing for change, we might never have known what happened to Ahmaud, Breonna, George Floyd, and too many other people.

I could not stop asking myself, *When these people lay dying, how was I squandering my own life in ways that I cannot even remember?*

What silly little thing was I complaining about when Ahmaud Arbery was killed on February 23, 2020?

What blessings was I taking for granted when Breonna Taylor lay dying in her own home on March 13, 2020?

In the last nine and a half minutes of George Floyd's life, while he begged to breathe and cried out for his mother, what was I doing with the privilege of my own breath?

What did I have to lose by venting my outrage on Instagram

when these people—some in their mid-twenties—had their lives brutally taken from them?

I learned that on May 8, runners across the country were going to run in honor of Ahmaud. At the request of his high school football coach Jason Vaughn, they would run 2.23 miles—marking the date he was murdered—on what was supposed to have been his twenty-sixth birthday. Whether alone, with family and friends, or with a run club, everyone was being called to run, jog, or even walk as Ahmaud would, rain or shine. Coach Vaughn asked people to record their runs and post to social media with the hashtag #IRunWithMaud.

After not having run for years and having never been a long-distance runner, I laced up my shoes and went out on a run for Ahmaud Arbery in Miami. As I was running, I saw all the other Black people running along with me. As we passed one another, we would give that nod that Southern Black folk do, acknowledging our common purpose. I began that trek filled with pride. But over time and with every step that hit the pavement, that pride gave way to sadness. By the time I finished my 2.23 miles and slowed to a walk, the grief overcame me. I bawled as I understood the profundity of Ahmaud's murder. I was running because he no longer could.

Every day people run because they want to take care of their bodies. They run to clear their minds. They run to honor their wellness, knowing that they need it to bring their best selves to the purposes and people that are important to them. They run because it brings them joy.

People run every day to live.

Ahmaud Arbery can no longer run because as a Black man, he was deemed unworthy of the right to health, wellness, and pleasure.

Three white men hunted him down and killed him in broad daylight because they decided he had no right to live. Simply because of the color of his skin. Still in 2020.

I've grappled with situational depression before, but never in my life have I struggled with such intense despair. I couldn't get out of bed. I couldn't shower. I couldn't eat. I couldn't take three steps without breaking down crying, and it had nothing to do with any life challenges unique to me, but rather the oppression of living in a world where anti-Blackness was relentless. As devastated as I was, I could not even fathom what George Floyd's family was feeling or how they were pulling through. I ruminated over what I could do to make things better for myself and other Black people.

In addition to feeling overwhelm and helplessness, the events of 2020 also left me feeling incredibly frustrated. Too many white people woke up as if Derek Chauvin invented racism on May 25 of that year. The United States was founded on white supremacist violence against Black people, Indigenous people, and people of color, and—the resistance of several social justice movements notwithstanding—that had continued unabated. We live with it while white people have the privilege to go about their everyday lives unaffected by it. Even I, who grew up privileged, am still Black at the start and the end of the day. My privilege doesn't greet people before I do. Before you know who I am and what my story is, you know that I'm Black, and depending on who you are, that can prove deadly for me or someone I love.

Knowing I wasn't alone, I continued to be public about my anguish. A week before Derek Chauvin asphyxiated George Floyd in Minneapolis, Van Lathan and I began a podcast called *Higher Learning*. In our first few episodes, I was crying so much that I could barely function. Stuck at home because of the coronavirus pandemic, we had no offices, parties, or movie theaters to escape to. The media coverage of each case became almost as relentless as the brutality itself. If you switched on the TV, every news station played the video of George's murder on repeat. If you turned on the radio, everyone was discussing it. And if you tuned in to a podcast like *Higher Learning,* we were processing it.

In fact, the podcast became therapeutic for me, pulling me out of that deep pit of despair. Talking about everything that I was feeling was a release for me. And because people were not only listening but asking questions, it gave me a sense of agency. Our listeners wanted to know what they could do where they were and with what they had available to them. One question at a time, I climbed out of the abyss that was dangerously close to swallowing me whole. Hearing that people wanted to learn more, do better, and contribute to change began rebuilding my fraying hope.

One listener is my lifelong friend Erin, whose grandmother feared she spent too much time with Black people, namely me. "Rach, as a white woman, what can I do?" she asked me. "I have no followers on social media, a platform, or anything like that."

"But, Erin, you actually have one of the most influential roles of all," I said. "You're a mother. Parents are raising the next generation, and many of the decisions they make have a great impact on the kind of citizens their children will become when they're adults. Diversify their friend group, take them to the library, and buy them books, introduce them to other cultures they may not encounter in their everyday lives. As a mother, you have so much power. Don't underestimate it."

The year 2020 proved to be a perfect storm. Had we not been trapped in our homes with only our televisions, radios, and phones to engage us, Black people and our allies might never have known what happened to George Floyd. We did not take our awareness and succumb to the devastation. Had we not become just as relentless in our demands for accountability, Derek Chauvin may not have ever stood trial and been convicted of second-degree murder.

Then, not a half hour after the Chauvin verdict was delivered, police in Columbus, Ohio, shot and killed sixteen-year-old Ma'Khia Bryant. And miss me with any *Well, actually*s about the circumstances to justify the shooting of this child. Knowing that Dylann Roof, Kyle Rittenhouse, and Robert Aaron Long not only were armed but had already shot other people, police still managed to take these white men into custody without firing a shot.

And this is why, in addition to podcasting, I also continue to protest. I joined people worldwide who took to the streets to demand justice for George Floyd. While this was not new to me, it was my husband Bryan's first protest. As I wrote in an essay for *Good Morning America*, Bryan was apprehensive about participating because of the negative portrayals of protesters in the media. I shared with him my lived experience at these demonstrations, and we discussed what kind of world we wanted to raise our biracial children in. These conversations were not new and have never been easy. Bryan and I often talk about our individual experiences of race and ethnicity—my being Black, his being Latinx—and how the world looks at us as an interracial couple. But the events of 2020—peaceful marches and violent uprisings alike—had raised the stakes. Honest and vulnerable communication is fundamental to our marriage, and we decided that we had to demand change not just for our own equality and safety but for that of our future children as well. While there might always be people who infiltrate an organized protest and hijack it for their own selfish end, we cannot let them silence us any more than we can the racists.

And on that June day in Miami, as I surveyed the crowd, I noticed something. Something very different from when I marched in downtown Dallas for Trayvon Martin a decade ago. As a Black person, I was in the minority. I knew I was angry and why I was there. I knew why my husband was angry, and why he was there. But I never expected to be among hundreds of people who did not look like me—white, Asian, Latinx, all out there, marching down the street and chanting in one voice for a common purpose: racial equality. If you've never participated in a protest, I strongly urge you to give it a try once. Like when the crowd at a live concert by your favorite artist sings along with their most famous hook or the moment the stadium erupts when your team makes the championship-winning score, there's an indescribably beautiful energy at a rally for social justice that you can only experience if you are there. I looked at Bryan, who, too, had become emotional. "I told you," I said. "It's powerful."

I'm aware that the majority of listeners to my podcasts are not other Black people, and so I take the podcasts as opportunities to speak about racial justice. Since I just might be the only Black person these listeners follow, I take these platforms as a responsibility to speak out. I understand the frustration that many Black people have with the pressure of educating non-Black people about racial issues. We all do what we can, and the way I see it, this is something I can do. I don't have to play this role . . . I *get* to. If my audience is looking to me to be a voice when it comes to these matters, then I want to provide it. In fact, because I'm not an activist, I use my platform to direct listeners to others whose work they should be following and supporting.

You read that correctly. Even though I use my platform for a purpose, I am *not* an activist. The activists are those who have dedicated their lives to the fight for racial justice, whether locally or nationally. What I am is the messenger or the connector who can make you aware of these courageous and committed people. On my podcast *Higher Learning* or blog *Honestly, Rach,* I've often felt the need to say, "Glad you're listening to me, but let me tell you who you really need to be listening to . . ." My social change role is to show you how you can acquire the knowledge you need so that you can act on it.

For example, knowing that many of my listeners are white, I often recommend Robin DiAngelo's *White Fragility,* because I understand the impact of hearing the hard truth about white privilege from an individual who looks like them and has had similar life experiences. A Black person cannot introduce white privilege to someone who woke up in 2020 to the fact that racism is still prevalent in our society. If you're a white person who can't believe that a person is racist unless they're wearing a white hood, burning crosses on Black people's lawns, and calling them niggers, I need you to understand that there are levels to this shit.

You need to understand that racism thrives through implicit biases embedded in all of our society's institutions and continues to hold my people down.

You need to understand what a microaggression is.

And for God's sake, you need to understand why telling me the color of my skin is so pretty, asking me if you can touch my hair (no, you cannot), and praising me for being so articulate is not a damn compliment.

Just don't. When it comes to covertly racist behavior, I think we all get that by now. The time is overdue for white people to move up a few weight classes in their anti-racist training.

The most downloaded episode of my *Bachelor Happy Hour*

podcast was the one released on June 9, 2020. The topic of my conversation with cohost Becca Kufrin was race. Cross-racial dialogue about racial injustice is usually painful, and this public discussion for several hundred thousand subscribers was particularly difficult because the person under scrutiny was none other than Becca's then fiancé Garrett Yrigoyen. Only when your relationship faces some challenges do you fully understand its potential and limitations, and a major test for Becca came in the form of racism. Garrett's racism was something that Becca did not contend with until 2020 woke her up. To her credit, she did wake up, which is why they're no longer together, and why to this day I consider her a true friend.

Becca and I intended for the conversation to be a sit-down where two women—one Black, the other white—would speak candidly, serving as an example for other people interested in having cross-racial dialogues with their friends. Or you could play the conversation for a friend who needed to hear it. Becca and I could have stuck to entertainment, kept *Bachelor Happy Hour* light, and chosen to have our conversation about racism privately. It would have been much easier for us to rationalize that what *Bachelor* Nation needed most from the podcast was an escape from all the racial strife. Especially for me, who is constantly reamed for "ruining" the franchise by depriving people of their guilty pleasure with my pesky calls for greater diversity.

But as always I was willing to take on the subject of racism, and because she is sincere in her commitment to becoming a better person, Becca took it on with me. The fact that it's the most downloaded episode in the history of the podcast—almost a half-million downloads—shows that many people are open and willing to at least listen. I'm not naive though and can imagine that while some people were drawn to the depth of the subject matter, others may have tuned in hoping to get the scoop on Becca's troubled engagement or itching for us to get in a catfight. Whatever drew them to episode fifty-one, they listened to a conversation about race when they could have pressed skip. And I did receive many messages from people who thanked us for having it. A few even wrote, *I don't even watch* The Bachelor, *but someone forwarded this to me.* Whatever brought them to the show, they listened. The response suggested that maybe if we remained committed to showing that level of realness and transparency, people just might be willing to continue to engage.

Unfortunately, the most basic people are the most vocal. They whine, "Of course, racial justice is important, Rachel, so why keep complaining about *The Bachelor*? There have been Black leads after you, so why don't you focus on more serious things? Even the producers call it 'this silly little show.'"

That silly little show you tune in to every Monday night involves real people. The cast members of the *Bachelor* shows are not characters or animations. We are real people with real issues offscreen despite the fantasy concocted for your entertainment every week. As real people, we can make a real difference if we choose to, and I choose to normalize courageous conversations about race despite the fact that they make you uncomfortable.

In fact, I do so precisely because they make you uncomfortable. Comfort comes after the change. The Rachel that once cared about making white people comfortable ceased to exist long before she followed a whim to audition for *The Bachelor*. I challenged the producers, and my authenticity got me on the show. Staying true to my values and intentions as the lead of *The Bachelorette* created the happy ending the show teases yet rarely delivers. In every moment, I had the choice to behave in ways that could make me more likable to the white people throughout the franchise—the decision makers, the other contestants, the fandom. You do not grow up Black in America without, at some point, making this choice, and the taking the risk if you choose yourself. Today I have a platform that extends beyond this "silly little show"—built upon moment after moment of choosing myself—and am now using it to move those more important things forward.

Think about what you're asking of me when you complain about the discomfort created by calling out the lack of representation of people of color in the *Bachelor* franchise. Ask yourself just how concerned with white discomfort the Black historical figure you post on Instagram every February was. Imagine if Martin Luther King Jr., Harriet Tubman, or Nelson Mandela—insert your fave here—had yielded to the white frailty of their time. If we applied that same thinking in every situation, where would our society be? We are hurting, but since you're having fun and being entertained, why don't I just shut my mouth and let things stay as they are?

You can miss me with your fragility.

The conversation about race that Becca and I had on the *Bachelor Happy Hour* podcast hints at the growth and healing that is possible with this "silly little show." If only the majority of the white people with influence on this franchise—from the decision makers behind the scenes to the fans on social media—were not so basic. I have always been willing to build with them, but the Becca Kufrins are the exception and not the rule. On the contrary, most of the people in *Bachelor* Nation's land of the carefree and home of the frail won't meet me even halfway.

Turn the page because I have time today.

NATION OF DOUBLE STANDARDS

Appearing on television provides a huge platform, but that platform also leaves room to be subjected to an astonishing level of racial violence from the public. Racist trolls are attracted to things that center Black women like bees to honey; no matter where we are in the mediascape and what we're doing, you can bet that there will be a swarm of people in the comments with something disgusting to say—an occupational hazard, if you will.

—Ineye Komonibo

Recapping the finale of my season, Eric Deggans of NPR's *All Things Considered* gave me the most ironic of compliments. "She expertly navigated the expectations of viewers in ways that made her seem like the Obama of *Bachelor* Nation. She remained authentic and compelling, even while challenging some people's notion of whom a Black woman could and should choose to love." Flattering comparison on the surface. However, the most potent thing that former president Obama and I have in common is how quickly many of the same people who patted themselves on the back for championing our selection turned on us when we attempted to usher in the change they claimed to support. Neither Obama nor I polarized our respective nations. We only exposed the cleavages that always existed as we drew the racists out of hiding.

Sidebar for those of you who might be hate-skimming this book at the bookstore: I dare you to read this chapter in its entirety. Don't expect any attempts to win you over. If you're set on disliking me, it might as well be the real me and not some angry Black Bitch stereotype you've subconsciously and overtly ascribed to.

One thing I learned quickly from being a part of *Bachelor* Nation is that I couldn't win. On the one hand, fans got mad at me for having an opinion and saying too much. On the other hand, they got upset with me for not saying anything. As a person of color, I would never be given the benefit of the doubt. I got this message early on, and it was reinforced repeatedly. Because of the social caste system in this country, if I had a disagreement with another white person in the franchise, the fans always cast me as the stereotypical angry Black woman.

The worst part was that the producers were aware of this racist strain in the show's viewership, and they had catered to it for decades. I first became aware of this when I had a conflict with Vanessa Grimaldi while filming our season of *The Bachelor*. The show brings out both the best and worst of you. It abruptly separates you from everything that is comfortable and comforting and thrusts you into a high-pressure environment. The intense competition stokes your insecurities as you compete with a houseful of beautiful and charming women for the one man in your world. Every minute of this experience is designed to fuel this competition, and you are constantly comparing yourself to your roommates. Few can cope with such drastic changes. Many act out their insecurities, namely by projecting them onto their competitors.

Because my relationship with Nick posed a threat to hers, Vanessa had been complaining about me. I gave her a wide berth, however, and so while we had tension between us, we didn't clash.

Without this conflict, however, there was no drama in the house, so the producers felt the need to fan the embers. They staged a confrontation between us and captured it on camera. At one point, Vanessa accused me of bullying her. I was livid but I had restrained myself. "You can't call a Black woman a bully on camera," I said. I asked for examples of said bullying, which Vanessa could not provide because it had never happened.

I wanted the show to air our conversation. Because of the way I carried myself, I made sure that what could have become an argument remained a debate. A debate I won. I believed that if my conversation with Vanessa aired unedited, the *Bachelor* audience would recognize that I was not a bully, but a producer made it clear that they would turn on me.

They were the *Bachelor* fandom. But the producers knew then what I only came to understand after years of racial antagonism from a segment of their viewership. They not only recognized who their audience was, they embraced them and had no qualms about giving them what they wanted. At the time, the decision to not air my argument with Vanessa seemed protective of me. After four years as a part of this franchise, I came to understand that efforts to protect me as their first Black lead also served their own interests. Before I came on *The Bachelor,* the show had spent fifteen years curating an audience that was used to a certain prototype as the lead. The ideal Bachelor or Bachelorette is beautiful, Christian, Southern or Midwestern . . .

. . . and white.

A few years after our season, Vanessa contacted me. I'm glad she did. We talked for more than an hour and let bygones be bygones. In response to the events of 2020, Vanessa reached out to me, and she continues to support me. It took reflection and courage for her to be the bigger person and initiate our reconciliation, and I commend and appreciate her for it.

Despite my being perceived as likable and making *Bachelorette* history, the viewership for my season dipped. The premiere pulled only 5.7 million viewers, a decrease of 14 percent from the previous year and the lowest ratings since 2010. Mike Fleiss, the creator himself, called it "disturbing in a Trumpish kind of way." He said, "How else are you going to explain the fact that she's down in the ratings, when—Black or white—she was an unbelievable Bachelorette? It revealed something about our fans."

I never gave Lee an additional thought until the show wrapped and his true nature was exposed courtesy of his Twitter feed. There aren't only racist tweets. There are misogynistic tweets. Homophobic tweets. And I started wondering: If Redditors could find this information on Lee so easily, how is it that the show had no clue? When I signed on to *The Bachelor,* a background person sat down with me and went through my social media profiles. How did Lee, with his problematic tweets, slip through the cracks?

Even when everyone started to say, "Oh my gosh, they cast him because he was racist for a story line," I didn't want to believe it. I kept giving the show the benefit of the doubt. Since they'd never had a Black lead, I fully expected some things would be mishandled and was willing to cut the producers some slack. But I could never shake the feeling that they knew Lee was racially ignorant (at best) and intentionally cast him. They knew the presence of this particular white man in the house would cause drama, and they allowed him to antagonize the Black contestants by spewing racial stereotypes that he'd learned through TV shows, music videos, or whatever. Because their lily-white lives are not impacted by racism, the producers are clueless about how exploiting racial tensions for a story line is triggering for Black contestants. Instead of the *Bachelor* bubble being the escape it is for white participants, these "social experiments" activate centuries of emotional trauma in the name of entertainment. This obliviousness is evidence of the systemic racism within this franchise and is perpetuated by its creators' refusal to learn. Beyond a story line, Lee's drama became the dominant narrative of my historic season.

To say I couldn't wait until the "Men Tell All" episode is an understatement, but that experience proved to be just as disappointing. In the moment, I was happy to have the opportunity to confront Lee and set him straight. I should have known better when Chris Harrison opened the show saying, "A lot of times the *Bachelorette* mansion ends up kind of like one big frat house, but this season was entirely different, with more conflict and angry fights than ever before. We even thought about beefing up security tonight." *Security? Are you fucking kidding me?* On the first season with a Black lead and the most diverse cast in franchise history, suddenly there's a need for security at the reunion. Meanwhile, no physical altercations occurred during my season, when previous ones with white leads depicted actual fights. Chris's language spoke to the subconscious of *Bachelor* Klan, where stereotypes of Black people fester.

The show dedicated almost a half hour—a third of the episode—of "Men Tell All" to recapping, analyzing, and challenging Lee's behavior to eke out a tepid admission from him that his social media posts and behavior toward Black men in the mansion were racist. More than once Chris commended Lee just for showing up, yet never acknowledged the Black men wringing themselves out to make him face his implicit bias. The commending should have been reversed.

Later, when I saw how differently the show handled race during my season compared to Becca Kufrin's the following year, I became even more upset. Becca gave Garrett Yrigoyen the First Impression Rose and eventually accepted his proposal. Several weeks into the airing of her season, however, fellow alum Ashley Spivey exposed that Garrett had liked several posts on Instagram that were far more egregious than anything Lee had written on Twitter. They mocked immigrants, Parkland shooting survivors, Black athletes who took nonviolent stands against police brutality, trans people, and more. That's where the similarity ends between my season and Becca's. Garrett posted an apology on Instagram in which he claimed not to realize the power behind a mindless double tap on Instagram. (Who hearts a picture of a soldier playfully swinging a small child with the caption *When a kid makes it over the wall and you have to throw him back* without understanding the point? Either he's a racist or a blithering idiot. You decide.) On the finale of Becca's season, they discussed the matter for less than five minutes. Whereas Lee's tweets were projected for the audience and dissected by the other contestants, Chris never challenged Garrett to clarify his views. Instead his questions centered not on the harm Garrett did but the impact of the public backlash on his relationship with Becca. Without a Black man as a convenient antagonist, the franchise skirted the matter to preserve Becca's happy ending.

Meanwhile, as a Black woman, I had no such luxury. In addition to carrying the show as a lead, I also had to be the resident expert on all racial matters. With no Black people as executive producers or in other key positions, the burden to educate decision makers on the Black experience fell entirely on me. At the reunion, I, Kenny, the other Black contestants, and a few allies spent much of the episode addressing Lee. It's at once amazing and frustrating to watch. He had already taken up too much space during my season, but that deeply ingrained impulse to handle him with kid gloves lest the franchise's white fan base dismiss us as angry is on full display. As grateful as I am to all the men who stood with me that day, I remain unsettled that Chris Harrison didn't step up to confront Lee the way he did Becca's racist, homophobic, xenophobic, transphobic, misogynistic, sexist fiancé Garrett. In fact, the show gave both Garrett and Lee opportunities to redeem themselves.

This is how they chose to deliver on their promise of my "historic" season. Not hiring a diversity consultant (oh, yeah . . . *I* was the consultant) but casting an openly racist, sexist, and homophobic contestant. I put my heart on the line for this show, and they did not hold in high enough regard the weight I carried as their first Black lead. Imagine the dichotomy of my having to do media as the face of the franchise's groundbreaking turn while also having to address the racism that occurred in my very public search for love. If it were not for the fact that it brought Bryan and me together and captured our courtship for posterity, I would have left the experience feeling broken and betrayed—in many ways I still do—and that's why I advocate so vociferously for change if they're going to continue to cast people of color as leads.

A sign of what—and who—was to come for me occurred after the show aired my breakup with runner-up Peter Kraus. From a place of honesty and vulnerability, I expressed to him my desire to be with someone who knew what they wanted to do—especially as it pertained to me. "Great," he responded petulantly. "Go find someone to have a mediocre life with." Despite this cruel remark, *Bachelor* fans attacked me on social media for not settling for Peter's ambivalence and instead choosing Bryan, who had no reservations about becoming my husband. This is the same audience that applauded me earlier in the season for telling a Black man who I believed had been deceptive, "So I'm really going to need you to get the fuck out." When he attempted to come back to the mansion and I refused to give him a second chance, they reveled in it. However, *Bachelor* fans let me have it again during the "After the Final Rose" episode for the crime of standing up to Peter simply by affirming that, to the contrary, I actually was living my best life.

As a white man from the Midwest, Peter is the perfect man in *Bachelor* Nation. Since that moment onstage with him, whenever I have a contrary opinion about a white man who's a fan favorite, they ruin me. If they're not unfollowing me on social media, they're accusing me of hating everybody and calling me angry, rude, and disrespectful. I'm so tired of these white women in the *Bachelor* franchise who coddle these piss-poor white men. "You don't know him," they post. "You don't know his heart." But then they want to tell me about myself. Do you know *my* heart?

Miss me with your mediocre white men.

The same fans who slammed me for choosing Bryan over Peter and having a questioning view of Colton Underwood made Hannah Brown a hero for standing up to Luke Parker's slut-shaming. Had she been the one to tell Peter that she was living her best life, her fellow white women would have jumped to their feet and cheered. You would think she procured world peace.

In fact, as far as *Bachelor* Nation is concerned, Hannah Brown can say "nigger," but I can't say that it offended me. In May 2020 in an Instagram Live, Hannah was singing along with the DaBaby song "Rockstar." She censored herself when it came to the word *fuck* but then proceeded to sing the word *nigger* as if it were nothing. Hannah's initial reaction, when fans watching the livestream called out her use of the slur, was to deny it and then blame her brother.

The next day I woke up to a barrage of messages. *Did you see what Hannah did? Are you going to call her out?* The irony is that this is an example of people believing that I'm quick to speak on anything and everything. I actually handled it differently.

Rather than jump on Instagram to call out Hannah, I reached out to her. Because she's also a Christian, I texted her a Bible verse: Matthew 18:15. *If your brother offends you, go and tell him his fault, between you and him alone. If he listens to you, you have gained your brother.*

Hannah replied, *Oh my God, thank you so much.* Then she called me crying. We spoke all day, calling each other back and forth. I said, "Listen, because you did this publicly, you should apologize in the same manner. And I'll support you. I'll come on IG Live with you and explain the weight and history of this word, and why it is so detrimental to the Black community." I was willing to do this because this was so much bigger than Hannah. She said a word that offended many people not only in the *Bachelor* community but across the world. With so many people who looked up to Hannah, this could have been a learning experience and an opportunity to use her platform with purpose.

Yes, Rachel Lindsay does have her Christian moments.

"Okay," Hannah said. "I'm going to talk to my PR team." Heavy is the crown, and with such a large audience comes a responsibility. Can you imagine the impact she could have had on the *Bachelor* audience as the reigning Bachelorette with the largest social media following?

She called me two hours later. I was deep into Peloton at the time and missed my ride, attempting to support her with this back-and-forth of phone calls and text messages so I could jump on this IG Live. Hannah informed me that her PR team told her not to apologize or go on a live with me. *We'll just put out a statement.*

"That just doesn't seem like me. I'm an outspoken person," Hannah cried. "I stand up for what I believe in. I don't run, and I don't hide. I don't feel like this is the right thing to do."

"You're right," I said. "It feels wrong because it is wrong. Don't hide behind the statement. Talk about how you truly feel."

But ultimately Hannah decided to go with her team's advice and put out the statement. She posted an apology on her Instagram story, which means it disappeared in twenty-four hours. You just offended an entire community, and not only could you not post it to your main page, your apology evaporates in the span of one day. Then Hannah herself disappeared for two weeks, because when you have white privilege you can do that.

But as a Black woman, I don't have the same privilege. I don't get to sit back while you offend me and stay silent. Because I have been a voice in this *Bachelor* community, I have to say something. People need to understand why what you did was wrong. So I put out a video explaining why saying this word cuts so deeply and warrants an apology.

Can you believe that more people criticized me for that video than criticized Hannah for actually saying the slur? Well, you've read this far. You probably can.

Please, Hannah didn't mean this. She's a sweet girl.
It was just an accident.
Y'all get to say it in songs. Why can't we?
Rachel, you're so quick to judge someone and take them down!

They were upset with me for not showing Hannah grace, understanding, and compassion, as if I had no right to be offended by her use of a dehumanizing slur.

Grace, understanding, and *compassion* were the same words that Chris Harrison threw at me less than a year later when Rachael Kirkconnell was criticized for attending a plantation party and liking photos of Confederate flags. He revealed to me how he truly felt when on *Extra* he demanded to know, "who the hell is Rachel Lindsay to demand an apology?" In our interview, he threw Hannah Brown in my face as an example of *Bachelor* Nation's lack of grace, understanding, and compassion. To make his case on camera, Chris acknowledged how we're both trolled on social media (as if he's been called racial slurs and given death threats) and claimed to enjoy talking to me about these difficult topics. But in reality he never once called me to see if I was okay when I was getting reamed on social media for calling out Hannah Brown's behavior. (The true test of a person's character in this media landscape is how they behave when the mics and cameras are off, and they believe no one is watching. Not once did Chris Harrison, who publicly called me his friend, check in on me during these attacks. Well, not until after I accepted his apology. Then I got an invitation to dinner.) And as we have both moved on to start new chapters in our lives, Chris removed me from his social media accounts similar to the way he removed the black square he posted for #BlackoutTuesday. Seems as if friending me publicly and on social media was performative, like the posting of that black square and the "listening and learning" televised apology. As his "friend," I am happy that he no longer has to pretend in this new chapter of his life. Only after things became so vile that I shut down my Instagram account did the producers issue a statement against the harassment.

Then *Bachelor* fans wondered why I shut down their demands to tell them the circumstances that resulted in ending a friendship with another contestant. In October 2019, I appeared on *Watch What Happens Live* with Andy Cohen, and a viewer named Lauren from Tennessee called in with a question for me. "What happened between you and your ex-friend Raven?"

"Number one question for you," said Andy. "We got this so much. What did she do to cause your falling-out?"

"I can't say." The audience groaned. "I promised I wouldn't say. But it was enough for me to not want to be friends with her anymore."

"And you're still not friends with her?"

"No, and I never will be."

Do you know I was dogged for saying that? *Bachelor* Nation had questions about the status of our relationship, then trashed me for answering honestly and diplomatically.

Rachel is so messy.
Why would she say something like that?
She's implying that Raven did something to her and not letting
Raven get a chance to speak about it.

They went so far as to call Raven the bigger person, as she did interviews claiming to have no idea why I was upset with her and that she missed our friendship. Even though it's clear that I'm the one who ended that relationship, I don't get the benefit of the doubt that I had a good reason to do so. One thing you can say about me is that I always speak my mind (whether or not you agree with what I have to say), and I do not lie.

And once again, there were red flags at the start that I chose to downplay. When we were living in the *Bachelor* mansion, Raven was always writing in her journal. One night she read aloud her first-night impressions of each of us.

"Rachel—she has black skin." *What the fuck? Who says that shit? Not only do you think it, but you actually say it out loud for people to hear?* "And she seems nice."

Of all the ways you could describe me, that's what you came up with? You ain't never seen a Black person before? Like, never seen one of us up close? Like I'm out here in the wild like a gorilla? I did not handle that moment as I might have in my normal life, because I understood that this was not the time or place to jump on someone. *She did say she was from small-town Arkansas,* I thought. *Give her the benefit of the doubt.*

Despite this inauspicious beginning, Raven and I did become close friends, a closeness that surprised even me. I wasn't cognizant of how much our friendship registered with *Bachelor* Nation until people noticed her absence in my life and commented on it. *What's up with Rachel and Raven? Why wasn't Raven at the bachelorette party?* When I was promoting my MTV show *Ghosted*, interviewers flat-out asked me about the status of our friendship.

Okay, *Bachelor* fans, I know how badly you want to know what happened between Raven and me. You probably picked up this book specifically hoping to get the tea. So let me tell you why . . .

. . . you can miss me with your intrusiveness.

When I ended the friendship with Raven, I made an agreement to not speak publicly about what occurred between us. I intend to honor that agreement. Other than to say that I found myself in a situation where I felt the need to protect and remove myself, these are the only details I'm going to provide. This is my business. This is Raven's business. This is not for anybody else to know. Your curiosity does not trump my integrity.

And even if I never promised Raven that I would not discuss the details of our falling-out in public, *Bachelor* Nation has already made assumptions about what occurred between us and has made me the one in the wrong, once again. I owe no one in this franchise my time, attention, or care. I especially refuse to give *Bachelor* Klan—forever thirsty to cast the white woman as a victim and the Black woman as her tormentor—any additional ammunition to take my words and use them against me. You knew how close Raven and I were. You could see the pain our estrangement caused her. And yet refused to acknowledge mine. Stay parched.

A PARTING GIFT

If your anti-racism work prioritizes the "growth" and "enlightenment" of white America over the safety, dignity and humanity of people of color, it's not anti-racism work. It's white supremacy.

—Ijeoma Oluo

I am not the first person to challenge *The Bachelor*. Back in 2011 two African American athletes sued *The Bachelor* for discrimination. Nathaniel Claybrooks and Christopher Johnson filed a class action lawsuit. Based on their audition experiences, the football players from Nashville, Tennessee, argued that despite all its public declarations about wanting to diversify its cast, the franchise actively excluded BIPOC contestants.

Denying the charges of racial discrimination, the defendants argued that even if it did elect to only cast white people, it had a right to do so under the First Amendment. You understood that correctly. They truly said, "We're not discriminating against anyone, but, you know, even *if* we were, we have a constitutional right to not want Black people or other racial minorities on our show." Mind you, this legal argument contradicted the producers' consistent efforts to point the finger at BIPOC themselves. Whenever challenged in interviews about the franchise's lack of diversity, Mike Fleiss would insist that we just don't audition for the show.

Remember, even in my own audition I was told that they did not get "quality people of color" to audition for the show.

Claybrooks and Johnson had hoped that the lawsuit would be a vehicle for change, but in October 2012 a judge dismissed their case. While sympathetic to the plaintiffs' concerns, Hon. Aleta Trauger essentially found that because the content of the show is inarguably protected by the First Amendment, then casting as a creative decision must be as well. She stated that this freedom of speech also applied to shows like *The Cosby Show* and *Jersey Shore*.

Reality TV shows like *The Bachelor* involve some scripting at every phase from casting to editing. While they do cast participants with genuine intentions, they also knowingly include people in the cast who only desire to be on television, or have preexisting conflicts with other contestants, or who have nothing to offer but gimmicks and drama. Sometimes while filming, they direct scenes to produce a certain effect, like when they encouraged Kenny and Lee to interrupt my conversations when one of them was with me, or when they nagged Will to dance with me when he had no romantic impulse of his own, or when they made an exception to their usual distaste for dates with a contestant's friends for Peter's hometown—all conveniently interracial couples. How a person responds to these scenarios is on them, but if I had been given a say, I wouldn't have agreed to participate in any of these situations.

Filming ends and contestants go home, but scripting continues in the editing suite. From ten weeks' worth of around-the-clock footage, a little more than two dozen episodes are made with scenes that are diced then spliced, cobbled together out of chronological order, or omitted in their entirety to build a story to their liking. The results can stray far from what actually happened. No amount of self-control in front of the cameras can make a contestant—never mind a lead—immune to these manipulations. My experience gave me a more nuanced perspective on the behavior of Black women who preceded me on reality TV. While I do not see anyone as powerless in the way they are portrayed, I have a better understanding of the limits on their ability to control their image. And for those for whom appearing on reality TV is a means of survival, they *have* to let Flavor give them those "disgusting nicknames" if they want to stay on the show.

The producers protected me at times, but often that protection was driven by self-interest. Set on my being the first Black Bachelorette, they did not want the fandom to turn on me. Sometimes they saved me from myself, such as when I drank too much. Other times, like when they pitted Vanessa and me against each other and our confrontation took on a racial charge, the producers had to rescue me from a scenario they concocted. They chose not to air the argument out of fear that fans would read me as the Angry Black Woman; this served them as much as it spared me. But it also implicates them—they were aware that they have viewers who would vilify me regardless of the restraint I showed. They know a segment of their audience is racist. They catered to that toxic element when they orchestrated that confrontation between Vanessa and me and were still coddling their prejudices when they decided not to air that footage. The decision was as much about protecting the investment they had already made by casting me as it was about buffering me from their toxicity. I should not have needed to be buffered.

The most troubling thing about this is how often they are crafting narratives through the filtered lens of their implicit bias. Without enough BIPOC behind the cameras and contestants at their mercy, they don't know the harm they cause even when they have no ill intentions. While also subject to producers' control of the narrative, white contestants at least have more freedom to focus on their emotional journey. They don't carry the burden of their depictions.

"Oops, I Blew Up The Bachelor." That was the headline of a cover story *New York* magazine ran in June 2021 about my experience with the franchise. The cover headline infuriated me so much I took to Instagram to make it clear that I had never uttered those words, nor was that clickbait a reflection of how I felt. You'd think that after revealing how the toxic wing of *Bachelor* fandom sent me death threats and that I had to consider hiring bodyguards, the editors would take better care than to suggest that I reveled in imploding the franchise, whether intentionally or inadvertently. Nothing could be further from the truth.

First of all, I doubt *The Bachelor* is going anywhere.

Two, as I state in the essay, the enterprise employs too many people for me to wish its demise, including many I care about. According to the data analytics firm Kantar Media, *The Bachelor* brought in $86 million in advertising revenue in 2017. *The Bachelorette* brought in a similar amount the same year.

Three, if the franchise folds under the weight of its own scandals, don't blame the Black woman.

The *New York* essay itself and the title used online at *Vulture,* however, nailed my sentiments—"Rachel Lindsay Has No Roses Left to Burn." It succinctly captures my major issues with how the franchise handles race—or not. However, I have more to say because, of course . . . While I'm no longer a part of *Bachelor*

Nation because of its ongoing racial problems, my prescription for elevating the franchise goes beyond *Hire more people of color* and *Transcend race:*

- **GAMBLE ON BLACK LOVE AND THEIR STORIES.** The casting department is looking for Black leads while being devoid of people of color. That means they choose whom they might be attracted to, and that usually results in casting the kind of Black person that is unlikely to choose a Black finalist. Meanwhile, no one blinks when, season after season, white leads choose white contestants. As a woman who herself is in an interracial marriage as a result of my appearance on the show, I support true love regardless of color. That said, the trepidation to cast Black leads who historically date within their own community caters to *Bachelor* Klan. According to several recent studies, they are also leaving money on the table. In 2021 McKinsey & Company released a study on the film and television industry that revealed Hollywood has the potential to generate an additional $10 billion in annual revenues by addressing racial inequalities. In other words, the racists the franchise would lose if it had the courage to depict Black romance would be far outweighed by the new viewers—Black and otherwise—who are open-minded enough to cheer on love no matter what it looks like. Highlight genuine Black stories instead of relying on stereotypes for story lines.

- **HIRE BIPOC CASTING DIRECTORS AND PRODUCERS ... AND LISTEN TO THEM.** I auditioned for *The Bachelor* on a whim. To diversify its cast, the show must actively recruit BIPOC contestants rather than hope they show up at auditions. BIPOC casting directors and producers have the connections to broaden the pool instead of waiting for hopefuls to come to them. Hire them and take their counsel seriously.

- **HIRE BIPOC EXECUTIVES AND SENIOR PRODUCERS ... AND LISTEN TO THEM.** Several times the franchise placed me in racially charged scenarios for the sake of conducting "social experiments" they lacked the racial literacy to understand. This is tantamount to putting BIPOC contestants in psychological jeopardy to appease their own curiosity. Our emotional lives are not your sociology workshop. Hire BIPOC producers, run these story lines by them, and heed them when they warn, "You don't have the range." The presence of diverse producers enables contestants of color to feel comfortable enough to open up. Behind that camera they need to see someone they know understands them and can trust with their emotions and experiences.

- **PUT ALL THE CONTESTANTS' EMOTIONAL WELFARE FIRST.** One of the things that makes me proud of my season is the emotional maturity that I and many of the men showcased. Our collective ability to connect to our emotions and communicate transparently about them generated drama that people could relate to. The stakes are real and higher than any catfight or macho headbutting the producers can orchestrate. For the *Bachelor* process to work, however, contestants have to feel reasonably safe to be authentic. That means less manipulation ... and less alcohol.

- **RECOMMIT TO THE PURSUIT OF THE HAPPY ENDING.** I understand how *The Bachelor* evolved into an ecosystem. Banking on spinoffs starring former contestants makes business sense, as audiences tune in again and again to follow their favorites. However, this also perpetuates the existing preponderance of white contestants and the tokenization of BIPOC cast members. It also betrays the premise of the show. Maybe if *The Bachelor* returned to the genuine pursuit of a happy ending while also diversifying its cast, it would attract a larger, healthier, and more reliable fan base.

As with any relationship, I gave this franchise my all, and I don't regret being its first Black lead. Nor do I pretend that I never made a bad decision on this journey. That said, I refuse to give the show credit for my marriage. Despite confronting additional challenges that no white contestant has to face, I navigated the process using skills and lessons I'd acquired long before I walked into that audition. *The Bachelor* gave me an opportunity, but *I* created my own happy ending. That's how it has always been, and that's how it'll always be.

WORKING GIRL

You don't need permission to live the life you want. You already have it.
— Marie Forleo

Although *The Bachelor* changed my personal life, I never expected it to impact my career path. I had no grand vision for my career after the show. Bryan and I finally had full control over our relationship, and I wanted to focus on building it. Save the obligatory promotional gigs, I wanted to normalize my life as much as possible. That included returning to my law firm in Dallas to practice civil defense litigation.

Being on the show, however, brought opportunities that reconnected me to my true career aspirations. Unlike my desire for marriage and children, which I readily owned and pursued, I'd spent much of my young adulthood attempting to reconcile two career paths rooted in strong but conflicting impulses: meeting my parents' expectations and becoming an attorney versus following my dreams to work in sports.

Part of the challenge was that for a long time, I genuinely wanted to become a lawyer. Except for a distant cousin who was an actor until he died at the age of nineteen, no one in my family has pursued a career in media. Not journalism, not radio, not television or film. Constance is a homemaker, while Heather works in the insurance field. Someone had to follow in my father's footsteps, and we all presumed that it would be me. Not just to please my parents, as important as that was to me, but also given how much I idolized him.

Television makes the public believe that the legal profession is one of constant excitement. Truth is, much of it is not. To be a lawyer, you have to enjoy being analytical, following protocols, and paying attention to detail. On the Myers-Briggs scale, I'm an ENFP—Extraverted, Intuitive, Feeling, and Perceiving. Perfect for journalists, TV anchors, and other kinds of media professionals. Lawyers not so much. I thrive on variety, need flexibility, and enjoy people. On the contrary, careers that require details and routines and offer little room for creativity and innovation are not the best option for me. Yet this is what practicing law entails, and whenever I felt unmotivated in my career, I came down hard on myself. *How could you feel that way after all the time and money your family and you have invested in this path?* Meanwhile, the law left me unfulfilled and uninspired. Deep down inside I wanted to veer from the traditional path—namely sports and/or communication, preferably both—but I was too afraid of disappointing my parents and others' expectations of me.

Meanwhile, I fit in the world of sports from the start. My first job in the industry was at a marketing company owned by Randy Rodgers, who ran training camps for high school athletes seeking to make it at the collegiate level. He taught them, for example, how to create their game tapes to increase the likelihood of landing a scholarship. Randy had connections at multiple universities, and I assisted him in organizing and marketing the camps. I mostly worked remotely from Austin but sometimes I traveled with him throughout Texas. He was a wonderful older gentleman who introduced me to the world of sports.

At one time I specifically set a goal to become a sports agent.

The idea of representing athletes struck me as a fulfilling way to apply my legal training and knowledge. My internship at the now defunct Capital Sports and Entertainment tore the bloom off that rose. They were launching a football division, and I worked for one of their agents, leveraging my friendships with players who were either playing for the league or destined to be drafted. I did research for and connected him to Texas ballers whom CS&E wanted to woo. They also allowed me to work on the entertainment side, such as on the Austin City Limits Festival, which essentially is the Southwestern equivalent of Lollapalooza. From running errands, handling logistics behind the scenes, or even working the reception desk, I did whatever they needed me to do; anything to build up my résumé and make connections. However, I also learned how much of being a sports agent is more babysitting than legal expertise. Less studying the market to negotiate a fair contract, more ordering a car service to get a client to the airport for his vacation. Or getting him out of trouble. I wanted none of that. And yet as I stated earlier, the legal work that did appeal to me was impossible to break into, and I landed in municipal law by default.

By the time I auditioned for *The Bachelor,* I was on my third law firm and had only been practicing law for four years. I thought that my unhappiness stemmed from my problems with Ed, but therapy made me realize that my career was also a factor. I enjoyed things about being an attorney—my colleagues, the compensation, the prestige, and most of all my parents' pride. But the law itself left me unsatisfied. The idea of walking away from it, however, was more than I could bear at the time. I struggled enough with walking away from my failing relationship without also attempting to abandon a successful career that garnered material comfort and social status.

On the contrary, I held on to my career even when I decided to go on *The Bachelor,* and I do not regret it. All contestants selected for the show are there to play a distinct role—from the drama queen who cries at the drop of a hat to the guy who yells ridiculous catchphrases. My role was the smart and sassy and, yes, Black attorney from Texas. But I broke the mold in ways besides race. Despite what is typed into the chyron beneath their names onscreen, most contestants have no real careers or professions at the time they're cast. Being unfamiliar with the show and having an established career set me apart from the typical *Bachelor* contestant.

People underestimate the huge risk involved in quitting your job to appear on *The Bachelor*. You can be a beacon of respectability while on the air, and still no one will hire you. Many *Bachelor* alums have been public about their difficulties gaining employment in their previous fields. (Go figure.) Only when the producers' offer surpassed my salary as an attorney was I willing to risk going on sabbatical from the law firm to be on the show.

Still I felt relieved that after my stints on both *The Bachelor* and *The Bachelorette,* my law firm, Cooper & Scully, P.C., welcomed me back with open arms. When other non-*Bachelor* opportunities in sports media came my way, I couldn't resist them. How could I when I had to fight for and humble myself for them? I seized the chance to guest-host *First Take* and *Football Frenzy* on ESPN, cramming them into my already jammed schedule.

Full-circle moment: After I became the Bachelorette, I met an agent at an event and mentioned how, years earlier, I had submitted my résumé to his firm. "Oh, we never read those," he said. "We just throw them out." (Later I would sit beside his partner—a well-known agent and head of the firm—on a plane and he was incredibly obnoxious and so shall remain nameless.)

Another burst bubble, another humbling experience. At twenty-two, I knew I was qualified to work there and had done what I thought I was supposed to do. That my qualifications would speak for themselves. Ten years later I realized that hard work might be necessary but was not enough; I also needed connections. Thank God I heard this at thirty-two. Had I learned this back then, it might have demoralized me.

Soon after the *Bachelorette* finale in August 2017, I received the invitation of a lifetime. ESPN called and asked to meet with me. The position: one of three hosts on a three-hour morning TV show. *ESPN recognizes my sports experience. And now I also have this platform. Oh my God, this is it!* I wake up every morning and watch ESPN, so to step foot on its campus was amazing.

I first met with the head of talent, who's a big fan of *The Bachelor* and gave it to me straight. "Listen, we love you, but the sports audience doesn't recognize who you are." Then I met with an influential showrunner, and he gave me a glimmer of hope. "You definitely have the talent," he said. "But you're just not there yet for the position we called you in for." In other words, I had to cut my teeth in local settings before I would be ready for the national stage.

They were a hundred percent right. Had they given me that job, it would have ended my career before it started. With no TV experience, I was unqualified to cohost a national show with thirty-year veterans of the game. The audience would have skewered me. *Why is she sitting at that table?*

Let me tell you how unready I was. My first sideline reporting gig was a disaster. While anchors and analysts comment from the booth, a sideline reporter is in the middle of the action. I was reporting a college basketball game in Murfreesboro, Tennessee, that Thanksgiving weekend. We were streaming live on Facebook, and I had to engage the audience. There are no commercial breaks.

In fact, as the sideline reporter, *I* was the commercial break. "We've got two analysts on the floor calling the game as well, but you're the intro," they told me. "When the red light comes on, go."

The red light never came on, and the earpiece to my interruptible foldback—the device that allows the crew to communicate with me—popped out. I stood there waiting until someone frantically waved and yelled, "You're on, you're on!"

When I tell you I never felt so alone in my life . . . like I was stranded on an island by myself.

I was still practicing law at the time and could have quit after that on-air fiasco. Instead I told myself, *You know what? You'll do better next time. You'll be more prepared.* And I did a few more games. It taught me that sideline reporting was not my thing, so I switched gears.

Life dealt me a major *No,* and it saved me. It's too easy to get caught up in the hype of *Bachelor* Nation. Everyone there tells you how much they love you. You're great. You're beautiful. You're smart. It makes you believe this is the way the world thinks about you *when they don't even know who you are.* Except for Trista Sutter, I spent thirty-one years of my life not knowing who anyone in the *Bachelor*-verse was. I could walk down the street and recognize not one of them. So why would anyone else outside of the fandom know who I am?

That necessary gut check from ESPN knocked me off my high horse. I still had to work to get to where I wanted to go and adjusted my mindset accordingly. How grateful I was to now have direct connections to major players at ESPN who were willing to work with me. But I had to be willing to start from the bottom and reinvent myself.

A month later, ESPN offered me another opportunity. The biggest sports show in the country, *First Take,* was coming to Dallas during Fashion Week. Why did Big Rach tell the head of ESPN talent that she was already booked? That's how green I was. Thankfully, my PR and manager at the time let me have it. "Are you kidding me? You don't say no to ESPN! You go do *First Take*, and we'll handle Fashion Week."

They brought me on as a guest to talk about the Dallas Cowboys with cohosts Stephen A. Smith, Max Kellerman, and Molly Qerim Rose, the top sports analysts in the industry. As he likes to do, Stephen A. tried to throw shade at me for my loyalty to the Cowboys: "I appreciate that because you know what that means, right?" he said. "You expect hard times."

I laughed good-naturedly then said, "Hard times are behind us. We're looking forward right now."

The crew loved it. *She got him, she got him!* Even Stephen A. said, "That was a good comeback!"

When I walked off the stage, a producer asked me, "What do you want to do?" Not only did he have no idea that I had been the Bachelorette, he thought I worked for ABC News.

I pointed back at the stage. "I want to do that."

He told me that in a year they could get me onto the show. In the meantime, I nurtured that relationship. I asked questions, met with him when I came to New York City, and otherwise stayed in touch. As he mentored me, I put in the work—writing for *Us Weekly,* appearing on the girl talk segment of *The Steve Harvey Show,* sideline reporting for *Stadium,* anything to position me to make a play when the next shot came.

About a year after my first appearance on *First Take,* that producer followed through on his promise and invited me to New York to serve as a moderator on the show. All I had to do was introduce the topic, toss a question to the guests filling in for Max, and allow them to debate. Wanting to offer more to the show, I spent all night studying the latest news in sports. The night before my first stint on live national television, the sports news of the year broke. LeBron James announced that he was leaving the Cleveland Cavaliers to play for the Los Angeles Lakers. Basketball fans across the nation were going to tune in for Max's and Stephen A.'s opinions on Bron's stunning decision.

The next day the producers told me that Stephen A. and Max were going to call in. I had not rehearsed for this moment and was terrified. This was live television, and I was now going to be talking to Stephen A. Smith and Max Kellerman on a screen while I sat alone at the *First Take* desk in the studio. I awaited the countdown before we went live.

"10 . . . 9 . . . 8 . . . 7 . . . 6 . . . We lost Stephen A. It's just you and Max. GO!"

"WELCOME TO *FIRST TAKE!*" I yelled nervously. I asked Max the question, and we chatted. In the back of my mind, I was freaking out. *At one point, he's going to stop, but we're on national television. I either have to debate him or throw him another question.* I threw Max a second question. In my earpiece was chaos. Apparently, losing one of their hosts before going live had never happened before, and they were too busy trying to put out the fire to throw me a lifeline. *Stay calm, Rachel. You're on live television. It's a two-shot of you and Max, so the viewers see you.* I gave Max another question, and about six or seven minutes into the show, they found someone to debate him. For my first time on live television as a host, I got thrown into a sink-or-swim situation, and by all accounts, I swam through it. I learned a long time ago that if you stay ready, you never have to get ready. That, coupled with several prayers, helped me sail through that moment and the rest of the week, and I secured a contract with ESPN. There I continued to work with the best in the business on various different projects in television, radio, and social media until I chose to leave to cohost the podcast *Higher Learning* with Van Lathan on The Ringer.

In November 2018, I went to see my hairstylist as I would every few months. "How are you, Rachel?" she asked as she whipped the cape around me.

And I gave her the same answer I had for the longest: "Girl, I'm exhausted." While taking on positions in media, I continued to put in hours at my law firm. As she combed my hair, I droned on about working myself to the bone. With frustration and despair, I recounted all the desires I had for my media career that kept eluding me no matter how much effort I made when not being a practicing attorney.

After letting me vent, my hairstylist paused and looked me in the eye through the mirror in front of us. "Listen, I'm hearing you talking about all these things that you want to do, but what are you actually doing in your life that is moving you toward where you want to go? You know what to do, so what's holding you back?"

My answer was simple and immediate. "My law career."

Satisfied with my response, my stylist resumed combing my hair. "Then you know exactly what you need to do."

And I did, but I was too afraid of giving up my identity as a lawyer. Folks knew me as either a Bachelorette or an attorney, and I drove myself ragged attempting to fulfill both roles while also pursuing what I truly wanted for myself. Despite becoming a part of the franchise with the intention of breaking the mold—or maybe even because of it—I was fearful of being perceived as someone who wanted to be famous. *Oh, for all her talk, Rachel's just like the rest of them.*

Also, if I gave up being a lawyer and failed because people could not see me as more than the Bachelorette, who would I be? Like the fear that kept me in a dead-end relationship and delayed my finding my husband and building a healthy partnership, I held on to my job at the law firm for so long because I was petrified of starting over and failing. Once again, I was putting other people's opinions above my own happiness, this time in an area of my life where I had a track record of getting results from my own best efforts.

That week I resigned from the law firm. I worked for the remainder of the calendar year, then never looked back. After being a jack-of-all-trades but master of none, I gave up the prestige and security of being an attorney and focused on becoming a media personality. I had been tethered to my legal career, but only when I unleashed myself was I able to fly. With a greater capacity to push myself came opportunities to learn, grow, and master my new field, and soon other things that I could not even imagine appeared before me.

To live your best life, you may need to learn some lessons twice. I'm so grateful to my hairstylist for posing the simple but powerful question that reminded me to apply what I had learned in my love life to my career goals. So regularly check in with yourself by asking, *What do I want and what is holding me back?* And find yourself a great hairstylist. Or life coach. If you're as lucky as I am, you just might find both at the same salon.

Some may say that I'm chasing the dream, but after living the life that someone else wanted for me for so long, my goal in life is not any specific position or title. It's to give myself the freedom to be who I authentically am and the permission to do what I genuinely desire instead of what any authority says I cannot or am supposed to do. If I'm pursuing what I truly want in the moment, I'm not chasing a dream. I'm living it.

RACHEL'S LIFE PLAN (AGE 36)

- **AGE 18:** Graduate from First Baptist Academy and move three hours away from Dallas to Austin to attend the University of Texas and major in government.

- **AGE 22:** Graduate from University of Texas with a BA in sports management. (Thank you, Mom and Dad, for hearing me out, trusting my choice, and supporting my change in major.) Take a year off to work as a substitute teacher and almost change the trajectory of my career due to the deep impact of those children. Then move to Milwaukee, Wisconsin, to attend law school. Nine Black people in a class of fewer than three hundred. Didn't choose Marquette for the diversity.

- **AGE 26:** Graduate from Marquette University Law School with a specialization in sports law. Fall in love with a former professional athlete and embark on an on-and-off-again, long-distance relationship that lasts almost five years.

- **AGE 30:** Start therapy, audition for *The Bachelor* on a whim, and finally end the relationship with the coach I was so desperate to marry. Get the First Impression Rose and make the final three.

Learn a hard lesson about needing to be emotionally vulnerable and expressive—on national TV.

- **AGE 31:** Become the first Black lead in the *Bachelor* franchise. Apply those hard-earned lessons about being emotionally vulnerable and expressive. Accept a wedding proposal from the man of my dreams—on national TV.

- **AGE 32:** Apply for my dream job at ESPN. Dream job denied. Because of my stint on *The Bachelor,* they don't believe people will receive me as a serious sports reporter despite my major, law degree, and career achievements, all deeply rooted in the business of sports. Use the rejection as motivation to reinvent myself yet again.

- **AGE 34:** Culminate a two-year engagement and marry Bryan Abasolo in Cancún, Mexico, in front of family and close friends both old, like Erin, Andrea, Jade, and Nika, and new, such as *Bachelor* alums Astrid, Kristina, Whitney, and Alexis. No wedding party, because who needs that stress? But as I planned at eighteen, we dance all night.

- **AGE 36:** Exit *Bachelor* Nation. I may not have full control over what opportunities my life may bring, but I do know I will make choices according to the life I want to live and not what others expect of me. Big Rach may not always get what she wants, but it'll never be because she doesn't know what that is.

THIS IS STILL NOT
A FAIRY TALE

Live your soul, not a role.

—Sonia Choquette

Checklists and plans are useful tools as long as we use them as guides and not rulebooks. As we journey through life, we are supposed to change and so should our goals. Throughout life we never stop receiving messages about who we should be, want, and have, and in every stage of our development, we shed another *should*. We find greater courage and more opportunities to be authentic and fulfill our purpose—the reason we are here. We need itineraries for a general sense of direction because the essence of who we are remains no matter how we may change, but we are meant to take detours and make discoveries not on the road map.

Ron Kirk was right. Today I am no longer an attorney but a businesswoman who makes more money and enjoys more fulfillment than I ever did practicing law. However, my legal training contributes to my success as an entrepreneur and played a factor in my becoming the first Black Bachelorette, which changed my life in ways I could not foresee. My fulfillment comes not from the income I earn but the impact that I have.

I am grateful for all the life desires I have been able to realize and look forward to experiencing more, including motherhood. I recognize that whatever comes my way reflects the relationship I have with myself. The inner journey creates the outer experience. Staying in alignment with my desires and values enables me to make the decisions that increase my shot at happiness. Connecting to my feelings and honoring my vulnerabilities give me the capacity to accept the things I cannot control and weather the storms that I would have rather passed me by.

So although I share some of my story with you in this book in the hopes that it can be of help to you, I don't judge younger Rachel's choices. While I used those experiences to understand myself better so I can make better decisions for myself, I don't dwell on what-ifs. *What if I had waited until marriage to have sex? What if I had not gone to law school? What if I had ended that relationship years earlier?* I work through the feelings these choices and their consequences spark, gather the insights, and move forward with my life, keeping the beliefs, practices, and relationships that serve my purpose.

To everything else, I say, Miss me with that.

ACKNOWLEDGMENTS

I do not even know where to begin so I will just start with a general THANK YOU. There is no way to remember every possible name and individual that allowed this moment and this book to happen. So, I want to thank those who have supported me, believed in me, prayed for me, and trusted me in writing this book. This is something I could have never done by myself, and it took a village of people and their support to get here. I am forever grateful for your dedication, love, and encouragement.

I want to of course thank God for guiding and ordering my steps as I stumbled across this thing called life. I may struggle with faith and question You at times but trusting and leaning on YOU has never led me astray.

Bryan. My dear, patient, kind, and overwhelmingly supportive husband. Thank you for loving me at my best and worst. Thank you for giving me a reason to live my best life because that means I get to do it with you. Thank you for taking a chance and putting your life on hold to join my journey and take a chance at love. Thank you for being you and for teaching me every day to slow down and appreciate life. Thank you for reminding me every day to take chances and to dream. Every page in this book led me to you; I am forever grateful.

Mommy, thank you for teaching me what it is to be a woman.

You have always provided me the best example even when I did not always follow it. Thank you for believing in me and always teaching me to trust my gut. Thank you for establishing and building a strong foundation that always made me feel safe and protected and loved. I have always aspired to be the woman, mother, and friend that you are and will forever continue to do so.

Daddy, thank you for not just being a father and teaching me what a man should be but also for being a mentor and a role model. I am so blessed to grow up with a father that was both. You taught me the essence of hard work and education. You were never easy on us, but it made me strong, independent, and resilient. It made me a Lindsay, and for that, I am forever proud and grateful.

To my sisters: I love you both so much. There is nothing better than having built-in best friends from the moment you are born. I will always look up to you both; you inspire me more than you know. You have always supported and encouraged me and believed in me, even when I could not see it.

To the Lindsays and Sheltons: I adore my family and love that my upbringing truly defines me as a person. Every aunt, uncle, cousin, and grandparent impacted me in ways you will never know. Your character, stories, and spirit define me and shaped the woman I am today. I am a well-rounded individual because I was raised as a Lindsay and a Shelton.

To my Glender: I adore you so much. You are a living saint. I will never forget our summer together and our random adventures throughout Houston. I did not get to grow up in the same city with you, but that summer connected us and bonded us in an unexplainable way. I stand on your shoulders every day as I represent myself as a woman and your granddaughter. You are the Thelma to my Louise. Thank you for loving me unconditionally.

To the Abasolos/Cohens: Thank you for taking me and accepting me into your family with open arms. I am so proud to be a part of your family. Bryan is so amazing because of how wonderful you all are. Grateful and blessed to call you mi familia.

To my friends: Just thank you for being there when I needed it. Thank you for being a mirror and checking me when I needed it the most. Thank you for picking me up when I was falling, holding me when I cried, listening to me as I complained, keeping my secrets, and giving me advice whether I wanted to hear it or not. Your friendships got me through some of the darkest times in my life. You know who you are and just know I love you. I am stronger because of you.

Thank you, Maryssa and Lauren: You changed my life forever.

Thank you, Michael Klein, Anthony Mattero, Alex Rice, Sara Weiss, Ballantine Books, and Penguin Random House for taking a chance on me and my story.

Thank you, Sofia Quintero. This was not possible without you. I connected with you and from the first time we spoke I knew we were destined to do something great together. Thank you for your honesty, patience, understanding, persistence, and for just being the amazing person you are. I learned so much from you in this process and am grateful to call you a friend.

Thank you to all my exes. My aunt Lisa once told me that people are in your life for a reason, a season, or forever. I think it is obvious that the reasons define me to this day. I am grateful for the lessons learned and I am a better person because of them.

Lastly, thank you to all that took the time to read this book. This is the most honest and vulnerable I have ever been. This book is the hardest thing I have ever done, and I am so blessed that you are here. I hope you learn not just something about me from this book but maybe a little something about yourself.

RACHEL LINDSAY is an attorney, media personality, podcaster, and speaker. She is currently a correspondent for *Extra* and cohosts The Ringer's *Higher Learning* podcast. Prior to her media career, she practiced law at Cooper & Scully, P.C., in Dallas. Lindsay has an exclusive newsletter called "Honestly, Rach" on Meta Bulletin where she talks about love, life, career, friendships, and social issues. An avid sports fan, Lindsay enjoys music, dancing, exercising, reading, and spending time with her husband, Bryan Abasolo, her dog, Copper, and her extended family. Lindsay is also an ambassador for the College Football Playoff Foundation and a member of the University of Texas at Austin College of Education Advisory Council. She lives in Los Angeles.

@therachlindsay